hRAC

A PREHISTORY OF THE CLOUD

A PREHISTORY OF THE CLOUD

Tung-Hui Hu

The MIT Press
Cambridge, Massachusetts
London, England

MIT Press books may be purchased at special quantity discounts for business or sales promotional use. For information, please email special_sales@mitpress.mit.edu.

This book was set in Gentium 10/14pt by Toppan Best-set Premedia Limited. Printed and bound in the United States of America.

Library of Congress Cataloging-in-Publication Data

Hu, Tung-Hui, 1978–
A prehistory of the cloud / Tung-Hui Hu.
    pages cm
Includes bibliographical references and index.
ISBN 978-0-262-02951-3 (hardcover : alk. paper)   1. Computer networks—History—Popular works.   2. Internet—Social aspects—Popular works.   I. Title.
TK5105.5.H79 2015
004.6—dc23

2015001899

10 9 8 7 6 5 4 3 2 1

CONTENTS

ACKNOWLEDGMENTS

Portions of this book were written while at the Michigan Society of Fellows and at the Stanford Center for Advanced Study in the Behavioral Sciences. Many units of the University of Michigan provided research funding and advice, including the Horace H. Rackham School of Graduate Studies, the Department of English, the University of Michigan Library, the Office of Research, and the College of Letters, Sciences, and the Arts. I thank these organizations for their support.

This book is for my correspondents: Megan Ankerson, Finn Brunton, John Cheney-Lippold, Victor Mendoza, and Lisa Nakamura. Thanks to Katy Peplin, whose work as a research assistant helped take this project in new directions. Ben Lempert's editorial advice has been indispensible and transformative. Karen Beckman, Linda Williams, Kaja Silverman, and Anne Wagner provided the intellectual scaffolding for this study—hopefully invisible to the reader, yet deeply felt nonetheless. Doug Sery, Susan Buckley, and Kathleen Caruso at the MIT Press brought this project to fruition. I'm grateful to the generous colleagues who read and commented on drafts of this book, including Sara Blair, Jonathan Freedman, Ilana Gershon, Roger Grant, Jeffrey Todd Knight, Petra Kuppers, Erica Levin, Kris Paulsen, Dan Rosenberg, Polly Rosenwaike, Ruby Tapia, Terri Tinkle, Damon Young, and Genevieve Yue; thank you. Last, for being there through the ends, and thus the beginnings: Elizabeth Bruch.

INTRODUCTION

Like the inaudible hum of the electrical grid at 60 hertz, the cloud is silent, in the background, and almost unnoticeable. As a piece of information flows through the cloud—provisionally defined, a system of networks that pools computing power[1]—it is designed to get to its destination with "five-nines" reliability, so that if one hard drive or piece of wire fails en route, another one takes its place, 99.999 percent of the time. Because of its reliability and ubiquity, the cloud is a particularly mute piece of infrastructure. It is just there, atmospheric and part of the environment.

Until something goes wrong, that is. Until a dictator throws the Internet "kill switch," or, more likely, a farmer's backhoe accidentally hits fiber-optic cable. Until state-sponsored hackers launch a wave of attacks, or, more likely, an unanticipated leap year throws off the servers, as it did on February 29, 2011. Until a small business in Virginia makes a mistake, and accidentally directs the entire Internet—yes, all of the Internet—to send its data via Virginia, and, almost unbelievably, it does. Until Pakistan Telecom inadvertently claims the data bound for YouTube. A multi-billion-dollar industry that claims 99.999 percent reliability breaks far more often than you'd think, because it sits on top of a few brittle fibers the width of a few hairs. The cloud is both an idea and a physical and material object, and the more one learns about it, the more one realizes just how fragile it is.

The gap between the physical reality of the cloud, and what we can see of it, between the idea of the cloud and the name that we give it—"cloud"—is a rich site for analysis. While consumers typically imagine "the cloud" as a new digital technology that arrived in 2010–2011, with the introduction of products such as iCloud or Amazon Cloud Player, perhaps the most surprising thing about the cloud is how old it is.[2] Seb Franklin has identified a 1922 design for predicting weather using a grid of "computers" (i.e., human mathematicians) connected by telegraphs.[3] AT&T launched the "electronic 'skyway'"—a series of microwave relay stations—in 1951, in conjunction with the first cross-country television network. And engineers at least as early as 1970 used the symbol of a cloud to represent any unspecifiable or unpredictable network, whether telephone network or Internet.

Figure I.1 provides an early example. Drawn by Irwin Dorros, director of network planning for AT&T, this diagram utilizes a series of three clouds to describe the network behind AT&T's new Picturephone service. Previously, network maps had been drawn as block diagrams—a series of boxes indicating either the exact telephone circuit or at least the possibility of finding the exact circuit. But Picturephone, a primitive videoconferencing system, was one of the first applications that worked across a mixture of analog and digital networks. Because Picturephone would operate regardless of the type of physical circuit underneath, Dorros illustrated the boundaries of the networks as an amorphous form.[4]

What we learn from the diagram is simple: the cloud's genesis was as a symbol. The cloud icon on a map allowed an administrator to situate a network he or she had direct knowledge of—the computers in his or her office, for example—within the same epistemic space as something that constantly fluctuates and is impossible to know: the amorphous admixture of the telephone network, cable network, and the Internet. While the thing that moves through the sky is in fact a formation of water vapor, water crystal, and aerosols, we call it a cloud to give a constantly shifting thing a simpler and more abstract form. Something similar happens in the digital world. While the system of computer resources is comprised of millions of hard drives, servers, routers, fiber-optic cables, and networks, we call it "the cloud": a single, virtual, object. To do so not only make things easier on users and computer programs, but also allows the whole system to withstand the loss of an individual part. (Most of the time, anyway.)

As a result, the cloud is the premier example of what computer scientists term virtualization—a technique for turning real things into logical objects, whether a physical network turned into a cloud-shaped icon, or a warehouse full of data storage servers turned into a "cloud drive." But the gap between the real and the virtual betrays a number of less studied consequences, some of which are benign and some of which are not. One's data trail grows with each website one visits and each packet one sends through the cloud. The results are used by both marketing companies trying to target an online ad

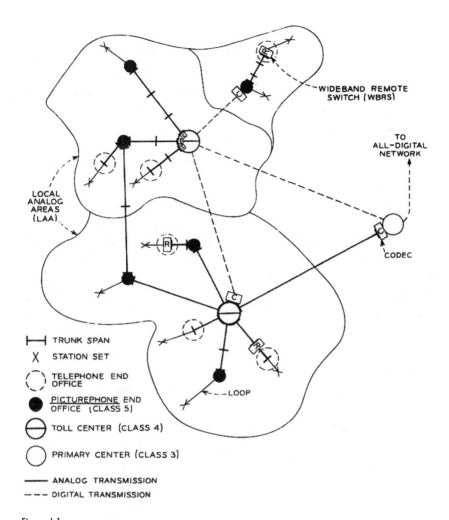

WIDEBAND REMOTE
SWITCH (WBRS)

TO
ALL-DIGITAL
NETWORK

LOCAL
ANALOG
AREAS
(LAA)

CODEC

⊢─┤   TRUNK SPAN

X   STATION SET

⌐ ̣⌐   TELEPHONE END
      OFFICE

●   PICTUREPHONE END
      OFFICE (CLASS 5)

⊖   TOLL CENTER (CLASS 4)

○   PRIMARY CENTER (CLASS 3)

──── ANALOG TRANSMISSION

─ ─ ─ DIGITAL TRANSMISSION

LOOP

Figure I.1

Illustrative local area configurations. *Source:* Irwin Dorros, "The Picturephone System:
The Network," *Bell System Technical Journal* 50, no. 2 (February 1971): 232. © 1971 The
Bell System Technical Journal. Reprinted with permission.

for, say, auto insurance, and government agencies trying to target terrorists for extrajudicial killings. We tend to perceive the two kinds of targeting as separate because online privacy appears to be a born-digital problem that has little to do with geopolitics. That gap, then, is crucial. The word "cloud" speaks to the way we imagine data in the virtual economy traveling instantaneously through the air or "skyway"—here in California one moment, there in Japan the next. Yet this idea of a virtual economy also masks the slow movement of electronics that power the cloud's data centers, and the workers who must unload this equipment at the docks.[5] It also covers up the Third World workers who invisibly moderate the websites and forums of Web 2.0, such as Facebook, to produce the clean, well-tended communities that Western consumers expect to find. By producing a seemingly instant, unmediated relationship between user and website, our imagination of a virtual "cloud" displaces the infrastructure of labor within digital networks.

This book is an attempt to examine what occurs in the gap between the real and the virtual. In this it offers two interrelated stories. On one hand, *A Prehistory of the Cloud* tells the story of how the cloud grew out of older networks, such as railroad tracks, sewer lines, and television circuits, and often continues to be layered on top of or over them. Today, of course, the cloud has become so naturalized in everyday life that we tend to look right through it, seeing it uncritically, if we see it at all.[6] To make this historical infrastructure more visible, this book turns back the clock to the clumsy moments when the cloud was more of an idea than a smoothly functioning technology. It examines a series of cultural records and events that shaped the cloud's "prehistory," including a group of microwave relay stations sabotaged near Wendover, Utah, in 1961 that sparked a furious debate about what a network actually *is*; a 1946 comic strip, *Bobby Gets Hep*, produced by AT&T that taught children etiquette for party lines and therefore helped construct our modern notion of privacy; and the US government's announcement of a National Data Center, a 1966 proposal deemed so dangerous to society that one scientist likened it to the development of a nuclear weapon.

Using these examples, the book tells a second story about the politics of digital culture. When commentators describe the nebulous Occupy Wall Street movements, the workings of global capitalism, the web-mediated resistance movements comprising the Arab Spring, and Al Qaeda and Associated Movements (AQAM) all as "cloudlike," or as "a network of networks," it is clear that the cloud, as an idea, has exceeded its technological platform and become a potent metaphor for the way contemporary society organizes and understands itself.[7] Responding to this shift, communications and media scholars have attempted to theorize the new forms and structures of power that result from networked societies.

One traditional model of explaining political power is known as sovereignty. Consider a hypothetical kingdom, in which its sovereign can coerce his subjects into doing what he wants. Power here is top-down: centralized in the throne room, it radiates out to the borders of the king's territories. Further, sovereign power is framed in the negative: it can punish unruly subjects, prohibit certain practices, and, in the most extreme cases, confiscate a subject's life. While many modern democracies no longer have monarchs, they nevertheless retain some aspects of sovereign power. The United States, for example, has clearly defined borders; it centralizes power into clearly defined federal institutions and agencies, such as the White House and the FBI; and many of those agencies exist to prosecute or punish violations of the law. Yet the Internet puts pressure on this model of power. In one case, the US government attempted to limit the export of strong encryption software, only to be confounded by a proliferation of foreign websites—easily accessible by US users—offering that software for free download. Explaining this difficulty, legal scholar James Boyle writes that digitally dispersed, transnational networks always exceed a sovereign state's ability to "regulate outside its borders . . . We are sailing into the future on a sinking ship. This vessel, the accumulated canon of copyright and patent law, was developed to convey forms and methods of expression entirely different from the vaporous cargo it is now being asked to carry."[8]

Boyle and his contemporaries use sovereign power as an example of what digital networks make obsolete. Yet, counterintuitively, what this book argues is that "the cloud" also indexes a *reemergence* of sovereign power within the realm of data. Sovereign power may seem worlds away from the age of the Internet, particularly given its antiquated elements, such as the monarch's power to arbitrarily kill. Algorithms and users seem to be running the world online, rather than there being a central decision maker; further, a topography of power based on borders or territories, instead of networks, seems out of date.[9] Indeed, the incongruity has caused media scholars to develop two main alternate models of power, which I explain below; I then return to why the cloud may actually effect a return to sovereignty.

Initially, scholars of surveillance and media turned to Michel Foucault's model of *disciplinary power*, which replaces a single source of power, the sovereign, with a series of institutions, such as a factory, prison, school, hospital, or even the family, through which power can be exercised and subjects managed. Disciplinary power is far less coercive than sovereignty; it instead operates according to a set of norms and rules. A school, for example, educates its pupils and in so doing produces certain formations of knowledge and self-understandings of what constitutes "good behavior." The school organizes pupils by classroom, grade, and daily schedule; evaluates each pupil through testing; and, occasionally, attempts to reform a wayward student by issuing detention. Disciplinary power, then, works as a kind of surveillant gaze, under which subjects internalize behavioral standards, learn to order their bodies, or are supervised through other social mechanisms. In his perhaps most quoted study, Foucault mobilizes Jeremy Bentham's 1791 design of a prison called the Panopticon to analyze a condition in which, as Foucault writes, "a state of conscious and permanent visibility . . . assures the automatic functioning of power."[10]

While the Internet is certainly a space of radical visibility—each and every packet of data that passes through the US Internet may be inspected by the National Security Agency, one aspect of surveillance that has led to Panopticon-like comparisons—digital networks complicate many other aspects of this theory. In the cloud, for example, there is seemingly no set of behavioral norms, hierarchies, or enclosed spaces, and any institutions involved in managing users seem purely incidental; the closest, it would seem, are Internet protocols, rather than organizations. And as computer networks seem to have become decentralized and distributed, power, too, seems to have become distributed on a microscopic level. For these reasons, over the last ten years, scholars of new media have generally coalesced around a second model: the *control society*.[11] If Foucault originally described a shift from sovereign societies to disciplinary societies, Gilles Deleuze extended this shift into a third phase, in which subjects are governed by invisible rules and systems of regulation, such as our credit scores, web history, and computer protocols. As Deleuze puts it, prisons and other disciplinary institutions are subsumed by these mechanisms of control: "Everyone knows these institutions are finished, whatever the length of their expiration periods. It's only a matter of administering their last rites and of keeping people employed until the installation of new forces knocking at the door."[12]

As an example of Deleuze's idea of the control society, consider the credit card. There are often no preset spending limits associated with the card, and because a computer determines whether a particular transaction is fraudulent by comparing it to the charges the spender usually makes, a cardholder does not even have to worry if someone steals the card. Yet—and this is the key difference—the very freedoms credit cards offer also require users to order and self-regulate their own behavior. Even if the card is issued with no preset spending limits, a new cardholder still cannot typically buy a $100,000 car using that card. Regardless of whether the cardholder can afford it, a computer will likely decline the charge based on the lack of prior spending behavior; a cardholder, in turn, is aware of that potential for embarrassment, as well as the fact that overloading one's credit line will likely impact one's credit score and future credit potential. (The cardholder may wish to buy a car or a house in a few years, for instance, and hopes to get a loan.) Yet this situation may change from day to day; perhaps after the cardholder buys a series of $1,000 meals over a period of time, the computer will decide that he or she fits the profile of a "high spender" and allow the $100,000 charge in the future.

Somewhere, a computer is calculating the impact of each spending decision and adjusting to it in real time, and, in turn, the cardholders adjust, too. "You" are a set of spending patterns, and that projected profile both enables the bank to extend credit to you as well as puts the onus on you to take responsibility for those spending patterns. Convenient, if a little creepy. The core idea behind a control society, then, is thus a continuous set of cybernetic systems, financial incentives, and monitoring technologies molded to each individual subject, that follow him or her even when "outside" an institution as such; and, precisely because there are fewer explicit institutions, spaces, or rules to restrict the subject's behaviors, these systems are often experienced as freeing.

Can the cloud be explained by this model of control? Most scholars would unequivocally say yes; Deleuze's description of data aggregation, the amorphous and open environment of computer code, and even the gaseous qualities of corporations within a control society map directly onto attributes of the cloud. If there is any problem with his theory, it is that his argument seems a little *too* easy to apply to the cloud. When he writes about a nightmare scenario—that an "electronic card that raises a given barrier" is governed by "the computer that tracks each person's position"—a present-day reader wonders what the fuss is about; much of what Deleuze envisioned, such as computer checkpoints and computer tracking, has come true already.[13] The widespread claim that we are in an era of biopolitics has largely been built on the strength of such evidence.

This book's goal is to think beyond this idea of the control society, to both acknowledge its influence and use the cloud to ask what this theory cannot account for. If we look at the cloud closely, we find the presence of phenomena that hint at other explanations. The all-but-forgotten infrastructures that undergird the cloud's physical origins, for example, often originated in a state's military apparatus; one of the earliest real-time computer networks was an early-warning system for incoming nuclear missiles in the 1950s. Today's cloud relies on a repurposed version of this infrastructure, among a host of other Cold War spaces. Internet providers reuse old weapons and command bunkers as data centers, while the largest data management company today, Iron Mountain, was founded as Iron Mountain Atomic Storage, Inc. Even as this militarized legacy begins to decay, its traces continue to haunt modern-day digital networks with their ghostly presence.

These traces are a clue that the supposedly anachronistic mode of sovereign power may be returning under different forms. Rather than consider sovereign power a historical exception or aberration within a wholesale shift to the systems of control, I suggest that it has mutated and been given new life inside the cloud.[14] As Foucault himself emphatically warns us: "We should not see these things as the replacement of a society of sovereignty by a society of discipline, and then of a society of discipline by a society, say, of government. In fact we have a triangle": a triangle where sovereign, disciplinary, and governmental power (or control) constitute the three sides.[15] What this book shows is that the cloud grafts control onto an older structure of sovereign power, much as fiber-optic networks are layered or grafted onto older networks. I term this new hybrid form the "sovereignty of data."

The cloud contains a subtle weapon, a way of wrapping sovereign power—torture, targeted killings, and the latest atrocities in the war on terror—in the image of data. By this I do not mean that sovereign power surfaces in new forms of "cyberwarfare," or (as others have argued) in the fact that war itself has become increasingly mediated by digital technologies.[16] Instead, the sovereignty of data comes out of the way we invest the cloud's technology with cultural fantasies about security and participation. These fantasies may be as simple as the idea that the cloud will protect our data from unsafe, "unfree" hackers; that data needs to be secured from disaster; or even that the cloud is a unique medium for user interaction. These ideologies are disseminated through routine interactions with applications in the cloud, such as tagging a photograph on Facebook. Even measures meant for our safety—marking messages as spam, for instance—construct a set of cultural norms that we internalize as "responsible" online behavior.

As users are increasingly aware, values such as participation are sometimes co-opted by market mechanisms that John Horvath originally described as "freeware capitalism."[17] Corporations, for example, ask us to "interact" as a form of marketing feedback. Even more subtly, however, by interfacing with the structure of sovereign power, these ideologies position the cloud's users within the same political economy as the acts of state violence performed in their name. The wars over resources and territory and extralegal torture after 9/11 may appear to be worlds away from the political economy of data. But, I contend, they point to a resurgence of a violence that is enabled by the cloud.

Seen correctly, the cloud is a topography or architecture of our own desire. Much of the cloud's data consists of our own data, the photographs and content uploaded from our hard drives and mobile phones; in an era of user-generated content, the cloud is, most obviously, our cloud (this is the promise of the "I" in Apple's "iCloud," or to use an older reference, the "my" in "mySpace"). Yet these fantasies—that the cloud gives us a new form of ownership over our data, or a new form of individualized participation—are nevertheless structured by older, preexisting discourses. As chapters 1 and 3 argue, the cloud's relationship to security can be traced to Cold War ways of thinking about internal enemies as well as nineteenth-century notions of a "race war," while chapters 2 and 4 show that its participatory impulse comes not just through new interactive technologies but also through economic liberalism's mechanisms for constructing a modern subject that is left to itself—the sort of subject we call the "user." The intersection of security and participation in the cloud can help us understand any number of individual cases: why we constantly invoke the specter of foreignness (e.g., China, Iran, Nigeria) when discussing hacker/spammer threats to the "free" Internet; why Cold War rhetoric has increasingly informed digital threats, as in the *New York Times'* invention of the phrase "mutually assured cyberdestruction";[18] why calls for digital activism (or "hacktivism") are often co-opted in a framework that already invites participation; why the so-called Internet kill switch reads (falsely) as a joke that involves no actual killing; and even why the NSA's facilities for decrypting intercepted calls are structurally similar to those used by digital archivists trying to preserve digital media from decay.

Taken together, my examples suggest that the sovereignty of data is ultimately what Achille Mbembe has called a "necropolitics," a politics of death.[19] It is the cloud's participatory ideology that motivates amateur data collectors to assist NATO in streamlining its F-16 bombing operations, for example: as I argue in chapter 4, war outsources its dirty work to volunteers by substituting a live, interactive representation of death for death itself. The perversity of the cloud is therefore not that it explicitly causes death. Rather, the cloud transmutes the mechanism of death and presents it to us as life.

How to View Emptiness

Of course, the idea that the cloud is inherently political may not be so new. Today one need not go far to find headlines like that on the February 2014 cover of *Popular Mechanics*: "Privacy Is Disappearing: How New Tech Tools Can Help You Fight Back." As ever more data moves into the cloud, the general public has increasingly become aware that the cloud is politically contested terrain; articles on data-veillance and cell phone tracking routinely run in the popular media. Yet typical responses to this debate invoke technological and legal solutions, such as do-not-track software or a new law; the *Popular Mechanics* article, for example, tells users to reclaim their privacy by installing encryption software and "practicing good browser hygiene."[20] The problem with this approach, however, is that it does little to address the wider political and social context from which these problems—and even the very idea of privacy—originate; nor does it take in account the logics behind technology itself that actually reproduce and redouble the problem of privacy. As I show in this book, for example, digital hygiene does not "fight" US government monitoring, as the article claims; indeed, digital hygiene is actually the goal of a Department of Homeland Security educational campaign that aims to have US users internalize correct (i.e., legal) online behaviors.

Scholars concerned about such issues have typically embraced the idea of materiality (or, more specifically, "platform studies") to recuperate the often invisible logics, algorithms, and apparatuses that structure digital culture. Focusing on digital culture's media-specific properties typically involves examining the technological platforms within: Internet Protocol, lines of Java code, network cables, or conventions for the Unix operating system.[21] In doing so, such scholars claim that an awareness of a medium's materiality will lead to a more effective understanding of its ideological content. Yet the cloud, I am arguing, inevitably frustrates this approach, because by design, it is not based on any single medium or technology; it is medium-agnostic, rather than medium-specific. As an inter-network, any type of communications network or technological platform can conceivably be attached to it, even analog ones; in 2001, one Norwegian enthusiast even implemented Internet Protocol with a set of carrier pigeons. (Observers reported a disappointing 56 percent packet loss rate: rephrased in English, five out of the nine pigeons appeared to have wandered off, or have been eaten.)

Further, one of the curious dilemmas that the cloud represents is that not even the engineers who have built it typically know where the cloud is, and, as a consequence, what part of the apparatus to examine. A personal anecdote: in my stint as a network engineer in the late 1990s, I would routinely travel to a handsome, terra-cotta-roofed building a few blocks from downtown Palo Alto, California. Unbeknownst to its well-heeled passers-by, perhaps one-fifth of the world's Internet traffic once flowed through this building. Back then, Palo Alto was one of five major exchange points in which the major national "backbone" networks, such as AT&T or Sprint, would connect with each other. Because of security concerns, engineers were never quite sure who or what was in the neighboring rack of network and computer equipment; my coworkers and I just knew that our cables ran somewhere into a cage in the floor below. I had a pretty good hunch, though—gleaned through a combination of the rumor mill, glimpses of router names punched on Dymo tape, and the Quebecois-accented English that some other workers spoke. Yet while I knew how to route packets to Deutsche Telekom, Nippon Telegraph and Telephone, and Teleglobe Canada over my computer screen, the network's physical presence still felt remote to me. One morning at 4:00 a.m., I decided to become better acquainted with it.

So, impulsively, I took a fiber-optic cable and unplugged it. Then I held it up to my eye and looked in. On the other side of the fiber, I imagined, was Japan. The light was red, and it winked like a star on a smoggy night. Because fiber optics were new at the time, what I had only read about, but not yet experienced, is that there are two kinds of fiber-optic cable: single-mode, for long distances, and multi-mode, for short distances. A single-mode laser would have lased a hole into my cornea and blinded me instantly. Multi-mode is often powered by LED light sources rather than true lasers. Single-mode is indicated by a yellow cable; multi-mode, orange. The cable I had grabbed was orange.

That I can still see today is a testament to both my dumb luck, and also, metaphorically, to the paradox that the cloud represents: that you can never see it by looking directly at it. Indeed, my naive desire to look into the cloud's fiber-optic network is a little like asking what a film is about, and looking into the most direct source of the image—the projector beam—to find out. You can get as close as you want to it, but the blinding light won't tell you much about the film, and it may even be dangerous for your eyes; it certainly involves turning your head away and not watching the film. The cloud is not unlike the changing shapes and virtual images cast by a projector. But to mistake the apparatus for the film makes us like those mythical "country rubes" of the 1910s who were said to have assaulted the projection booth, looking for the real movie star shown by the film.

Analyzing the cloud requires standing at a middle distance from it, mindful of but not wholly immersed in either its virtuality or its materiality. For this reason, this book does not adhere to the cloud's current technologies— for instance, by dissecting the lines of code in a network protocol implementation. Nor will this book begin with the story of an invention. There are no scenes of apartment windows in Cupertino or cubicles in Seattle lit late at night, where an Apple worker realized something about accessing e-mail applications over the web, or an Amazon engineer became aware that excess computing capacity could be resold to other companies. Because the "cloud" is, properly understood, a cultural phenomenon, I mobilize three categories of primary sources that address this larger sense of the cloud:

1. Representations and anticipations of the cloud in US popular media, legal and political records, corporate advertisements and ephemera, and the like. To be sure, the prehistory of the cloud is not only an American story; there is a need for parallel scholarly studies on, say, the French online service Minitel and specifically non-Western network cultures.[22] But the United States wields considerable veto power over supposedly international bodies for Internet standards as well as infrastructures such as domain name service; the Department of Justice has even used its jurisdiction over the Virginia-based registrar for the .com, .net, and .org domains to seize and prosecute non-US websites. And, more metaphorically, the book's focus on

the United States also responds to the cloud's own rhetorical framing as "the cloud." President George W. Bush was widely mocked for using the plural "Internets" when he referred to "rumors on the, uh, Internets" during a 2004 presidential debate. But in pluralizing the term, Bush was dead-on in a strict sense: there are multiple private Internets and clouds that parallel or shadow the public Internet, run by research universities, militaries, and even foreign countries that have built or are building "walled garden" Internets. Instead of recognizing this, however, we typically internalize the fiction that there is only one Internet, and one cloud.

The use of the cloud's singular form—"the cloud"—not only condenses a wide multiplicity of network forms and clouds into a single vision that encompasses all networks, but also reflects a universalist world view that tracked closely with American political ideals as they developed through the 1950s on: that the cloud would stand in for a "free" Internet and liberal civil society. For that reason, texts drawn from US culture offer a unique perspective for understanding this sensibility.

2. Examples drawn from the culture of computer science itself: the terms, metaphors, and diagrams that show how scientists and hackers understood their subjects—descriptions, to be clear, which often failed or succeeded purely by practice rather than technological superiority. What does it mean, for example, to name (and therefore to think of) a nonfunctional link to another website a "dead link" (rather than a "404 error"), or to mark each data packet with a "time to live" stamp? To think of multitasking as "intimacy," and debugging as a form of "peeping"?

In revisiting subjects whose stories have been partially told by computer historians, my goal is not to recycle existing narratives of invention, but to examine discourses that are typically hidden within these narratives. Part of this aim is to avoid the presentist bias that often confirms successful technologies at the expense of the myriad of alternate ways that scientists imagined the future. Interactive computing was, for example, not developed for interactivity at all, but rather for more efficient debugging. For a while, the word "computer" did not even designate a machine, but rather a laborer—generally a low-paid female worker. Nor was computer science thought of as an independent discipline worth serious academic study until the 1950s and 1960s, when the first computer science programs were founded at the University of Cambridge and Purdue University. Lacking their own discipline, early computer scientists were by necessity in dialogue with urban planners, sociologists, businessmen, and even members of the counterculture; they were amateurs as well as professionals who were part of, but did not have the final word over, their cultural context.

3. Photographs, drawings, videos, and even games that offer insight into how visual culture functions in the cloud: what the cloud looks like on-screen; how we draw or map its shape; how the cloud grew out of TV/ video networks. Crucial to this enterprise is the belief that visual culture does not merely reflect or represent beliefs; it also anticipates and shapes it. As Marshall McLuhan put it, artists serve as a "Distant Early Warning system" for societal change,[23] and the artistic avant-garde offer us a window into the bleeding edge of how new media might be used. The art objects I consider— by Ant Farm, Trevor Paglen, the Raindance Corporation, and others—bring into focus key moments of the cloud's development, and allow us to think through historical problems of power and visibility. Because visual culture tracks the minor mutations of power that shape the cloud, the question of power's visibility may be best interrogated by artists.

Collectively, these works of art also pose an important, if unanswerable, question: what tactics can we use to challenge a diffuse, invisible structure of power? Increasingly, artists and activists have used new media techniques to critique the myriad of problems raised in and by digital culture. As a form of electronic protest, for example, "hacktivist" groups have used distributed denial-of-service software to overwhelm target websites. Perhaps the best-known example occurred in 2010, when Visa and MasterCard refused to process donations for WikiLeaks, the site that positioned itself as a secure drop box for massive floods of leaked information; in response, pro-WikiLeaks sympathizers flooded, and shut down, websites such as Visa.com and Mastercard. com. In turn, the quantity of info on the WikiLeaks site, such as the 109,032 field reports of every death in the Iraq war, spurred another set of hacktivists to develop a parallel tactic: the construction of data-mining and data visualization tools for mapping and "seeing" the cloud of data (figure I.2).

Taken as a whole, these heterogeneous groups of "tactical media" artists have suggested that electronic problems should be opposed electronically.[24] Whether through activism, art, or simply the narratives written about it, the cloud has offered a platform for unconventional modes of critique and dissent, a medium for loosely organized, decentralized modes of protest. Yet as productive as these strategies may be, many of them assume that the electronic medium they work in is a neutral one; as we see in chapters 3 and 4,

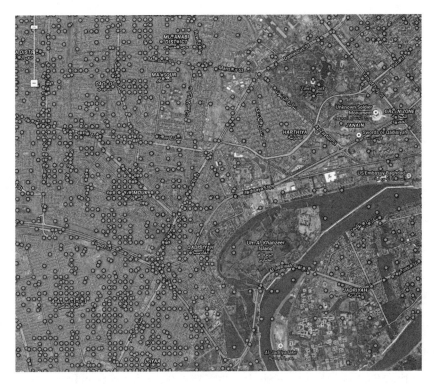

Figure I.2

Simon Rogers, *Wikileaks Iraq War Logs: Every Death Mapped*, data interface, *The Guardian Datablog*, 2010–. Map data: Google Imagery; Cnes/Spot Image; DigitalGlobe; Landsat. Courtesy of Simon Rogers.

their protests often reproduce the system of values (of, say, "participation") embedded in the cloud.

This is a thorny problem, doubled by a historiographic one: the lines between newer and older forms of resisting power are typically drawn more sharply than usual, because the field of new media studies is typically built around finding and writing about the new. At the least, the term "new media" contains within it an implicit opposition to old media, just as digital media implicitly rules out or excludes the analog. (Even in the field of media archeology, a field oriented to studying dead media, the phrase "dead media"— and, as a result, media's "deadness"—is too often taken for granted.) In discussing these artists, it may be more productive to set aside the impulse toward defining what is new about their work. For the battles over digital media are often reflected in other, older medias, such as Portapak video, that were once new. The call to reconfigure the structure of the television net-work in the 1970s using community access television (CATV), for example, is strongly reminiscent of the early debates over broadband Internet; both technologies briefly seemed to offer an alternative to the network's central-ized structure before they were quickly commercialized and recentralized.[25]

Though such strategies may have failed in their utopian idealism, they offer a perspective on and a way of working through problems of contempo-rary media. To be clear, I am not suggesting that there is nothing new about new technology. Instead, I am offering an alternative to the kind of histo-riographical model reliant on a series of technologically induced epistemic shifts or ruptures that often pervades media studies.[26] The analog technolo-gies within the cloud periodically return to view, even if in spectral form. As a result, analog sources will allow us to think through digital problems, and, in turn, challenge the implicit separation between analog and digital.

To challenge this separation is to realize that the cloud is a historical, fragile, and even mortal phenomenon with its own timespan. Over the last twenty years, the Internet has been variously described as a "series of tubes," an "information superhighway," an "ecosystem," a "commons," a "rhizome," a "simulacra," a "cloud" (note the title of this book), and even, as the director of the MIT Media Lab once put it, a "flock of ducks." Each term brings with it an implicit politics of space: if the Internet is imagined as a "public com-mons" being walled off by regulations such as the Digital Millennium Copy-right Act, this serves as potent rallying point for those who would defend it from such incursions; but if the Internet is a "rhizome," then such incursions are already part of the network's anarchic structure: "The Net treats cen-sorship as noise and is designed to work around it."[27] These metaphors have therefore served as flashpoints for political debate. As Tiziana Terranova has shown, prominent neoconservatives such as Alvin Toffler and Newt Gingrich used the image of a network as a self-regulating "ecosystem" to repudiate the Clintonian metaphor of an "information superhighway" that, presum-ably, needed government construction and maintenance.[28]

"The cloud" is only the latest in this series of metaphors. Because it repre-sents a cultural fantasy, it is always more than its present-day technological manifestation (which has, at any rate, already changed since the moment I set these words to paper). If we come to see the cloud as a historical object, we might realize that the story of the cloud is largely unwritten on two fronts: the past and the future. As its title indicates, this book puts forth a prehistory of the cloud. But it also attempts to open up a set of methodological tools to imagine the cloud in the future, meaning both the cloud's impending obsolescence as well as its barely foreseen consequences. For the legacy of the cloud has already begun to write itself into the real environment. As one of the largest consumers of coal energy, for example, the cloud's infrastructure was responsible for 2 percent of the world's greenhouse gas emissions in 2008, and data centers have grown exponentially since then. The long-term consequences of the cloud are worlds away from the seductive "now" produced by its real-time systems. It is our job to catch up with this legacy.

Mapping *Cloud*/Mapping the Cloud

To make a book about something as formless as the cloud is inherently a quixotic objective. Every book is a technology that imposes its own spatial terms on its subject: it's generally linear in form, contains a certain number of pages, and is operated by flipping (or swiping). Within that container, my own four-chapter structure lays out the following question: if the cloud is a cultural fantasy (chapter 1) of participation (chapter 2) and security (chapter 3), what happens when users participate in their own security (chapter 4)? My argument is constructed by examining the cloud's networks (chapter 1), virtualization (chapter 2), storage (chapter 3), and data-mining interfaces (chapter 4).

To understand what the chapter subjects in A Prehistory of the Cloud have to do with each other, it is first worth explaining one concept from computer science, which typically divides a technical apparatus into a series of so-called abstraction layers. These layers move progressively from the least abstract to most abstract. In the case of networks, for example, the physical link on the bottom—fiber-optic cable, Ethernet copper wire—forms the layer of least abstraction. Various protocols in between (Internet Protocol, then Transmission Control Protocol on top of IP) form the middle layers, with the application layer on the very top (the software built on networking protocols, such as streaming video) being the most abstract. This model also describes other technologies, such as operating systems or algorithms, usually through three to seven layers of abstraction.

The idea of layered abstraction is readily visible in our day-to-day lives: you can send an e-mail without worrying about if it travels over a wireless or wired connection, or store a file without knowing whether it is on a USB

Table I.1

The book understood as abstraction layers

4: Application	Data mining	Seeing the Cloud of Data
3: Data access	Data storage	Data Centers and Data Bunkers
2: Platform	Virtualization	Time-Sharing and Virtualization
1: Infrastructure	Network	The Shape of the Network

drive versus a magnetic drive; it is just "the network" or "the drive." The idea thus offers a spatial model of understanding and even standardizing computing: each layer depends on the more material layers "below" it to work, but does not need to know the exact implementation of those layers. Cloud computing is the epitome of this abstraction, a way of turning millions of computers and networks into a single, extremely abstract idea: "the cloud."

The chapter structure of *A Prehistory of the Cloud* evokes the spirit of its subject's abstraction layers (table I.1). This book begins with the earliest vision of the cloud as a "network of networks"; moves to the virtualization software that allows networked resources to be abstracted, and therefore shared; continues to data storage and security delivered through those virtual machines; and, last, examines the data-mining algorithms that "see" through, and rely on, cloud-delivered data. This layer of abstraction may be useful for readers more familiar with a traditional platform studies approach: for instance, someone who has read Matthew Kirschenbaum's work on hard drives and storage might refer directly to chapter 3, while someone interested in material infrastructures might find chapter 1 of interest.[29]

Of course, from a different perspective, my division of the cloud into four layers is arbitrary, and omits any number of other possible technological layers that could have been examined—for instance, the relational database, or web application architecture. Further, because the technology of the cloud is relatively young, the relation between layers is likely confusing: a consumer may think of "cloud" as the cloud drive on his phone (layer 3); a software developer may use "cloud" to mean "software as a service" (layer 2), while a network engineer may continue to use "cloud" to mean a "network of networks" (layer 1). Yet this confusion may also be an opportunity. One of the reasons that a network engineer thinks of a cloud in this way is because the cloud signified a network in the 1970s, while cloud storage did not explicitly declare itself "the cloud" until the late 2000s. In other words, as each infrastructure becomes naturalized, we tend to refer to it with increasing amounts of abstraction, talking about its use (cloud storage) rather than the infrastructure itself (storage servers in data centers). Thus each level of abstraction is a sort of archeological deposit that records the idea of what we thought of "the cloud" at a certain moment in time—however problematic that "we" is. This chronology is neither linear nor exact, but instead testifies to the multiple discourses and prehistories that form the cloud today.

Begin, then, with the cloud's base layer: the network. How did the cloud come to be shaped the way it is? Chapter 1, "The Shape of the Network," answers this question by examining a highly charged moment in 1961, when the Bell System was targeted by a series of bomb attacks that tore through Utah and Nevada, at the same time that engineer Paul Baran began to develop his theories on distributed networks. Reviewing Senate hearings on the bombing, I conclude that the perfect network is an ideological fantasy, one that has, at its core, the principle of deviance: of having a break or a rot somewhere in the network, of having circuits—or people—that are unreliable and untrustworthy. From this, I turn to the architectural collective Ant Farm, which offered a very different vision of an information highway in 1970 and 1971—one reliant on trucks circulating on the interstate highway to carry packets of data—to suggest that in order to approach the perceptual effects of the cloud, one must first think of the network unobscured by the effects of technology.

In chapter 2, "Time-Sharing and Virtualization," I examine the prehistory of what we now call "cloud computing," the idea that computer power—along with the software programs and networks associated with them—could be "piped" into a user's home, like electricity or other utilities. This vision came out of the early 1960s, with the invention of a technology called time-sharing, which allowed the million-dollar cost of a computer to be shared and the computer multitasked. Though mostly forgotten, time-sharing not only invented the modern idea of a user—a personal subject that "owns" his or her data—but also positioned that user within a political economy that makes a user synonymous with his or her usage, and encourages users to take (even steal) computer resources for free. The freedom that results, however, is a deeply ambiguous one, for the same technologies that allow files and user accounts to be made private in the cloud—known as virtualization software—also represent a subtle form of control. This chapter uses the metaphor of an ancient technology, the sewer system, to understand how the cloud keeps each household's private business private even as it extends the armature of the state or the corporation into individual homes.

Chapter 3, "Data Centers and Data Bunkers," traces the cloud of data back to the data centers that store them. These massive warehouses at the heart of the cloud cost up to $1 billion each to build and contain virtually every form of data imaginable, including airline tickets, personnel records, streaming video, pornography, and financial transactions. Interestingly, a number of data centers enclose data inside repurposed Cold War military bunkers. This suggests an unexpected consequence: the sovereign's rationale for a bunker or a keep, to defend an area of territory, has now become transported to the realm of data. Digital networks do not transcend territorial logic; even as data bunkers allow networks to be divided into logical zones of inside and outside, they raise the specter of attack from those that might be "outside" to network society, such as Chinese hackers or Iranian cyberwarfare specialists. By revisiting Paul Virilio's classic text *Bunker Archaeology*, I suggest that the specter of a disaster that the cloud continually raises also carries within it a temporality of our imagined death. This temporality animates a recent series of digital preservation projects, such as the "digital genome" time capsule, intended to survive the "death of the digital."

In chapter 4, "Seeing the Cloud of Data," I continue the discussion of data-centric tools by examining the ways that companies, users, and states navigate the piles of data by "targeting" information. As I show, targeted marketing campaigns online come out of the same ideological apparatus as military targeting, and I take up this militarized aspect to offer a more complete picture of data mining. Two oppositional groups provide case studies for this chapter. First, I examine a group of radio-frequency hackers who started data-mining the 2011 NATO intervention in Libya, in effect turning war into a problem of "big data." Next, I turn to artist/geographer Trevor Paglen, who has obsessively used data-gathering techniques to photograph what he calls "blank spots on the map"—reconnaissance satellites used to spy on us, and covert desert airstrips used to run the CIA's extraordinary rendition program, which secretly transferred foreign prisoners to torture sites outside of US soil. However these "hacktivists" may posit a mode of countersurveillance, their tactics mimic a militarized state's own operations; for this reason, these tactics may only end up reanimating the very structures of power that they purport to expose or overturn. This duplicative structure is part of a logic I call the sovereignty of data, which co-opts the opposition's participation and gives practices such as torture and extraordinary rendition new life within the cloud.

Writing about violence within the cloud is difficult because the violence is largely displaced elsewhere. Rob Nixon, for example, has incisively pointed to the contrast between the supposedly real-time nature of the Gulf War and what he terms the "slow violence" of its aftermath.[30] The story of the Gulf War—so critics and writers tell us—is one of networks and screens, of virtually instantaneous strikes by computer, of what one journalist dubbed the "Hundred Hour War." Yet the story of the depleted uranium munitions released during combat (and their 4.5-billion-year lifespan) is not as easy to tell. Environmental problems, Nixon concludes, are difficult to narrate through conventional forms: "Stories—tightly framed in time, space, and point of view—are convenient places for concealing bodies."[31]

Nixon's insight is applicable beyond the realm of environmental activism (and the environmental footprint of the cloud); the cloud, too, enacts its own form of slow violence. The constantly changing platforms of digital technology seem to call out for, as Peter Lunenfeld puts it, "doing theory and criticism in real time"—namely, responding to each event of digital culture as quickly as possible.[32] Yet the cloud, this book argues, causes a double displacement: the displacement of place itself from sight, but also a temporal displacement. *A Prehistory of the Cloud* attempts to reframe this discussion. It places the digital cloud in dialogue with objects and spaces on the other side of the analog/digital divide. Both interacting with and stepping back from the current moment, it explores the limits and potentialities of a slower form of writing that takes seriously the temporal disjunctions and dislocations within the idea of the cloud. In doing so, I hope to shed light on the hybrid construction I have called the sovereignty of data, a construction that joins war and security, users and use value, participation and opposition. As I argue in this book, looking at the cloud's technology is not enough to tell the story. In truth, the technology has produced the means of its own interpretation, the lens ("cloud") through which power is read, the crude map by which we understand the world. That is the tail wagging the dog. Begin with space, power, and the combination we call history. Then the cloud will follow.

1   THE SHAPE OF THE NETWORK

The Graft

Here is how you tear up railroad track. "The jaw of a giant loader plucked up railroad ties in its teeth. A wheelbarrow-like contraption sucked up bolts and spikes, and spit them out. Guys in hardhats snipped off power cables and yanked down wire fences."[1] Stripped for metal during World War II, railroads are now stripped for tax reasons. Gradually, thousands of miles of track have been abandoned since peaking at 254,000 miles in 1916;[2] the pace has only sped up since deregulation in 1980. In photographer Mark Ruwedel's *Central Pacific #18* (1994), you can see the track bed exposed and eroding (figure 1.1). A pile of bent trestles along the side disrupts the symmetry of the composition. The familiar parallel lines of a railroad track heading to the vanishing point seem to signal another vanishing: the railroad, that technology of the machine age, itself heading for obsolescence.

But the relatively recent gouges and tire marks in Ruwedel's photograph suggest that the railroad has not been swept aside entirely by new technologies. In fact, the relationship between old and new is a complicated one, because beneath the abandoned railroad bed from the nineteenth century lies fiber-optic cable, technology of the twenty-first century. In 1978, the track's owner, the Southern Pacific Railroad, realized that it could sell excess capacity on its network—heretofore used for internal communications, such as train signaling—to corporate customers. A few years later, the Southern Pacific spun off this telecommunications division, the Southern Pacific Railroad Internal Network; its new acronym was SPRINT. Around ten years later, it spun off a second company, Southern Pacific Telecommunications Company, later renamed Qwest, to run fiber beneath its rights-of-way. Together,

Figure 1.1
Mark Ruwedel, *Central Pacific #18*, from the series *Westward the Course of Empire*. Gelatin silver print, 8 × 10 in., 1994. Courtesy of Mark Ruwedel.

the corporate descendants of a single railroad company comprise two of the six major fiber-optic carriers of the US Internet (figure 1.2).[3]

This chapter begins by contending that new and old medias are layered on top of each other, just as the railroad track is layered with fiber-optic conduit. The process of media change causes "old media" to be forgotten in our cultural memory, almost as if a box has been buried, and then the map or route to it abandoned. We know or remember it is there somewhere, but are unable to see it. Though digital technologies seem to change faster than the observer can record, its physical traces are slower to change. By examining the physical geography of digital networks, we can see the spaces where the old has been displaced, and where new media, such as that of the Internet, are layered, adjacent, or even intertwined with far older mediums. Buildings and built landscapes, such as railroad tracks and other infrastructures, are the slowest medium of all, taking years to construct and then an order of magnitude longer to decay. Paradoxically, because space is arguably

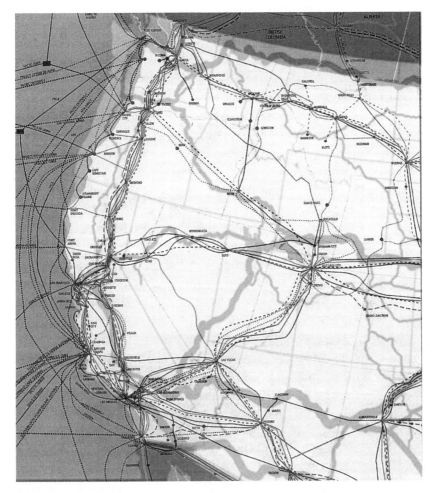

Figure 1.2
Overlay of fiber-optic routes and railroad routes. *Sources:* KMI Corp., "North American Fiberoptic Long-Haul Routes," 1999; U.S. Department of Transportation, Federal Railroad Administration, 2010. (KMI was acquired by CRU Group, crugroup.com, in 2006.)

always being made obsolete by the daily practice of bodies walking through and interacting with space, the built environment may be an ideal location for observing displacement and media change.

It may appear odd to begin a book about digital networks by following the transcontinental rights of way granted in the 1860s by the Pacific Railway Acts. I do so, however, to offer a puzzle: even as digital networks seem to annihilate or deterritorialize physical space, space seems to continually reappear, often as an unwanted flaw in the system.[4] A new $1.5 billion fiber-optic cable across the Arctic will shave between twenty and sixty milliseconds off the route from Tokyo to London for stock market traders, but the toxic metals used in their electronics inevitably end back up in the bodies of laborers manning poorly regulated disassembly plants in China.[5] Their bodies are absent from the picture, just as the Chinese bodies of railroad workers are absent from nineteenth-century railroad photographs.

When cloud computing enters into the picture, this puzzle becomes particularly complicated, because the cloud buries or hides its physical location by design. The cloud is so named because the Internet has traditionally been represented as a cloud in network diagrams: it "has no fixed topology and typically covered varying geographic areas."[6] The cloud thus offers a vision of globalization that follows the dictates of a multinational corporation—a coalition of geographic areas that move capital and resources through the most efficient path. Just as it is cheaper for Apple to use Ireland as its tax domicile to avoid paying US taxes on its French operations, for example, it is more efficient for Facebook to serve some of its Japanese customers from a Singapore data center.

But if the cloud has turned geography into the virtual flows of market capital, it has also spawned a number of equally virtual political movements that challenge this vision. At the same time that networks describe the newly dematerialized corporate structures, they also have shaped capital's seeming opposite: antiglobalization protests. The loosely organized Occupy Wall Street protests seemed, like the Internet, to be resistant to the "hierarchical centralization of 'the mob,'" even creating, one political scientist claims, a new form of "cloud protesting."[7] Yet as much as the Occupy protests were enabled by social media, they have also been very much about occupying specific buildings, public places, and locales. As Etienne Balibar points out, any sort of deterritorializing communications technology is dialectically related to its opposite: "the constitution of a network is also of course a reterritorialization."[8]

If the cloud represents a new reconfiguration of the relationship between place and placelessness, it is clear that relationship directly affects the organization of contemporary power. What this chapter attempts to do is to offer a more precise structure of the cloud, one that accounts for both aspects of this dialectic. It starts by asking a simpler question: where is the cloud's network in physical space?

Because of geographic limitations, the route from Salt Lake City to the San Francisco Bay Area has been the final leg in a number of American transcontinental networks, and therefore it offers a rich site for exploring the layering or copresence of multiple technologies. That route was the last segment of the railroad and telegraph systems, joined at Promontory, Utah, in 1869; the telephone system, joined at Wendover, Utah, in 1914, which AT&T, referring to the railroad's Golden Spike, celebrated as the "Golden Splice"; the national television network, dubbed the "electronic Pony Express" and completed in 1951; and finally the ARPAnet, a predecessor to the Internet, which joined the University of Utah to the Stanford Research Institute in 1969. (A transcontinental communications system was, as one might expect, impeded by the difficulty of the terrain; harsh weather, even the lack of available water, made this route the last to be constructed. Salt in the air corroded telephone electronics, while gophers were reported to have attacked coaxial cable casings.[9])

The location and extent of the network fundamentally affected the network's shape and structure. Before the transcontinental system came into place, each type of network contained pockets of isolation or asynchrony: nineteenth-century mail networks were unreliable and, consequently, western states were often out of date with news in the East; midcentury television stations showed primarily local programming and broadcast local news; even ARPAnet's research nodes were built for different computing capabilities: Utah's facilities were for computer graphics, while the Stanford Research Institute specialized in databases.[10] In almost every case, the completion of the network across the desert had profoundly centralizing tendencies: the railroad tied the nation's goods and passengers together, standardizing clocks in the process by creating "railroad time"; telephone service gave rise to the largest and wealthiest monopoly on earth, the Bell System; television broadcast schedules were coordinated to deliver a uniform American audience to advertisers.

Yet ARPAnet and the eventual Internet seemed to be different. With its distributed structure, it seemed to resist centralization; indeed, its structure held the potential to radically transform the shape of communications. In his seminal paper "On Distributed Communications Networks" (1962), computer scientist Paul Baran offers a diagram that illustrates three major network topologies, from centralized ("star") to decentralized ("tree") to distributed ("mesh" or "cloud") (figure 1.3).[11] It has become virtually an article of faith among scholars of new media that network design has progressed from the

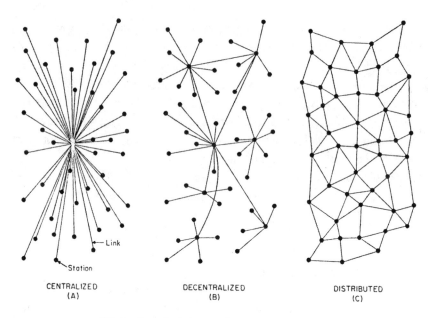

FIG. I — Centralized, Decentralized and Distributed Networks

Figure 1.3
Paul Baran, "Centralized, Decentralized and Distributed Networks," 1962. Reproduced with permission of The RAND Corp.

first to the last shape over time, resulting in a distributed network called the Internet.[12] As evidence, these scholars cite the movement away from the centralized, command-and-control structures of US Air Force computer rooms to ARPAnet and the contemporary Internet. This model of rupture remains a seductive myth because it explains the dispersion of power through the formal qualities of the computer networks that supposedly enable it.

One problem, however: the distributed network, as designed by Baran, was never built. Stephen Lukasik, former director of ARPA, points out that Baran's proposed system "had many features still sorely lacking in the public Internet forty years later: redundancy to withstand heavy attacks yet fail gracefully as links were severed; high reliability; security."[13] Indeed, a truly distributed network is almost impossible to create, because of economic, political, and even geographic considerations (it is hard to run fiber-optic cable across mountains). As a result, virtually all traffic on the US Internet runs across the same routes established in the nineteenth century, a point that is readily visible when looking at network diagrams, which have changed remarkably little since Baran's day. It is worth remembering that the fiber-optic cables that run from Salt Lake City to the San Francisco Bay Area are in the same position they always have been, since the telegraph: in the immediate vicinity of railroad tracks.

(I have been using the case of the US Internet because it is both the largest and most-developed network and also the network that most scholars describe as "open" and distributed. In cases such as the Chinese Internet, described as the Party-controlled "Great Firewall of China," it should be clear that there is nothing inherently decentralizing about Internet technology. As I suggested in my introduction, the relative lack of attention to non-Western Internets results in the elision of place from "the Internet," and the collapse of a multitude of networks into a single, monolithic cloud—itself an ironically centralizing ideology.)

What we realize is that the structure of the US Internet is bifurcated. On a logical level, we see communication patterns that may resemble a distributed network—although the fact that cloud computing concentrates our files into the data centers of a few underlying service providers, such as Google and Amazon Web Services, complicates this theory.[14] This seemingly distributed network is built, however, on top of a layer that can only be centripetal in nature, whether approached from the question of access—one or two broadband companies per population center, such as Comcast and the local telephone monopoly; the market dominance of a handful of wireless carriers, such as Verizon and AT&T—or from the level of infrastructure, where six telecommunications companies control the vast majority of the routes.[15] And so the introduction of interoperable protocols such as Internet Protocol, or IP, is like the situation of railroad barons: when they began to widely adopt standard gauge after 1863, interoperability between their networks only increased their concentration of power.

Seen properly, the structure of the Internet resembles a *graft*: a newer network grafted on top of an older, more established network. In this metaphor, preexisting infrastructures, such as the rail network, are like rootstock, while the newer fiber-optic cables resemble the uppermost portion, known in horticulture as the scion. Neither half, rootstock or scion, describes the full story; yet it is almost impossible to look at the whole. Looking at the shape of the more recent and more visible part, the distributed network, is like looking up at tree branches silhouetted against a bright sky in a low-angle shot of a forest. From below, looking at the newest growth, the branches appear to resemble a series of loosely but densely interconnected structures—possibly even a rhizome, a mesh, or a cloud. (Looking at the older part, we see only a single, centralized trunk.) But these two parts are integral and interconnected: the scion takes life and nutrition from the grafted rootstock, and the qualities of the rootstock (sturdiness, survivability, its connection with terrain) transport themselves in indirect ways to the scion. To look at the middle point of union, to think both parts at the same time, is not just "arboreal"; it is historical.[16]

As a graft, the Internet is always already a historical object, and the next stage of its development is never a complete rupture from its past. As such, when scholars liken the shape of power to the shape of the network, citing its manifestations in protest movements or terror groups,[17] they inevitably refer to the distributed network, the top layer, or the scion. But territorial politics also threaten to periodically erupt from below, entering the root structure of the present in the way that the Latin *terrere* enters the etymology of both territory and terror.[18] Rather than dismiss these threats as aberrations from a now-forgotten past, we might understand them as part and parcel of the structure of the graft. For one increasingly begins to suspect that the rapid proliferation of networks may be common cause of both "electronic" and "territorial" wars.

It is this book's contention that the graft may have more than a descriptive use; the graft may also serve as a method of analysis, a way of uncovering a structural relationship between power and networks. To understand the irruption of war (specifically, the older, nominally obsolescent variety concerned with territory) into network culture, I will move between the present day and the Cold War era when the Internet's predecessor networks were designed. Looking for the legacy of electronic wars in the empty spaces of the desert West, we will find our first case study in 1961, the first documented moment of the American telecommunications network coming under attack; after that, we will briefly consider another Cold War infrastructure that has shaped the Internet: the interstate highway system.

But let us first set the table for this discussion by reviewing the historical claims that surround the Internet's origins, one that Alexander Galloway sums up as follows: "the Internet was invented to avoid certain vulnerabilities of a nuclear attack."[19] The old shape of war, exemplified by cities such as Hiroshima or Nagasaki, is a "strategic massing of power," easily targeted in an atomic strike. But for Galloway as for other scholars including Hardt and Negri, the "Internet has a different diagram than a nuclear attack; *it is in a different shape*. And that new shape happens to be immune to the older."[20] Like the just-so stories of how tigers got their stripes, or rhinoceroses their horns, there is something captivating in this story of how the network got its shape. The idea of the bomb appears to explain a number of things: the network lacks a central location because a center would make a good target. Urban planners responded to the atomic threat by dispersing industrial targets away from urban centers;[21] and this dispersion also seems to influence an entirely new invention: the network as Internet.

Indeed, the claim may even appear self-evident when one reads Paul Baran's first paper (1960) on survivable communications networks, a paper published two years before his now-famous diagram of network shapes (figure 1.3). In it, Baran imagines how to maintain some continuity of government in the worst-case scenario, and describes, as an example, a distributed network of congressmen scattered across the country. Some—many, even—are killed in a nuclear strike, but the surviving members of Congress may be able to cast votes from their home offices. This paper opens with a steely evocation of survival after the mushroom clouds dissipate: "If war does not mean the end of the earth in a black and white manner, then it follows that we should do . . . all the things necessary to permit the survivors of the holocaust to shuck their ashes and reconstruct the economy swiftly."[22]

It is because of Baran's 1960 paper that one of the most widely held beliefs about the Internet began to propagate. Yet by now, this claim has been well debunked; it comes out of a series of confusions, between Baran's 1960 paper and a paper written two years later, and between the Internet and its earlier incarnation, ARPAnet. (ARPAnet scientists cited, but did not implement, Baran's 1962 paper, and even in that 1962 paper, Baran had moved away from the nuclear rhetoric of his previous paper. Weapons salvoes were now merely a special case of a more general principle, that of link reliability and interference.[23]) Baran's network was never built, and we are several generations removed from its nuclear logic.

If the Internet never had this nuclear-proof shape, then why do scholars continually tell or write this idea back into existence? In other words, I'm interested less in debunking the myth than in the reason that it persists in digital culture, reanimated in the popular imagination of a digital cloud shaped like the elegant mesh of Baran's diagram. There is, in short, a collective desire to keep the myth alive despite evidence to the contrary. This desire, after all, is symptomatic not only of how media historians explain the Internet's origins, but is, more generally, symptomatic of our method. To want another opinion; to doubt received history; to read history against the grain; these are all signs, in academia, of good scholarship.

I purposely bring up the question of media scholarship rather than the network itself because it's important to recognize that scholars are implicated in an intellectual quest that is not far from paranoia—a word that is not meant as a pejorative. Where else can one find the belief that a single idea, the network, links "drug cartels, terror groups, black hat hacker crews," with "corporate management techniques, manufacturing supply chains, advertising campaigns," except inside a Thomas Pynchon novel?[24] But on a more general level, how else can we take the act of interpretation—the act of finding meaning within disorder, the "reflex of seeking other orders behind the visible," as Pynchon once glossed paranoia—that scholars of digital culture, myself included, so often engage in? I am surely not the only teacher who has been accused by a student of engaging in conspiracy theories when I read too much between the lines of a text or shots of a film, or when I piece together information from disparate sources and disciplines to weave a web or a network.

Let me pause here to underscore a semantic point. I'm intentionally engaging in some slippage between network as a physical object (the Internet) and network as a metaphor for knowledge, because, I'm arguing, the network is always more than its digital or physical infrastructure. The network is a primarily the idea that "everything is connected," and, as such, is a product of a system of belief. The reader will readily observe that when I use the word "network," I mean something a little different from its common definition. Because reality can never match up to that system of belief, because, in fact, not everything is connected, the network exists primarily as a state of *desire*.

Studying the metro Detroit area in 1972, the architect and urban planner Constantinos Doxiadis declared: "Our child, our city is sick. We look only at the symptoms and we do not understand the causes. We are frightened. The mother goes out in the street and screams."[25] To illustrate his point, this architect printed photographs of a spider's web before and after ingesting amphetamines; the second picture, taken twelve hours after ingestion, is compared to Detroit's road network, one of the symptoms of postwar dispersion from an urban core. A bad network is likened to a bad drug trip. The messy road network demands, for Doxiadis, a single solution. "We must coordinate *all* of our Networks *now*. All networks, from roads to telephones."[26] Yet the solution—a network of networks, the same desire that led to what we now call the Internet—is itself a malady; it is Doxiadis's case that causes critic Mark Wigley to retroactively label him as one of the first patients suffering from "network fever."[27] Network fever is the desire to connect *all* networks, indeed, the desire to connect every piece of information to another piece. And to construct a system of knowledge where everything is connected is, as psychoanalysis tells us, the sign of paranoia.

In other words, network fever cannot be separated from the network, because the network is its fever. The cloudlike nature of the network has much less to do with its structural or technological properties than the way that we perceive and understand it; seen properly, the cloud resides within us. It is crucial to keep this in mind as we enter the Cold War era in the next section; there, we will examine the first moment when the American communications network became part of the nation's critical infrastructure, something to be protected against foreign (even nuclear) attack. While I have put paranoia on the table as a potential lens through which to understand the network, I'm not trying to establish that a Cold War network was paranoid—a tautological definition if there ever was one. Rather, I hope to understand how a specific way of thinking networks and connectivity in 1961–1962 has continued to structure our vision to this day, long after the physical network has been dismantled and replaced by a new one. Just as abandoned railroad tracks have left a barely visible channel across the desert West, these Cold War forms linger inside the cloud but are visible only in their absence. It is to these ghosts that I now turn.

"Strange and Unusual Fits," 1961

There was, in fact, one recorded attack on the network, but it did not come from a missile hurtling through the air, or anything nuclear-related. On May 29, 1961, an edgy nation woke up to discover that three microwave towers had been dynamited by unknown saboteurs the previous morning. Crucially, these relays, located in remote locations in the Great Salt Lake desert, not only glued together the transcontinental telephone system, but also formed part of the national defense circuit. For a tense four hours, the explosion affected everything from the Strategic Air Command and the Conelrad emergency warning system to Associated Press teletype and civilian radio circuits. Various rumors suggested that it could have been the work of Soviet agents—General Maxwell E. Rich, commander of the Utah National Guard, thought that the Soviets might be monitoring how fast the nation responded to an emergency, while an unnamed military officer on the scene recalled that Soviet trawlers had once dredged up submarine cables.[28] Air Force General Curtis LeMay cited a published report stating that the perpetrators bore the hallmarks of training from an East German school of sabotage.[29]

Whoever the culprit was, the reaction was swift and immediate. Six states deployed soldiers and national guardsmen to their relay stations and signal towers; as a precaution, Bell facilities as far away as Illinois received armed sentries. In Los Angeles alone, a nervous sheriff summoned all seven thousand deputies to report for duty. The governor of Utah rushed to inspect the scene of destruction, which left concrete and aluminum debris twisted into the volcanic rocks, a sharp smell of battery acid in the air, and—most oddly—a white field of Styrofoam bits, a result of the microwave lens's unusual construction.[30] *Newsweek* captured the scene well: "The desolate wastes of the Great Salt Lake Desert suddenly swarmed with investigators—civil and military."[31] Meanwhile, temporary circuits had to be installed: a Globemaster cargo plane landed the same evening at Wendover Air Force Base carrying more personnel and portable microwave equipment; so much equipment, in fact, that the phone technicians wondered how they would load them onto their company trucks.

This was the first act of sabotage directed against the nation's transcontinental communications circuits, and it signaled a shift in the way the nation understood communications: previously invisible lines in the desert had suddenly been exposed. The centralized Bell System upon which the nation relied had begun to exhibit cracks, even if its officials rushed to assure the nation that defense circuits had been rerouted within ninety seconds. (The actual response time turned out to be far longer.) More important for our story, the bombing of the Bell System occurred during a moment when scientists were designing distributed networks to survive similar attacks. In other words, the bombing made real a largely abstract fear—that war might destroy a centralized communications network. Because this was front-page news, Baran almost certainly read about it as he was revising a paper that he would publish as "On Distributed Networks" a year later.[32] So two things

happened that year: the technological network came into being, simultaneously with another kind of network—network understood as conspiracy.

A group calling itself the American Republican Army eventually took
credit for the attack. It was later discovered to be an army with a "rather
slim" membership of two, namely, Jerome Brouse, age fifty-one, a construction worker with a grudge against AT&T's monopoly, wearing a fake six-
shooter in his holster, and a partner, Dale Chris Jensen, age thirty-three. Yet
because the bombing affected the system as a whole, the 1961 event seemed,
at the time, to result from something rotten in the political system. Writing
for the *New Republic*, journalist Gerald Johnson saw the bombing as symptomatic of a national "atmosphere of conspiracy." Why shouldn't a nation see
everything as a "counterplot" or "plot," Johnson asked, when it had been told
by its government that "half the world is engaged in a great and infamous
plot against it, and that it can trust nobody?"[33] The secretive atmosphere of
government breeds a corresponding rise in secret societies, Johnson wrote;
the supposed left-wing plots by Communists create a corresponding rise in
right-wing groups such as the American Republican Army.

Before the culprits were caught, another rumor circulated that the
bombing was a test by another branch of the government: a rumor almost
too strange to believe outside an "atmosphere of conspiracy," yet a rumor
matched and even exceeded by later conspiracy theories on the supposed
governmental origins of the Kennedy assassination and 9/11. Yet there was
something specific about the Bell System as the locus of conspiracy. Conspiracy, by definition, is concerned with systems; it connects seemingly
unrelated pieces of information, weaving them into systems. In 1961, the Bell
System was not only the largest and wealthiest corporation in the world (as
Life proudly noted the following month), but it was also the technological
system by which corporations, governments, and individuals spoke to each
other. The bombers in the American Republican Army called AT&T a "cartel,"
but it turned out to be far more: AT&T *was* the Pynchonesque system of paranoia in which "everything is connected."

Push a little further into the story of the bombing and we begin to see
something unexpected. A seller of janitorial supplies sporting a Castro-style
beard and imagining himself as an entire army triggers the actual army
to respond; there is an almost comical relationship between the very routine business of AT&T and the gravity of a national emergency. As the legal
records show, accident and emergency are intimately connected, and the two

ends of the spectrum can be flipped at any moment. To see what I mean, let us turn to the halls of the Senate.

On June 7, about a month later, the Senate Internal Security Subcommittee (SISS) took up a bill to safeguard defense communications, which had almost certainly been rushed to the docket because of the attack. Bill 1990's sponsor, Senator Thomas Dodd of Connecticut (who would later be indicted for corruption by the same committee), was absent, but submitted a written statement opening with an ominous description of "a person or persons unknown" who had sabotaged "3,000 interstate communications" circuits in Utah and Nevada, many of which, Dodd continued, were essential to military and civilian defense.

Dodd's bill was a relatively simple one that extended the anti-sabotage law to all defense-related circuits, not just federally owned ones; in fact, it was a resubmission of a bill that hadn't made it to the Senate floor the previous year because of time limitations. But it was a strange hearing: with the bombing on everyone's minds, photographs of the attack were appended to the Senate record. What ought to have been routine business became a matter of grave national security, yet, at the same time, the senators wondered what to do if the destruction turned out to be the result of a worker on strike or even a prankster: "some boy that likes to hear something pop off," or who might "stub the toe of a Western Union messenger."[34] Comical scenarios, perhaps, but to this day, crucial communication lines are disrupted accidentally all the time, typically by a farmer or a construction worker digging with a backhoe: in 2009, the *Washington Post* reported on the phenomenon of black Chevrolet Suburbans arriving at construction sites. Suited government agents tended to show up minutes after an accidental cut of a classified (and thus unmarked) fiber route.[35] The *Post* even offered a name for classified cable routes: "black wire." So the distinction between the emergency and the accident was already wearing thin in 1961, and fifty years later, it seems to have eroded away entirely.

Moreover, in the hearing, it wasn't clear what defense system—or what circuits—they were talking about securing. The senators and the military men approached this question first with a list of examples and acronyms, among them the Ballistic Missile Early-Warning System (BMEWS), the mid-Canada line, the Distant Early Warning (DEW) Line, the Missile Defense Alarm System (MIDAS), etc. But the confusion was an epistemological one: General DuPlantis testified that "it is impossible to define 'what is operated and controlled by the United States.'"[36] For if a law is written to protect engi-neered military circuits, that same law "could be interpreted to extend to the entire communications systems" of the Bell System, Western Union, and any other company. Any circuit could, at any moment, become a military circuit. In the event of an emergency, one circuit may take an alternate path; a Des Moines outage might affect both St. Louis and Kansas City. Responding to a question by Senator Roman Hruska—what *is* the network?—DuPlantis testi-fied, in dialogue reminiscent of a Beckett play:

> *General DuPlantis:* Sir, you would never be able to define the system that you had reference to since it is subject to call. As I tried to explain in this rerouting process which goes on all the time, you can't put your finger on the circuits that you will call up. You know where the terminal ends are, but these circuits will take devious paths from minute to minute . . .
>
> *Senator Hruska:* And if some damage to any part thereof occurred, it would be considered damage within the meaning of the law, would it not?
>
> *General DuPlantis:* If you could define which ones you had reference to.
>
> *Senator Hruska:* Well, if they are so comprehensive that it could be any of them.
>
> *General DuPlantis:* This could be true, but it would be very difficult.
>
> *Senator Hruska:* I understand the circuitous business.
>
> *General DuPlantis:* That it goes round and round and you don't know where it goes from minute to minute.[37]

One imagines a slight note of exasperation from the general. Because of the new design for switching networks, the circuits varied from "minute to minute." Thus, for DuPlantis, as it is for scholars of contemporary networks, it was impossible to pin down what the system "is"; the system reroutes itself depending on the need. It is a logical overlay, rather than a physical thing; it is a process, not a static moment; it is a matter of what should not be cov-ered, rather than defining what it does cover. The network is an idea that is resistant to knowing.

The practical result, for DuPlantis, was that the law *must* apply to all cir-cuits, because this is the very design of the network. Concerning the question of "what our requirements for seizure would be," DuPlantis testified: "This, of course, is very nebulous, but . . . we can say we have a requirement for all of it."[38] What could conceivably count as part of the network is "very nebu-lous," echoing the word's Latin origins in *nebule*, cloud: a cloudlike vision that is simultaneously vague and also universal. In the 1950s, AT&T successfully sued an undertaker who gave away a plastic cover for its telephone books for violating its monopoly on telecommunications: it claimed that its network extended even to the act of picking up the Yellow Pages.[39] Like the AT&T lawyer who stumbled across the plastic cover by accident, the committee, too, saw the network in everything that could conceivably be involved in communications, from AT&T lines to Western Union messengers. "All of it": the prime symptom of network fever.

What we take from this hearing is that war circuits are indistinguishable from civilian circuits, because, in a time of emergency, everything will be part of a war circuit. Although the modern packet-switched network had yet to be invented, the idea of the network was beginning to radically reconfigure the relationship between military and civilian spheres, the state of war and the state of exception. And while the rest of this book will explore this issue in more detail, I want to dwell on the implications of DuPlantis's testimony. For there is something richly evocative about his description that "these circuits will take devious paths from minute to minute."

What did DuPlantis mean by "devious"? Attempting to explain this to the senators, the counselor remarked that he had once made an emergency call from Washington to Seattle that needed to be patched through via Atlanta and Minneapolis.[40] In fact, DuPlantis responded, it is even more devious than the counselor's example; machines automatically route calls around broken circuits, so that paths deviate from the norm all of the time. A physical route is suppressed in favor of the logical route; the networked path deviates from the straight path. It is indeed a "circuitous business," as the senator put it.

But there is another context, of course; one that will go a long way toward explaining why the network is a matter of internal security, rather than international security; why there are no discussions of nuclear strikes but plenty of discussion on the limits of regulation. For the word "devious" has a peculiar resonance in the context of the Internal Security subcommittee. Recall that this is the same committee that had become notorious for its inquisitions of "subversives" and communism; the deviant, in this context, would have referred to those who chose a political path deviating from the norm. Serving as the Senate counterpart to the House Un-American Activities Committee (HUAC), the SISS had originally been chartered to investigate acts "including, but not limited to, espionage, sabotage, and infiltration of persons who are or may be under the domination of the foreign government or organization controlling the world Communist movement or any movement seeking to overthrow the Government of the United States by force and violence."[41]

In today's digital culture, deviance is commonly associated with sexual deviance. This is what animates Wendy Hui Kyong Chun's study of the "cyberporn" scares of the 1990s, where anxiety about the network comes from the twenty-first-century paranoid subject, who metaphorically understands fiber-optic cable as nerves of light that penetrate his body and produce a deviant sexual response.[42] And this direction may be a productive one to pursue, as SISS had spent a good part of the 1950s investigating homosexual "deviants" in the State Department as part of the so-called Lavender Scare.

But what the Senate record shows is perhaps less expected: fully half of the June 7 hearing on network security was taken up by a discussion of another kind of political deviation, organized labor. Indeed, the final two witnesses called to the hearing were the president of the Commercial Telegraphers' Union and the counsel for the American Civil Liberties Union. The witnesses were concerned that telecommunications workers exercising their legitimate right to strike might, under the new law, be detained for national security reasons, even as they pledge to suspend those rights, out of patriotism, during a time of war.[43] And the last time the Bell System had been disrupted was during a period of labor unrest—the only time before Wendover that the robustness of defense circuits had been tested. During a 1957 Communications Workers of America strike, a worker acting on his own had dynamited Southern Bell lines in Jackson, Mississippi; this, General Bestic remembered, was the last time he testified about defense communications. The same committee's investigations of alleged Communists in Southern labor unions were undoubtedly still on his mind.

The network that the committee saw was the network within the network, as it were: the shadow of organized labor over the telephone lines, what filmmaker Caroline Martel, in her documentary on female phone operators, called "the phantom operator." And, indeed, there was a long-standing connection between the threat of labor and the misrouted message. In 1907, *Le Cri Postal*, the newspaper of the Postmen and Telegrapher's union, made this fear explicit: "What you will never be able to prevent is that some fine day the letters and telegrams from Lille take a little stroll around Perpignan. . . . What you cannot avoid is that the telephone wires be simultaneously tangled and the telegraphic instruments take strange and unexplainable fits. What you will never prevent is that ten thousand workers remain at their places, but with their arms crossed."[44]

The crossed signals of a network become the crossed arms of labor; the "strange and unexplainable fits" that indicate a technical glitch are the paths that the wires will take absent the maintenance that labor puts into it. Though the histories of labor and telecommunications have been intertwined from the start, the former tends to drop out of its telling, and infrastructure has come to exclusively stand for computer machinery. Even as labor itself has been written out of the network's history, however, the tangled wires haunt the senders of the signals. Signals are sent to one place only to reappear elsewhere; the counselor's emergency calls travel through Atlanta to eventually get to Minneapolis. The goal of the distributed (or "self-healing") network is that circuits will automatically reroute themselves without human intervention—a design that is at the very heart of the cloud, where networks, servers, and applications alike can crash or fail without requiring intervention. But behind this is an ideology that the tangle of wire with worker can be permanently separated.

I have used the example of labor to correct a mythology that focuses on the network as a Cold War weapon against Soviet threats. But the larger issue at stake is that what I am calling the network—a way of thinking the connectedness between individual events—is always an "internal affair," a matter of thinking internal deviations. Whether this is the State Department worker suspected of homosexuality, or the worker suspected of belonging to part of a devious network, the network is always already internally focused. This is a complicated point because, again, I am using the network as a specific epistemological stance: one that, as Chun has argued, "does not respond to an overwhelming, all-seeing power but rather to a power found to be lacking—rotten and inadequate, always decaying. Paranoid knowledge similarly responds to technologies' vulnerabilities, even as it denies them."[45]

Earlier we observed that epistemological difficulty—the "very nebulous," cloudlike nature of definitions—is what led the committee to define everything as part of the network. The perfect network is where everything is connected and the network is omnipresent; "network fever" afflicts military planners and media scholars alike. This fantasy of the universal network has, at its core, the principle of deviance: of having a break or a rot somewhere in the network, of having circuits—or people—that are unreliable and untrustworthy, of not being able to know for sure "where it goes," or who is breaking it.

What I mean by the network's nebulousness is the opacity through which any given circuit is seen, a usage that recalls the well-known phrase "the fog of war." This opacity means that the paranoid subject can't tell friend from enemy, and is threatened by that which allows friend and enemy to mix. If friend can appear as enemy and vice versa, then the paranoid subject may lash out against certain manifestations of this phenomenon. But the ultimate target of her anger is the system behind these phenomena. In other words, the paranoid subject's goal is to bring down this system. Yet to expose this system is also to unravel the system of paranoid knowledge—the connections between two seemingly unrelated persons, ideas, or events—that she has laboriously woven together. Because creating the system of connections is synonymous with exposing or unraveling the system, creating the system is synonymous with the act of pulling it apart.

But the irony, of course, is that this is a system that she has herself constructed: it is a way of mapping the external world onto an internal system of knowledge, a cognitive map that attempts to explain the world's totality. This map is deeply self-referential; at its center is a dot that always reads YOU ARE HERE, for the map is ultimately a way of translating the external world into the paranoid subject's own body. Or as Richard Hofstadter wrote in his now-classic essay on paranoia in American politics, "It is hard to resist the conclusion that this enemy is on many counts the projection of the self."[46] This is what makes paranoia a type of autoimmune disease. It would be one thing if the system were external to the paranoid subject; but the system is *her* system of knowledge. Only she can see the connections, and only she can unravel it. So what the paranoid subject seeks to destroy is something entirely internal to her; it is her worldview, indeed, her body, that is destroyed.

As rumor went, the 1961 bombing was a symptom of one branch of government attacking another. As outlandish as this fantasy was, it nevertheless revealed the paranoid logic taken to its extreme, in which the state attacks itself, as if ridding itself of its internal diseases. The paranoid principle, in which everything is connected, is intimately related to its opposite, a world where nothing is connected. In extreme cases, a paranoid system of knowledge will attack its own system of connectivity—most literally, the communications network that it had once built—in order to unravel this world of connectivity. Paranoia, by definition, contains the seeds of both radical connectivity and radical disconnection.

Just as certain autoimmune diseases, such as multiple sclerosis, attack the body's nervous system—the body's communications network—we might expect the target of a paranoid structure of power to be its own telephone networks, or even the Internet. Theory is not intended to have predictive value, but one recent case is nevertheless suggestive. When Egypt's rulers found themselves threatened by mass protests in the winter of 2011, they dispatched the intelligence service to the Ramses Exchange in Cairo, a building that housed a data exchange for Egypt's leading Internet service providers, to shut down the Egyptian Internet. The popular media surmised that its providers were coerced through various technological weapons, such as attacking the BGP routing tables that direct Internet traffic. But it appears that the security services took a simpler approach: on January 28, 2011, at 12:28 a.m., breaker switches were thrown and routers powered down; phone calls to the providers convinced any less-connected holdouts to terminate service. (In other words, the most-connected providers were the most vulnerable to this shutdown.) Cell phone service was also cut, though it was restored the next day, and the Internet was not operational until February 2, six days later.

During those six days, many businesses could not function; banks and the stock exchange had trouble processing electronic transactions. *Forbes* later estimated that the country had lost roughly $110 million in direct revenue, including call-center jobs that were shifted to New Zealand; the total economic damage was something closer to $1 billion.[47] Warigia Bowman reported that, in the absence of the network, "people were forced to rely on traditional means of communication, including knocking on doors, going to the mosque, assembling in the street, or other central gathering places"—places such as Tahrir Square.[48] Far from tamping down the protests, the regime's Internet shutdown may have inadvertently hastened the regime's downfall.

Jacques Derrida has suggested that the common logics after 9/11, such as "terrorism," have increasingly begun to align otherwise disparate movements into a paranoid system. This paranoia, Derrida argues, is ultimately a type of autoimmune disease in which "repression . . . ends up producing, reproducing, and regenerating the very thing which it seeks to disarm": the war on terror, for example, only produces the very terrorism it is meant to eradicate.[49] It would be incorrect to consider terror a new phenomenon that has arisen since the weakening of nation-states after the Cold War. Perhaps the first historical moment of modern terrorism, Derrida argues, was the Reign of Terror, carried out in the name of the French state. Since terror, in other words, is an integral part of how a state wields sovereign power, terrorism after 9/11 must be understood within that context.[50]

Thus when scholars write about a new form of distributed power invented to immunize us from the nuclear strike, and, more generally, from the older forms of war that it represents, something seems to go awry. The supposed immunity of the Internet instead leads to what Derrida calls "that strange behavior where a living being, in quasi-suicidal fashion, itself makes to destroy its own protection . . . its own immunity."[51] Years after the Internet supposedly immunizes us from nuclear threat, that threat returns in the form of networked viruses that target the turbines of Iranian nuclear reactors, a cyberwarfare tactic that the New York Times described as a first step toward "mutually assured cyberdestruction."[52]

The implication of Derrida's analysis is that the most extreme cases of repression may produce the most extreme response. Seen in this light, the Egypt case become even more interesting. Numerous commentators claimed that the so-called Internet kill switch in Egypt could never happen in more democratic and networked environments, such as the United States. Set aside, for a moment, the rather patronizing nature of these proclamations. What I want to argue is the opposite: precisely because the United States is more interconnected, it is more prone to extreme responses. Take perhaps the most networked region in the country, the San Francisco Bay Area, where proximity to the giants of Silicon Valley, such as Cisco, Google, Apple, and so forth, has caused it to be a test bed for technical and government experiments on pervasive networking.

Planners noticed one hole in the network, though: the underground, and specifically the underground transit system. The Bay Area's public transit system, BART, installed wireless antennae in underground stations as early as 2004. Later, it expanded the network to the tunnel beneath San Francisco Bay, so commuters could check their e-mail or make phone calls while crossing from San Francisco to Oakland. But the excess of network connectivity resulted in a familiar scenario. On July 3, 2011, a BART policeman fatally shot a forty-five-year old homeless man wielding a knife. A previous incident, where a white BART policeman fatally shot an unarmed African American man in 2009, had sparked region-wide protests and riots and had resulted in an eventual manslaughter conviction; this time, inflamed citizens gathered on online message boards to discuss protest actions. This chatter made BART officials nervous. Early on the morning of August 11, the day of another planned protest, BART spokesman Linton Johnson sent an e-mail to his transit police: "A whole heck of a lot their ability to carry out this exercise is predicated on being able to communicate with each other. Can't we just shut off wireless mobile phone and Wifi communication in the downtown stations? It's not like it's a constitutional right for BART to provide mobile phone and Wifi service."[53]

Later that morning, after overcoming some dissent, BART's general manager decided to hit the kill switch. In an unprecedented move, cell phone service was shut off system-wide, from the airport through downtown stations. And tactics that had originally come from labor, sending the network into "strange and unexplainable fits," had now been co-opted by management. For contractual reasons, Verizon, Sprint, and AT&T, the three carriers then inside the BART system, were forced to comply. The protest never occurred.

One of the main rationales for the existence of BART's wireless network was that an earthquake might strike while commuters were trapped in the underwater tunnel.[54] BART deployed the network in the name of public safety and then disabled the network in the face of the protest, again in the name of public safety. The BART case may be the first in a series of autoimmune responses to network fever. Rather than reading this shutdown as a one-time exception or an overreaction, I am suggesting that it reveals something systemic about the way that paranoid imagination of networks manifests itself, when the network of Internet-enabled protesters is again conflated with the communications network. Over half a century earlier, a similar flare-up of network fever had authorities wondering whether they could cite a wartime law preventing the disruption of interstate communications to quash a San Diego labor strike against Pacific Telephone and Telegraph in 1947—because Congress had not technically declared the war over, nearly two years after V-J Day.[55] Just as labor strikes were once conflated with the invocation of war, the present moment has increasingly seen different political scenarios flattened into a sparse set of terms: war, terror, protest, network.

The logic that ties the "network of networks" represented by Al Qaeda–affiliated movements with the "cloud protesting" of Occupy, for example, is a sad reminder of this sparseness of language. What we urgently need is a richer vocabulary that captures the complexity of each social movement, a language that is less interpretive than phenomenological. To see what I

Figure 1.4
Still from Francis Ford Coppola, *The Conversation*, 1974.

mean, I offer a fictional example that captures both the extremes of paranoia and possibly a way out.

Francis Ford Coppola's 1974 film *The Conversation* tells the story of a surveillance expert who monitors other people's phone calls and picks up acoustic signals with a boom mike to reconstruct their conversations. This expert is an interpreter who pieces together the network of people supposedly involved in an assassination plot. In the final sequence, he receives a telephone call containing sounds of him alone in his San Francisco apartment, and realizes he has been deceived; he is the one who has been under surveillance (figure 1.4). The camera shows Gene Hackman tearing his own apartment apart looking for the bug, an autoimmune response to the paranoid gaze (or the paranoid ear, in this case). Hackman has hit the breaking point and crossed over to madness.

Commentators have often focused on the madness and on the camera that pans back and forth, like a surveillance camera, as some sort of morality tale: the coldness of technology, or the emotional deadness of the main character. But I'm most drawn to a minor detail, to the question of why Hackman plays a saxophone solo for the surveillance camera. I'm resistant to any claims about the ontology of jazz, but I do think that the contingency of Hackman's alto sax offers a poignant way out of the double-bind of networks and paranoia. To be clear, the music doesn't suggest a way of opting out of the network—indeed, he plays for the camera, and, by implication, for the people watching him. On the soundtrack, there is a simple chord sequence, which Hackman hears as a sort of delusion. And we hear the sequence, too, a sign that we are also implicated in his web of paranoia. Hackman improvises to the chord sequence on the soundtrack, and as improv, there isn't a score; there isn't even a professional musician as such, since Hackman himself is playing the music as an amateur: a strange intrusion of live performance into a canned soundtrack. Hackman's character is still clearly mad; the piece he plays is a deviation, a nonlinear path. Yet he no longer follows that path to make meaning. The reason that the solo is almost completely ignored by film critics is probably because there is nothing left to interpret. It is simply an act of madness.

Instead, the solo is, like the title of this section, full of "strange and unexplainable fits." Partially released from the desire for interpretive meaning, the solo serves to produce only one thing: pleasure. And perhaps that is enough of a lesson to us. If we are not able to escape the throes of network fever, we might as well take pleasure from its deviances.

Truckstop Networks (Portola Valley, California)

Take pleasure, or at least make art. In the 1960s through the 1970s, several groups of engineers from California were trying to find an alternative to the centralized network. Not all of these engineers were working for RAND or other military-funded laboratories, however; many of them were artists. And for them, as for much of the rest of the country, the networks they were designing did not necessarily involve digital data. Instead, at that moment, *television* was the centralized system that needed to be subverted or at least radically redesigned. Network television was a monolithic schedule of programming pumped out by NBC, CBS, ABC, and, until it folded, DuMont: national broadcasters that homogenized the flow of information. The studios broadcast content to the home; information flow was a one-way street—at least before a 1969 Federal Communications Commission decision allowing community access television (CATV), better known as cable. Television delivered the network. But video and cable had the potential to hijack it.

In 1970, the same year that computer scientist John McCarthy asked whether home computer networks could lure TV viewers away from the tube with alternative sources of information, an artist group called Raindance Corporation proposed a "Center for Decentralized Television."[56] A playful parody of the RAND Corporation's 1964 design for a decentralized digital network, its name suggested the design's paradoxically centralizing tendencies. Formed in response to news that the RAND Corporation had begun to study cable networks (or, as one contributor speculated, was developing mind-control techniques), the video collective wrote: "We believe culture needs new information structures, not just improved content pumped through existing ones," and their unrealized "Center" would have served as a regranting agency for video artists.[57] An early issue of the collective's newsletter, *Radical Software*, suggests the thrill of imagining new information structures: the typography of Frank Gillette's piece, "Loop-de-Loop," depicts arrows twisted to form loops that lead nowhere. Claude Ponsot illustrates an article about the structure of cybernetics and guerilla tactics with whimsical mathematical diagrams dubbed "Klein worms," after the topologically impossible Klein bottle. We are still within the ballpark of Baran's network diagrams, but just barely (figure 1.5).

These earlier moments of reconfiguring the network structure hold uncanny parallels to modern-day digital networks. The first page of *Radical Software*'s first issue is an excerpt from Gene Youngblood's book, *The Videosphere*; a later advertisement summarizes his book as a description of a "single unified system, a 'decentralized feedback communication network'" that would unite five different mediums: cable TV, portable video, storage networks, "time-shared computer utilities," and "the domestic satellite system." Youngblood's videosphere is often understood metaphorically, as a reiteration of Marshall McLuhan, but here Youngblood turns his attention to specific networks: the FCC's decision to allow MCI (then called Microwave Communications Inc.) to compete with AT&T by renting CATV circuits; a "'quasi-laser' broadcasting system . . . [that] transmits up to 15 miles," a technology pioneered by MCI that will anticipate fiber-optic cable; the US Defense Department satellites, along with Soviet and the commercial Comsat networks. Youngblood's union of heterogeneous networks is eerily similar to the union of satellite, land, and radio networks that was dubbed, five years later, the Internet. Add in the "time-shared computer utilities" and storage networks (considered in the next two chapters), and you have the cloud.

Excited by the potential of this new technology, the late 1960s and early 1970s became a test bed for questions that would preoccupy network culture: If you could design a two-way, "feedback network," could you even out the structures of power and create a more participatory media environment?

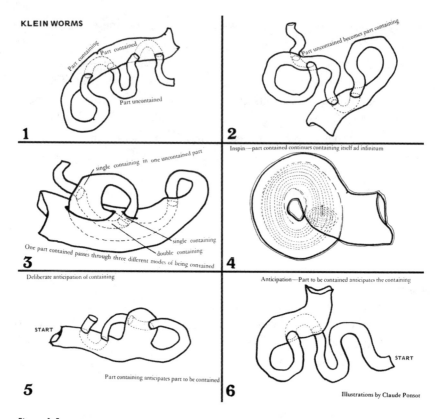

Figure 1.5
Paul Ryan and Claude Ponsot, "Klein Worms," in *Radical Software* 1, no. 3 (1971); Labadie Collection, University of Michigan Library.

And if you could change the media, would its viewers see differently? These are large questions, but ones that have lost their potency over time because so many of these structures have come into fruition: viewers feed back images and videos to television shows all the time, as with citizen-generated videos that regularly air on CNN, and YouTube has become an even more eclectic repository for images than cable ever was. We take distributed networks, and their properties, such as two-way interaction, for granted; the rhetoric of the artists is too utopian to be taken as more than a product of its time. And as David Joselit reminds us, while video and cable may be a "cautionary tale regarding the Internet's claims as a site for radical democracy," it is an embarrassing lesson to learn—particularly given how quickly cable, like the Internet, became commercialized and assimilated into the system of power it once claimed to subvert.[58]

These artistic attempts to critique and reconfigure the network of television at the same time as ARPAnet and the Internet suggest that a larger, generalizable discourse about networks was at play in the late 1960s and early 1970s, and that it wasn't limited to computers and digital technology. Essayist Joan Didion aptly summed up the massive social upheaval in the late 1960s by invoking Yeats: "The center was not holding."[59] Despite a smoothly functioning marketplace and a high GNP, the gravitational pull of these economic mechanisms no longer seemed enough. That decentralized networks were created in response—whether as alternatives to the centralized system of information distribution, or as buttresses meant to uphold the center by dispersing its power—does not strike me as a coincidence.

While the publics of the Internet were not yet present in the early 1970s, the publics created by television—the network user, here understood as a viewer of television and video—nevertheless registered the shifts in the network's shape. For the advent of new media in the late 1960s and early 1970s was felt primarily as the advent of news media—for instance, recall news reports from the 1972 Democratic and Republican National Conventions by the amateur group TVTV (Top Value Television), wielding the new Sony handheld video recorders named Portapaks. We tend to lose sight of this because a scholarly focus on the specificity of the network's *mediums* (its wires or logics or apparatus) has led to its inevitable separation from the network's *media*, the sense of mass or communications media.[60] To recuperate this larger discourse of the network, I turn to one of *Radical Software*'s collaborators, the San Francisco–based collective Ant Farm (Chip Lord, Doug Michaels, Hudson Marquez, and Curtis Schreier). Ant Farm's proposal for a media distribution structure called a "Truckstop Network" allows us to see how fertile the ground was for alternate network structures. The caveat is that my abbreviated consideration of a single Ant Farm project misses not only the rest of their work, but also contemporaneous examples from the rich history of video, such as artist Dan Graham's "feed-forward" cable network (ca. 1972); Austin Community Television (ACTV, 1972–), which fed directly into the cable's "head-end," or distribution center; Stan VanDerBeek's live performance/call-in piece for WGBH-Boston, *Violence Sonata* (1970); or the Videofreex pirate TV station in the Catskills, Lanesville TV (1972–1977), that attempted to hack or reconfigure the shape of the network system. For interested readers, I direct them to books that take up this subject in more depth.[61]

With this caveat in mind, let us move to 1970, when a modified Chevrolet van with a clear plastic bubble and a distinctive antenna hit the road. Serving as Ant Farm's temporary home for a year, it contained a TV window, a video-tape setup, silver roof-mounted speaker domes, and a dashboard-mounted camera, all hardware "reminiscent of a B-52."[62] It was quickly named the Media Van, and it became an integral part of what they eventually dubbed the Truckstop Network. Ant Farm bought several of the new Portapaks and went on tour, stopping at several colleges, shooting video of "dancing chickens, an okra farmer, a ground-breaking in Scottsdale, aspiring pop singer Johnny Romeo belting out a ballad in the Yale School of Architecture."[63] If commercial television refused to broadcast these video images, the Media Van would bring the network directly to the audience's door.

This van drove off during a moment of transition for highway culture. Through the 1960s, Jonathan Crary argues, the automobile and the television worked hand-in-hand in popular culture to conceal the growing complexity of capitalist representation. A highway route had an effect much like television, acting as a sort of TV channel that seemed to enable a driver/viewer's autonomy by giving him or her the power to choose—even as it cloaked the mechanism of capital behind it.[64] In the 1970s, Crary continues, television "began to be grafted onto other networks . . . the screens of home computer and word processor," and the computer's window replaced the car's window as the predominant space of the virtual.[65] Though the ideal of car culture had begun to sour—a matter brought to a head by the 1973 oil crisis—it was precisely the highway's identification with Cold War surplus and rusted roadside attractions, and its lack of newness, that made it fertile ground for artistic reappropriation.[66]

Thus Truckstop Network was more than a road trip tour; it was also a statement about mobility itself. Standing on the hinge between auto window and computer window, it proposed a countrywide network of truck stops for "media nomads." Placed just off the highway, each truck stop would offer an array of services for those living on the road: housing, electricity, and water; truck repair and a communal kitchen; and also communications services—computers and video equipment—seen, "like food and gas, as nutrients necessary for survival."[67]

Indeed, the computer aspect was essential to this plan: not only would it link all the truck stops, or "nodes," in Ant Farm's parlance, into a nationwide "communication network," but it would also direct the visitor to the services

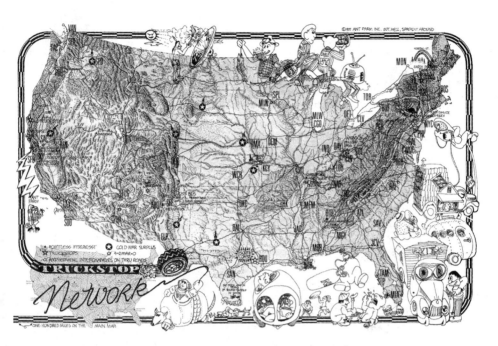

Figure 1.6

Ant Farm, *Truckstop Network Placemat* (recto), 1971, Ant Farm, offset printing on paper (2-sided); 17 × 11 in.; University of California, Berkeley Art Museum and Pacific Film Archive. Photo: Benjamin Blackwell. © Ant Farm. Courtesy of Chip Lord.

available at other truck stops—a woodworking shop, or astrology lessons, for example.[68] Truckers could be sent to other nodes via several highway directions; a placemat passed out to audiences on the Ant Farm tour maps several of these cross-country routes, including the "Overland Route" (Chicago to Salt Lake City to San Francisco Bay) and the "Sunset Route" (Los Angeles to New Orleans) (figure 1.6). On the flip side of the placemat, a star identifies potential Cold War surplus sites that could be reused as nodes, an act of reappropriating what Mark Wasiuta describes as the nation's "expanding computerized military network and its underground command centers."[69] A sketch for one of these sites, identified as a former desert missile silo near Wendato (likely Wendover, Utah), contains plans to transform layers of the silo into various layers for maintaining software (film/video) and hardware (auto/bus), all wired via a solar dish to its nervous system/core.[70]

For Ant Farm, the interconnections turned each node into a "physically fragmented . . . 'city'" of media.[71] Distributed across the country in places where "land is cheap and codes are lax in between the cities"—one thinks of the arid wheat field in Amarillo, Texas, where they executed their most famous piece, Cadillac Ranch, or the California deserts where they set up inflatable structures—the Truckstop nodes would be connected by the simplest yet most robust piece of Cold War infrastructure, the interstate highway.[72] And by placing the nodes at the side of the highway, it was possible to build an existence where the journey was the destination, and where the motion of the network was the point of the network. Cars traveling between the nodes thus became packets; remaining in constant motion, each packet would not stop at one node for long before traveling to another node. In other words, packet-switching.[73] Without a centralized node (although at one point Ant Farm envisioned a central computer to direct traffic), the network would constantly move information from point to point while avoiding the concentration of information in any one place. Moreover, the nodes were cheap, inflatable, and flexible. In effect, Ant Farm had envisioned an anarchic, distributed network for mobile living.

We may be tempted to dismiss this plan for "mobile living" as New Age artist cant. But Truckstop Network articulated an idea of mobility that would soon profoundly shape cloud computing. For the first Internet protocol was not developed through ARPAnet, as one might expect, and as most network historians claim, but through the physical act of driving on the open road. With its fixed nodes of bunker-sized computers and fixed links, ARPAnet was the quintessential piece of "closed-world" infrastructure. Instead, military researchers envisioned soldiers going mobile. Though there is no evidence that researchers at the Stanford Research Institute (SRI) saw any of Ant Farm's media productions, they nonetheless shared a similar vision: media would need to be produced and consumed on the road.

For SRI's engineers, this meant retrofitting a "bread truck" style van to test the difficulty of broadcasting and receiving network signals on the move. They wanted to see if, for instance, their packet radio connection would remain intact if the van went under a highway overpass.[74] (Packet radio is an early version of today's cellular networks.) Rigged on the inside with a DEC LSI-11 computer and two packet radio transmitters, the SRI van (figure 1.7) ran its first successful test in August 1976, six years after Ant Farm's own Media Van (figure 1.8). The test was of a protocol that would bridge the aerial network—the Packet Radio Network, or PRnet—with the ground-based ARPAnet. It was the first time two disparate computer networks were

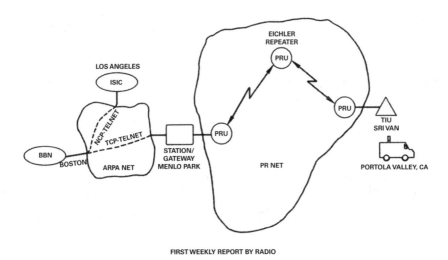

Figure 1.7

Diagram of first two-network Internet transmission, August 27, 1976. Originally published in "Progress Report on Packet Radio Experimental Network," September 1977. © SRI International, Inc. Used with permission.

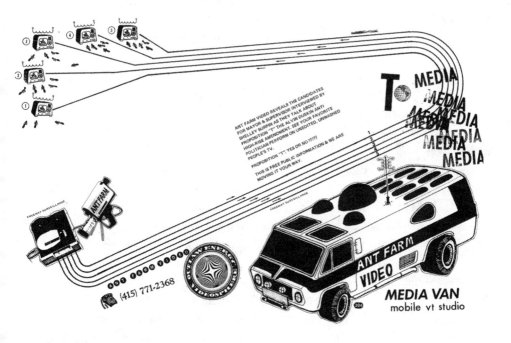

Figure 1.8

"Media Van: mobile vt studio," 1971, Ant Farm; ink, stamp marks in black ink, sticker, and collage elements on paper; 11 × 17 in.; University of California, Berkeley Art Museum and Pacific Film Archive. Photograph: Benjamin Blackwell. © Ant Farm. Used with permission.

bridged, and as a result, it is considered the first inter-network, or Internet, transmission.

In this inaugural test, the van is clearly visible on the right side of the network diagram, connected to two clouds labeled PR NET and ARPA NET. What is perhaps missing from the diagram is the texture of the setting, of the van's driver—protocol engineer Jim Mathis—trucking down Northern California's Bayshore Freeway, and the van's final stop, which was chosen because it was a "'hostile environment'—in keeping with relevance to military application": "This was the parking lot of Ross[o]tti's biker bar in Palo Alto, still well in reach of the repeater units at Mt. Umun[h]um and Mission Ridge—and with good supply of local bikers who gave the appearance of hostility after the requisite number of beers."[75]

There is an improvisatory aspect to SRI's van test. The inter-network they built was by definition an "amalgam of wire and radio networks"; it was a way of allowing a highly mobile, even ethereal network—packet radio—to tap into a preexisting, fixed network infrastructure.[76] The van also reveals a third infrastructure that is only implicit: the highways in what is now known as Silicon Valley where the researchers circulated to test their van, which also delighted the bikers and video freaks with whom they mingled. A few miles down the street from Rossotti's, you could buy a catalog containing Ant Farm's latest inflatable architecture projects or video schematics from the "Whole Earth Truck Store." The first node on the intermedia network was a truck stop, or, in the case of SRI, a biker bar.

The two media vans soon went into storage, SRI's to a forgotten back lot, Ant Farm's to a bunker in Marin County, California. But the inter-networking protocol tested in 1976, TCP, would cement the growth of what would be christened the "Internet" in 1983, and the networks' shapes would resemble the possibilities—the freedom of the road; a constantly moving, physically fragmented existence—once offered by the highway. No matter that American highway culture itself had gone into decline. The potentialities that the highway once represented—the idea of the highway without the highway itself, simultaneously decentralized and yet an infrastructure from the Cold War—remained.

The "information superhighway" articulated a new kind of lifestyle, where media processors could go mobile, feeding information (often in the form of video) back into the cloud. Yet the shift from the media of the van to digital media was not a particularly hard one to envision. In "Truckstop

Fantasy Number One," Ant Farm had even mused that "EVENTUALLY WE WILL ABANDON PHYSICAL MOVEMENT FOR TELEPATHIC/CYBERNETIC MOVEMENT (TELEVISION) AND OUR NETWORK WILL ADAPT TO THE CHANGE."[77] For Ant Farm, computer links were merely one of many forms of communication, and the specific medium (telepathy or television!) was somewhat beside the point. In the bottom of their network diagram for Truckstop Network, Ant Farm asks: "How many ways do you communicate/ inter truckstop."[78] And then they list "linear" mediums, such as the mail, next to "electronic" mediums (radio and telegraph and computer) and land and aerial transportation mediums (cars, trucks, blimps). A single anomalous dotted line in a mesh network appears to indicate, of all things, a telegraph line.

The inspiration for Truckstop Network was as much the new technology of the Sony Portapak as the well-worn technology of the postal service. As Chip Lord recalls, "Before we went on the road, we were doing mail art and we tapped into this network of people doing mail art."[79] Kris Paulsen has additionally uncovered a buried history of guerilla television within its lo-fi distribution network: videographers swapped half-inch videotapes by advertisements and mail order.[80] The point is that the cloud is always an amalgam—a "network of networks"—that can only come into existence when it is not tied to a specific network or medium. This is why there are multiple clouds in the SRI diagram, and even some internal debate at SRI on how many networks—two or three—are needed before the project can officially be termed an "inter-network."

To think about the digital network, I am arguing, one must first think about the network in the absence of individual technologies. This is what I have tried to do with the example of the two media vans. In the late 1960s and early 1970s, the rhetoric behind the creation of new information structures was often overblown; the utopianism of their claims are so sweeping that they are sometimes hard to take seriously (Youngblood's videosphere that envisioned an "Intermedia network" that will unite all media). But we dismiss their rhetoric at our own risk. Strip away the technological layer— the artists' concern with television, for example—and we see something very similar to what we have now: the cloud as a place where all media seem to converge; the cloud as an enabler of supposedly distributed publics.[81] The universalist fantasy of the cloud remains as ubiquitous now as it was forty years ago.

There is a second reason why I have brought the vans into the story. If we only imagine the network as a product of the military, working with their contractors, to "invent" ARPA and the Internet, then the network that we take away is a deeply paranoid one—a vision of nuclear strikes and distributed tanks. There is a hole in that narrative. By their own admission, the engineers at SRI were trying to convince the military that their interests in packet radio could eventually have a military application. Inside the van were several other projects, including a computer program for encoding speech run by the "Network Speech Compression and Network Skiing Club," that reflected a more utopian heritage within SRI of using computers to augment human capabilities. Yet the story they told to the military is the one that is inevitably retold by computer historians.

Precisely because many of the claims in the late 1960s and early 1970s are strange—precisely because they are unexplainable—is grounds for why we should embrace them. SRI used a Mickey Mouse phone inside its van to test phone service over the packet network; this research in digital speech resulted in the decidedly unmilitary Speak & Spell toy for children. Meanwhile, Ant Farm sketched an ink diagram of Television America, its prime-time audience reimagined as a slice of prime—prime meat, that is. In their specificity, in their improvisatory strangeness, they rub against the grain of universalism. A dancing chicken broadcast from the Media Van undercuts any sort of sweeping claims for a new Media America. By their very refusal to be assimilated into useful categories for Internet history, they stake out a space for the autonomy of their production. In contrast to understanding network culture as a paranoid world system, one that encompasses all networks, these weird and unexplainable moments offer the potential for an alternate, reparative reading.[82]

It is unknown whether the video freaks and the network engineers in Portola Valley rubbed shoulders over a beer at Rossotti's, though Ant Farm did visit the Xerox PARC archives in the early 1970s to research an upcoming exhibition. In either case, there was a rich relationship between the counterculture and computer scientists of the San Francisco Bay Area. Theodore Roszak and John Markoff have identified a shared interest in political dissent, communalist, and consciousness-expanding practices by members of the counterculture and computer researchers living in San Francisco and the Stanford area, respectively.[83] And as Fred Turner has shown, Stewart Brand served as a key hinge between the two worlds, acting as a cameraman during

Douglas Engelbart's 1968 demonstration of personal computing, and as a publisher of the seminal Whole Earth Catalog (an outgrowth of the Whole Earth Truck Store)—a kind of World Wide Web in print that indirectly led to the establishment of the Berkeley Homebrew Computer Club.[84]

These histories, however, typically trace inventors and researchers within or on the peripheries of computer science. As I have tried to show, network culture properly resides in a vibrant debate—one that preceded the 1960s, and continues to this day—about the proper configuration between media and power. Computer scientists were a part of this debate, but they were not the only ones to weigh in. Years before ARPAnet's existence, sociologists, urban planners, government bureaucrats, privacy advocates, epidemiologists, computer scientists, and, of course, the aforementioned artists, were keenly aware of the centralizing tendencies of networks. Would the computer network become a "natural monopoly," like all of its predecessor utilities, asked Baran in a 1966 Congressional hearing, and if so, how might concentrating data inside such computer monopolies affect privacy?

The next chapter tells the story leading up to that first federal hearing on computer privacy, and the effect it had on shaping what we now call cloud computing. Before I turn to that story, which begins just across the Stanford campus from the SRI engineers, it is worthwhile to remember that similar questions had already begun to percolate in the fierce debates over television. Only five years earlier, Newton Minow, the incoming FCC commissioner, warned about television's monopoly over its viewers in his famous "wasteland" speech by describing the flatness of television: "You will see a procession of game shows, formula comedies about totally unbelievable families, blood and thunder, mayhem, violence, sadism, murder, western bad men, western good men, private eyes, gangsters, more violence, and cartoons . . . And most of all, boredom."[85] This distaste builds to the commissioner's larger point: "I am deeply concerned with concentration of power in the hands of the networks." The network was then, as it is now, a potent manifestation of aesthetic questions. Aesthetic—which is to say, political.

2   TIME-SHARING AND VIRTUALIZATION

Intimacies of the User: From the Stolen Look to Stolen Time

It is October 1972, and *Rolling Stone* is visiting Stanford University. Although accredited as a sports reporter, journalist Stewart Brand is not there to watch a traditional college sport; instead, he is there for the computer game Spacewar (figure 2.1). Ushered into the computer lab, Brand watches as long-haired programmers in front of a glowing TV-like tube grab their joysticks, maneuver their spaceships, and fire photon torpedoes, "joyously slaying their friend and wasting their employers' valuable computer time."[1]

Brand's description would have been unfathomable for a typical reader of the early 1970s. Not only were the programmers not using computers—office machinery that cost hundreds of thousands of dollars apiece—for work, they were using them interactively. The usual way of using computers at the time was called batch processing, in which users would submit punch cards or magnetic tape to an operator and receive the results in hours, even a few days later—a process Brand derided as "passive consumerism: data was something you sent to the manufacturer, like color film."[2] Instead, at the Stanford AI lab, a console would ask a programmer questions ("HOW MANY SPACE MINES DO YOU WANT?"), and he or she would type back an answer. Then, a fraction of a second later, the computer would draw the mines on the console—no punch cards involved.

For today's critics as much as Brand, Spacewar represented a historical turning point toward personal computing. In his 2003 book, for example, historian Paul Ceruzzi writes that "the way it was being used was personal: for fun, interactively, with no concern for how many ticks of the processor one was using."[3] Appropriately, the *Rolling Stone* article on Spacewar opens his chapter on the personal computer, for in Ceruzzi's reading of it, this moment

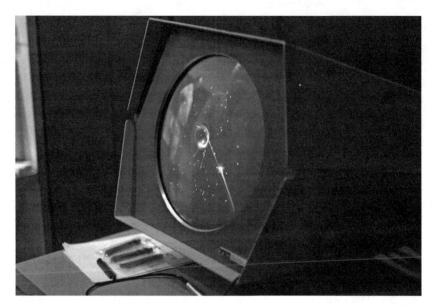

Figure 2.1

Spacewar! running on a PDP-1. (The Computer History Museum in Mountain View, California runs a demo of *Spacewar* every first and third Saturday.) © Joi Ito, reprinted under Creative Commons BY 2.0 license.

would offer the first "mental model" of a user of personal computers. This model meant that computing could be used for 'personal' matters, such as dating, gaming, and so on. But personal computing would also mean something that may seem odd to a contemporary reader: the illusion that a person would be "given the full attention and resources of the computer."[4]

We might find that statement a tautology: of course each person has the full 'attention and resources' of his or her own computer! At the time of Brand's article, however, only a single computer served the dozens of programmers at the Stanford lab, a PDP-10 next door to the room where the competitors were playing Spacewar. It was far too costly for any single individual to own a computer—but new software known as time-sharing made it seem as if this were in fact the case. Time-sharing technology, theorized in the late 1950s and deployed by the early 1960s, allowed the tremendous cost of a computer to be shared by dividing the computer's time into infinitesimal increments. By spending a fraction of a second on one user's program, switching rapidly to other users's programs, then immediately moving back to the first program, it appeared as if the computer were responding instantly to each user's commands. The position of each person's spaceship showed up on-screen in a split second, rather than several hours later; each user could think of the $250,000 computer in the back room as his or her own.

Contemporary scholars agree that the user was a modern invention; time-sharing systems, and the applications written for them, such as Spacewar, would invent the personal user.[5] But what is often lacking in these accounts is a description of the way the user's subject position is created not just by software, as media theorists would assert, but by the economic system that undergirds whatever relation any of us have with technology. If we take a closer look at the second part of Ceruzzi's sentence—the space warriors played "with no concern for how many ticks of the processor one was using"—we can sense the complexity of this economic model. Even as time-sharing allowed a new imagination of computing as a utility that could be billed down to each tick of a computer's clock, the game player would be encouraged to forget about that bill. Why bill and then erase the bill? It is an interesting paradox that is fundamental to today's digital culture, where downloads, storage space, e-mail, video, and so forth are free by default. Computer power is now so plentiful that we've stopped counting, and the minimal cost of computation seems to enable a sort of personal freedom. Computers are cheap enough, in other words, that we use them for blogging, playing games, personal expression, and so on—not just for work.

The paradox cannot be explained by software alone. We need another explanation, and this chapter revisits the history of time-sharing not to retell a well-worn story of inventors, technologies, and dates, but to show how time-sharing seemed to restructure the very boundaries between work and leisure, public and private. I analyze both the rhetoric invoked by computer scientists to describe their own work, as well as political, legal, and nonspecialist documents that set out a broader cultural imagination of what time-sharing could do. As I argue, time-sharing was part of a larger and more fundamental economic shift away from waged labor and toward what Maurizio Lazzarato terms the economy of "immaterial labor"—an economy of flexible labor that encompasses even seemingly personal or unpaid tasks, such as writing a review for a favorite product on Amazon.com.

By focusing on the time-shared user as an economic subject, we can understand many of the attitudes that structure present-day digital culture. For the irony is that though the word "time-sharing" went out of fashion with the advent of mini- and personal computers in the 1980s, the very same ideas have morphed into what seems to be the most modern of computing concepts: cloud computing. In cloud computing, time on expensive servers (whether storage space, computational power, software applications, and so on) can be rented as a service or utility, rather than paid for up front. Even the software housed on the Stanford PDP-10 has profoundly shaped the cloud: the mechanisms that once gave Spacewar players the illusion of having their own computer now gives a cloud's client the illusion of having a "virtual machine"—even when there are actually hundreds if not thousands of virtual machines all running on the same server.

After a roughly two-decade hiatus in which computing costs were generally bundled into the price of a new computer or a new software package, charging by computer time is back in vogue.[6] Cloud computing providers are again billing in computer-hours, and cloud software such as Office, Adobe Creative Suite, and so on is again rented in monthly or yearly subscriptions— —a process pioneered by long-forgotten time-sharing businesses such as Allen-Babcock and Tymshare in the 1960s. In the first time-sharing systems, the $1.6 million cost of an IBM 7094 system in 1963 could be fractionalized to the tune of a mere $450/hour. As of 2014, Amazon was charging 45 cents per computer-hour on its Elastic Computer Cloud, or EC2: a thousandfold reduction from 1963 in nominal terms, and yet a service that is far more profitable for Amazon than books, DVDs, or groceries.[7] When futurists predicted that time-shared computers could become a public utility for millions, they were very nearly right; they were just several decades too early.

To understand the history of time-sharing, this chapter's first two sections follow two closely related tracks on the themes of intimacy and privacy. I begin by asking: how did computing come to feel personal? As I suggest, a sense of intimacy with the computer resulted from a user's flirtation with a series of transgressions: what was initially a voyeuristic relationship with an off-limits computer behind a glass wall (metaphorically, a "stolen look") set the stage for a modern operating system that accounts for each tick of "stolen time." Again, this shift was not simply the result of technological innovation; time-sharing was symptomatic of a postwar economic shift toward multitasking and freelancing. It is this larger context that explains why cloud computing deliberately confuses "free" time with liberal freedoms, and why it produces a quasi-illicit economy that encourages users to take (even steal) things for free. By positioning users as intimate partners of the computer, time-sharing yoked users to a political economy that made users synonymous with their usage, and allowed them (or their advertising sponsors) to be tracked, rented, or billed down to each tick of the clock.

To make the intimacy of the user work, a user must be made to feel individual and private—even as millions of users share the same hard drives, computers, and data pipes underneath. A vast and unseen layer inside today's cloud, known as virtualization software, ensures that the data jumbled within the cloud's data centers and networks appear as individual streams of data (and each person's slice of a shared server appears as his or her own "virtual machine"). But individuation is also an ideology that plays a role far beyond the cloud's internal mechanism. For example, companies employ complex algorithms to filter content according to browsing history; when two people Google the same word, the algorithm will return different results to each, results that are meant to correlate to demographic information about each user.[8] As a result of this individuation, each user can be billed for actual computer usage—or, more commonly, each user's computer usage (now in the form of web history, clickstream data, etc.) can be turned into a commodity by advertisers. This ideology, to paraphrase artist Richard Serra, "delivers people";[9] the cloud has replaced television as the premier mechanism for sorting the public into private users.

How time-sharing systems "delivered" individual users and made them private is the subject of this chapter's second section. As part of this story, I explore how computer scientists working behind the scenes transformed the risks of many users sharing the same computers—whether computer viruses that afflicted overly "social" users, or garbage and unclean objects left behind in computer memory—from a set of catastrophic failures to an ongoing problem to be managed (and even, in today's "sharing economy," embraced). This mechanism is, however, a double-edged sword, for that mechanism also allows the cloud to exert a soft form of control over today's users. As I argue, the best way to understand how this power is deployed is not through surveillance cameras, web trackers, or cryptographic algorithms. Rather, it is an ancient technology, the sewer system: centuries before computers were invented, sewers kept each household's private business private even as it extended the armature of the state into individual homes. Using the case study of data leakage and leaking in general, the final section examines a possible way to reimagine this topography of control.

a

b

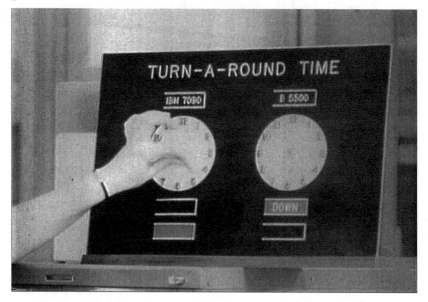

Figure 2.2a, b

Stills from Art Eisenson and Gary Feldman, *Ellis D. Kropotechev and Zeus, A Marvelous Time-Sharing System* (1967), 16mm film. Courtesy of the Computer History Museum; used with permission of Gary Feldman.

In a slapstick film produced by two Stanford graduate students in 1967, we are introduced to a mustachioed computer scientist Ellis D. Kropotechev, "a man with a problem, a girl, and a deadline."[10] Said girl, a painter, awaits him at a picnic, but because Kropotechev is stuck waiting for his punch cards to be processed, he is left in various stages of limbo: pounding the side of a jammed IBM punch machine, smoking in the cafeteria as he waits, and running down a never-ending hallway. After intertitles reading "Later" and "Still Later" and "Later Still" break up shots of Kropotechev's growing anxiety, we finally see the computer output returned to him. The printout shows the seconds of processing time billed, then an error message: the program has crashed. As we see a shot of the girl about to leave, Kropotechev races to deliver the next set of punchcards. But he slips and the punchcards fly out of his hand, Charlie Chaplin–style, fluttering uselessly across the screen. It is only through the intervention of a quasi-divine time-sharing computer named "Zeus" that our hero is saved—and his girl won.

The film is a humorous and brilliant introduction to the difference between batch processing and time-sharing. Filmed to the soundtrack of the Rolling Stones' "Cool, Calm, Collected" ("Well she's very wealthy . . ."), Kropotechev's object of desire, the painter, seems out of reach. What stands in Kropotechev's way is another woman: a computer operator, who collects the punchcards and sets a clock marked "Turnaround Time—IBM 7090" (figure 2.2a, b). This second woman metonymically recalls the fact that the word "computer" had originally designated the female operator of a machine, rather than the machine itself. As Jennifer Light explains, a computer was typically a low-paid laborer who initially served as a human calculator for wartime problems, such as ballistics, and soon took on the physically demanding work of programming circuits and fixing the machines herself.[11]

The manifest message of the film is an economic story: eliminating the middleman, speeding up the programming operation, and replacing the drudgery of low-paid labor with better technology so that pleasurable, higher-status activities—courting a "very wealthy" girl, painting—can occur. But there is a more complicated subtext, for if the goal of time-sharing is to free up time to get the girl, the real question is: which girl, the computer (operator) or the painter? The film pairs the two women so symmetrically— one the timekeeper, one the expiring deadline—that the economic benefits of time-sharing are embodied in sexual terms. One computer delays and prevents climax; the other (named, by delightful coincidence, after a Greek god known for his many dalliances) enables it. The virility bestowed by the time-sharing system allows Kropotechev to bypass the drudgery of batch processing, fend off a romantic rival, and reclaim his girl. (This nominally heterosexual narrative becomes a bit queer in the substitution of machine for flesh, as when the Zeus computer demonstrates that it, too, has a drawing and painting program, just like Kropotechev's object of desire.[12]) These tangled sexual undercurrents within real-time programming aptly illustrate why Fernando Corbató, deputy director of MIT's Compatible Time-Sharing System (CTSS), described interacting with his time-sharing system as "programming intimacy."[13]

Corbató was not the only computer scientist to think about time-sharing in these terms. J. C. R. Licklider opened his seminal article "Man-Computer Symbiosis" (1960) with a parable about the "very close coupling" of an insect that lives in the ovary of a fig tree and in turn pollinates it; man and computer, he writes, are two creatures "living together in intimate association, or even close union."[14] The word "intimacy" has now been superseded in contemporary parlance by terms such as "interactivity," but it is a useful one, as it allows us to recover a largely sublimated sense of desire within the concept of the user. This relationship between human and machine predates the computer: the typewriter, Friedrich Kittler similarly observed,[15] once designated a female secretary and now refers to a machine. And it occasionally becomes explicit, as in the crude joke that "programming is like having sex: one mistake and you have to support it for the rest of your life." But this sensibility has largely been lost or disavowed.

I use the lens of intimacy to revisit time-sharing, an approach that allows me to examine how the always unstable desire for the computer—whether (human) operator or machine—creates the subject position we now call the user. To explain the subjectivity of early computation before time-sharing, one might find an analogy to cinema, which constructed a spectacle for viewers to look at—but always at a remove. If the quasi-illicit pleasure of cinema is peering in on a scene, as if through a keyhole, the computer user initially occupied a similar position. For their programmers, the batch-processed computer was visible but physically out of reach: at Stanford, as *Ellis D. Kropotechev and Zeus, A Marvelous Time-Sharing System* illustrates (figure 2.2a), the IBM 7090 was inside a glass room guarded by computer operators. Sometimes called the "glass house," this machine room (cold, noisy, and a generally forbidden space) both walled off the computer even as it occasionally revealed it; though programmers were required to submit program requests to the staff, they could often steal looks at the computer's internal registers through the glass.

The idea of looking was also a long-standing metaphor for the act of programming—which is to say debugging—itself. As computer historian Martin Campbell-Kelly writes, before the time of the IBM 7090: "There were, of course, no software debugging aids whatever on the EDSAC at this time [1949], so the program had to be debugged on a naked machine, by 'single-stepping' through the program and observing the contents of the memory and registers on the monitor tubes. This process was known by the rather charming name of 'peeping.'"[16]

Put differently, debugging in the era of batch processing was an explicitly voyeuristic act. The act of "peeping" into a computer in the middle of its routine constructed a scopophilic relationship between user and machine. Even today, debuggers occasionally use the word "peeping": one guidebook to Visual Basic .NET announces that the "Watch window also allows you to be a peeping Tom."[17] (The window of modern graphical operating systems is therefore conceptualized not just as a portal into a virtual world elsewhere, but also a window into the inner secrets of the machine.[18])

As a sort of voyeur, the batch-processed user's exact identity was not particularly important: each user was interchangeable with another from the standpoint of the computer. Consequently, there were no individual user names, and the user was merely a number recorded for billing purposes. The gap between man and machine thus remained a perverse distance, one whose occasional crossing recreated the enjoyment of a Peeping Tom.

This gap, however, began to be bridged in a series of technologies that culminated in time-sharing. The first of these technologies came in the 1950s, when crashing programs triggered a small routine known as the "post-mortem dump." After the death of the user's program, this trigger printed out the previously interior contents of a computer's memory so that the user could study why the program produced an error. As an automatic if indiscriminate way of inspecting the computer's interior, the dump was a literal manifestation of both waste and a user's time wasted. Waiting for the operator to load the next program, the user waited several hours before trying again, in a cycle that represents a failure of consummation, or at least, of elimination: "Several attempts must be made before all errors are eliminated. Since much machine time can be lost in this way a major preoccupation of the EDSAC group at the present time is the development of techniques for avoiding errors, detecting them before the tape is put on the machine."[19]

If "peeping" positioned the user as a voyeur who secretly gazed on the computer's inner operations with a stolen look, improved debugging technologies reshaped this relationship through a newly transgressive pleasure: that of "stealing" computer time. Early experiments in the late 1950s by John McCarthy, Steve Russell, and Herb Teager explored the potential of what they called "time-stealing."[20] This process allowed an important professor's job to temporarily interrupt an existing computer program. After the success of this demonstration, McCarthy and others convinced computer manufacturers at IBM and Digital Equipment Corporation to modify their memory systems to support time-sharing, and the first systems began to arrive at MIT in the early 1960s.[21]

As time-stealing technologies matured into time-sharing, they seemed to miraculously recover time that was hitherto wasted, allowing each user to steal computer cycles out of thin air. In 1966, for example, Douglas Parkhill devoted a chapter of *The Challenge of the Computer Utility* to estimating the unused capacity of government computers. Sixty percent of computer time is wasted, he speculates, resulting in a potentially gargantuan $550 million of savings if time-sharing were deployed.[22] Parkhill probably did not count on home-brewed programs filling these empty cycles. Yet time-sharing led to an explosive growth in these informal and unanticipated uses. Because cycles could now be run on the side, this "two-timing" aspect of time-sharing opened a variety of ways for users to furtively acquire time. One could bill one's program to the operator account, forge the books, or zero out one's billing account.[23]

Surprisingly, managers at MIT did not clamp down entirely on users' ability to use time-sharing systems for themselves. Instead, they came up with a way of regulating the system that is now so naturalized as to seem obvious, but was completely novel at the time: naming each user. As we saw earlier, users were simply problem numbers or terminals in a batch-processing system, but time-sharing put forth a mental model of the user who had both a username and a password. The goal, Corbató recounted, "was to make it personal so that we were dealing with individuals . . . we also needed accounting. It wasn't so much for charging but [to] keep track of usage at least."[24]

To make computing "personal," to be "known as a person when you logged in," the user had to be radically refashioned. Crucially, the user was not yet personal in the sense of personal computing; rather, this process made a user's personhood synonymous with his or her *usage*. It mapped the identity of the user onto his or her time spent using the computer. Many hackers took umbrage at what they saw as a managerial intrusion: "People had to get accounts and had to pay attention to security. It was a benign bureaucracy, but nevertheless a bureaucracy."[25] Making this need to register a user's identity explicit, a 1968 ARPA study tested twenty-one programmers on a mix of time-sharing and batch-processing systems to gauge whether time-sharing would help with programming error. The scientists carefully logged and tracked each user's person-hours worked "by close personal observation," and compared the figure with the number of computer-hours used; "discrepancies . . . were resolved by tactful interviewing."[26] The study thus indicates an early attempt to reconcile the "real" number of hours worked with the hours used by the computer.

By making the user equivalent to his or her usage, time-sharing yoked the user's labor to the labor of the computer itself. In doing so, human–computer interaction initially functioned as a management technique, as a way to fashion an efficient worker capable of flexibly managing time. (It is no coincidence that multitasking, a concept that originally came out of time-sharing, now refers to this kind of flexible work.) This new kind of worker resulted from a broader economic shift away from factory-based work and toward immaterial labor, in which "workers are expected to become 'active subjects' in the coordination of the various functions of production, instead of being subjected to it as simple command" (Lazzarato).[27] This type of economy most fully manifests itself through a cybernetic model of control, in which user and computer jointly make decisions in real time. Thus, scientist Licklider explains, the user would be asked to "fill in the gaps . . . when the computer has no mode or routine," and similarly, the computer would perform "clerical operations that fill the intervals between decisions."[28]

Despite naming it "real time," the mode of time that Licklider describes is neither "real" nor unmediated; real time actually functions as an ideology of economic productivity. By splitting a problem into thousands of increments, and then stitching these intervals of computer and worker time alike back into a seeming whole, the computer disavows unproductive moments with "no mode or routine," and turns our attention away from these gaps, stutters, and freezes and toward more productive modes of work.[29] Yet to do so is to subtly refashion the subject brought within the domain of real time. To understand this, consider a parallel example of a film spectator, which is also subjected to numerous gaps within and surrounding the film: for instance, a cut from one scene to the next, the inactive and unseen moments between two moments of action, or even, in the case of analog film, the black leader in between film frames.[30] Even as we are repeatedly subjected to these gaps, a set of methods, termed "suture" by film theorists, creates a subject position that offers the illusion of unity.

"The operation of suture," Kaja Silverman explains, "is successful at the moment that the viewing subject says, 'Yes, that's me,' or 'That's what I see.'"[31] Similarly, with a program sent into limbo and then reanimated every fraction of a second, a computer's operating system also employs techniques to ensure a user does not notice the gaps. Thus, when a computer user can stand in as an "I"—as a unified subject—the operation of real time succeeds. And yet, in actuality, a computer's "real time" is a process of reassembling thousands of seconds of time "stolen" from other programs. Because time-sharing equates a computer user with the amount of work done by the computer, the user is actually an assemblage of economic value—with the time spent using a computer a commodity to be tracked. Though similar to marketing methods that monetize a viewer's television watching time, there is one seeming difference: the user is expected to interact, to actively "use" the computer.[32]

Like a sleight-of-hand trick, then, time-sharing performed two things simultaneously: it created a sense of personal intimacy with the computer, even as it masked the economic mechanism that supported it. To recall Spacewar, it made users feel as if they were playing "for fun, interactively, with no concern for how many ticks of the processor one was using." This trick was not necessarily a bad thing; time-sharing was often experienced as a permissive and even freeing system, for it asked users to think of the computer's time as their own time. Still, by connecting each user to a central computer, and by implication, the work of the computer, the link that bound the two in unison would increasingly function as a subtle tether, a motif that will recur throughout the remainder of this chapter.

From a contemporary perspective, the intimacy experienced by a computer user may seem to be the first step toward liberal subjectivity—with computers as "cyborg partners, second selves, a new subjective space that included the machine" (Paul Edwards).[33] It may also appear that this intimacy was an inevitable result of technologies for human–computer interaction.

But this is an oversimplification; time-sharing was initially developed for debugging, not for interactivity.[34] Moreover, time-sharing was not universally acclaimed; some programmers resented the need to be present at the same time as their programs. (Time spent waiting for a batch-processed computer to return results undoubtedly provided a welcome break from the routine of work.) And most important, we shouldn't forget that time-sharing was first and foremost a new way of conceiving and accounting for one's own time in relationship to productivity. Any sense of the "personal" relationship that began to develop between people and computers was a symptom, a secondary and holographic effect.

As part of this shift, time-sharing normalized and even promoted the transgressive potential of time stealing. Because typewriters or TV-like displays now connected users to the computer, there was no need to steal looks at the computer itself; accordingly, the real computer moved out of the glass-walled rooms and out of sight. Users could now "steal" computing power when needed—both taking processor time while doing something else, as if stealing away from work to run a personal errand, and also taking advantage of processor time as if it were free. In this, time-sharing anticipated the way that the contemporary cloud encourages its users to take things free of charge. By making each online resource freely available—computer storage, processing time, content, even software—the cloud encourages the pleasurable and quasi-illicit feeling that we are getting away with something: that we, too, have stolen time.

To unpack this idea, let us return, once again, to Spacewar. Recall that the Stanford gamers played "for fun, interactively, with no concern for how many ticks of the processor one was using." Their knowing disavowal of the cost of computing time—a PDP-10 may still have cost half a million dollars in 1972, when Brand wrote his article—evokes the contradictory resonances of the word "free." On first glance, free may suggest a space located outside the marketplace—as merely "for fun," with no commercial value.[35] But free also takes on the sense of the phrase "free time": time off from work, perhaps, but only within a labor market where play can pay off and work may seem like play. Thinking of his employees playing Spacewar, Les Earnest, executive director of Stanford's AI Lab, commented: "Sometimes it's hard to tell the difference between recreation and work, happily. We try to judge people not on how much time they waste but on what they accomplish over fairly long periods of time."[36]

Earnest's words remind us that, in today's Silicon Valley, recreation and personal interests have become subcategories of work, with even recreational activities and time often seen as ways of furthering a company's productivity.[37] By agreeing to work in real time, the user enters a flexible economic framework in which she is free to choose how to spend her time, as long as time is understood as something to be spent. While the batch-processed user was primarily an accounting method that counted the number of computer hours to be billed for each problem, time-sharing asked users to *account for themselves.*

As a consequence, what we think of the "user" confuses personal intimacy for economic intimacy. This confusion may explain why so much of digital culture is powered by user labor and user-generated content. Laboring in a time-shared economy—everything from tagging a photo on Facebook to reviewing businesses on Yelp to answering product questions on Amazon—is performed for the love of the task, for personal reasons and during "free time," even as this labor generates value (if not profit) for the company that administers it. Theorist Tiziana Terranova enumerates this sort of work: "Simultaneously voluntarily given and unwaged, enjoyed and exploited, free labor on the Net includes the activity of building web sites, modifying software packages, reading and participating in mailing lists and building virtual spaces."[38] To be sure, free laborers are by no means dupes; indeed, the gentle tether of a time-sharing economy most closely resembles the freedom of a freelancer—the ability, in other words, to decide for themselves which projects to take on, which activities will pay off, and which projects are personal ones.[39] Once again, this flexibility can often be genuinely experienced as liberatory. But this flexibility comes, as they say, at a price.

The bargain is thus: to be a user, you must continually act (and act within this framework). As Lazzarato comments, postindustrial capitalism takes as its slogan "Become an active subject": "one *has to* express oneself, one *has to* speak, communicate, cooperate, and so forth."[40] Conversely, the one user of no value to online companies is the user who fails to "use," who registers with a website and then never returns. This failed user, the user that doesn't participate or produce content, represents the queer stoppage of technological (re)productivity.[41] Consequently, much of the free storage or free offerings in today's digital culture is structured to entice and reward (if not compel) participation. As time-sharing's successor, the cloud is the fullest manifestation of phenomena described as "freeware capitalism": "[Free stuff] makes you just consume more time on the net. After all, the goal . . . is to have users spend as much time on the net as possible, regardless of what they are doing. The objective is to have you consume bandwidth."[42]

Regardless of how much bandwidth costs, and how much actual money is spent, the underlying logic of freeware capitalism is consumption—of time. While it is far too easy to critique today's monetization of the Internet user, these arguments imagine an originary Internet gift economy that is purely fictional. The reality is that ever since time-sharing systems bestowed names upon users, those users have been interpellated as units of economic value.

This brings me to a closely related point. Complaints about monetizing the Internet user inevitably raise the specter of a user's privacy being violated: buying and selling clickstream data, tracking, and so forth. Privacy debates typically invoke the rhetoric of intimacy to explain this sense of violation. Pictured as an algorithm "peeping" into a computer user's bedroom, surveillance in the cloud seems to involve the interplay of voyeurism, watching, and stolen looks. Meanwhile, the metaphors of sexual relationality are displaced on the realm of technological reproducibility: for example, the promiscuous proliferation of copying and file sharing.[43] When privacy advocates invoke a so-called "right to privacy" online, they reenact and reanimate the libidinous circuits of desire that run through US Supreme Court decisions on "whether to bear or beget a child . . . personal decisions related to marriage, procreation, contraception, family relationships, child rearing, and education."[44] The topics of the landmark privacy cases cited as a precedent for digital privacy law therefore range from contraception (*Griswold v. Connecticut*, 1965) to viewing pornography (*Stanley v. Georgia*, 1969) to abortion (*Roe v. Wade*, 1972) to homosexuality (*Lawrence v. Texas*, 2003).

Fixated on these problems of the stolen look and personal intimacy, these debates misread the digital user as a liberal subject. But in the vast majority of the cases, users negotiate their privacy "freely" (which is to say as freelancers): working within the confines of private contracts, such as software licensing agreements. These matters therefore fall within the realm of tort law, rather than constitutional law. Asked to manage ourselves as users, we are also asked to manage our own privacy online by negotiating with private companies: by taking on liability for copyright infringement on reposted images, by managing whom our posts can be shared with, and even by opting in to restrictions on search results for children, in what Raiford Guins terms a culture of self-imposed filtering.[45] The subtext here is that in return, we generally expect some say in how our data should be monetized: when to run advertisements, for instance, on our "personal" blog. When this contract seems to fall apart—when a social media company sells an image that we have produced, without our permission—we feel it as a violation of personal intimacy, even when the damage is, in actuality, an economic one.

The irony is that many digital privacy debates are attempts to resurrect a Victorian ideal that imagines a separation between the private and the public spheres.[46] But the idea of privacy on a time-shared system would have been difficult to comprehend in the 1960s, when mechanisms to produce a sense of user privacy were not yet fully developed. After all, despite a user's intimacy with "his" or "her" computer, that same computer was shared with tens to hundreds of other users (and now, in the cloud, thousands). As technology journalist Steven Levy wrote, "The very idea that you could not control the entire machine was disturbing . . . you would just know that it wasn't all yours. It would be like trying to make love to your wife, knowing she was simultaneously making love to six other people!"[47] The separation with public and private did not yet exist; the boundaries of intimacies first needed to be built. Analogous to the technologies of government and economic management that produced a conception of the self in the period we now call modernity, the user itself had to become a "modern user," one that seemed private and individual even as it was positioned wholly within a time-shared economy.

In what follows, I circle back to time-sharing's origins in the 1960s to offer a second story, of how the "benign bureaucracy" of system managers made users private. This narrative will closely track the one we have just considered on development of a time-shared economy. These two methods for governing users—first, by promoting computer usage as a vehicle for economic intimacy, and second, by preventing too much intimacy between users—both do their work behind the scenes. They act, like a carrot and stick, as a hidden layer of control within the mechanisms of cloud computing.

"The Victorians Built Magnificent Drains": Waste, Privacy, and the Cloud

Almost as soon as they were deployed, time-sharing systems began to reshape the social compact between their users. There were other people around at the same time, and in response, users quickly began to test the boundaries of social acceptability. Scientist Alan Kay describes the early days of MIT's Project MAC (Multiple Access Computer), circa 1963: "One of the guys wrote a program called 'The Unknown Glitch,' which at random intervals would wake up, print out I AM THE UNKNOWN GLITCH. CATCH ME IF YOU CAN, and then it would relocate itself somewhere else in core memory, set a clock interrupt, and go back to sleep. There was no way to find it."[48]

The best symbol for this new era was therefore less Spacewar than Core Wars—battling a glitch, bug, or infection from someone or something within the computer. Still, in university labs, these actions did not yet rise to the level of a violation. In a single phrase, Baran perfectly captured this inchoate sense of digital privacy as fooling around under the covers: "hanky-panky."[49]

All this would change in the mid-1960s, when the secret of time-sharing left the labs and burst onto the public's attention. Time-sharing systems had expanded so rapidly that leading computer scientists envisioned it would become a public utility, like the telephone system.[50] (This vision remains almost unchanged today, except that cloud computing is more accurately described as a series of *private* utilities.) Martin Greenberger had presciently predicted the "computer utility" in a 1964 essay for *The Atlantic*, and a 1965 issue of *Time* was among the first to tell businessmen that "'time sharing' is part of a growing trend to market the computer's abilities much as a utility sells light or gas."[51] Early 1966 saw the publication of a profile of MIT's Project MAC in *Scientific American* and Parkhill's full-length book *The Challenge of the Computer Utility*.[52] In the same year, the chairman of the US Service Commission excitedly informed the public that his agency was planning a new National Data Center that would collect and centralize data from twenty-two government departments, such as the Census Bureau, the Internal Revenue Service, and Social Security, in the name of efficiency and automating government.[53]

This last application seemed to merely extend moves by local government into time-sharing. Municipal areas such as Alexandria, Virginia, Tulsa, Oklahoma, Little Rock, Arkansas, Fort Worth, Texas, Denver, Colorado, and Detroit, Michigan, had already established "Metropolitan Data Centers" and other urban data banks to share demographic information, while the groupings only expanded: "a central time-shared computer system for twenty San Gabriel Valley (California) cities with sharing of data of common interest to several cities."[54] But something about the federal government taking charge—and the mingling of criminal, tax, census, and Social Security records—struck a nerve. Only a few weeks after the article announcing the

National Data Center hit the newsstands, an alarmed congressional subcommittee convened hearings on "The Computer and Invasion of Privacy" with a rapidity that caught even computer scientists by surprise.[55]

Held over three days from July 26–28, 1966, the hearings featured law professors, sociologists, computer scientists, and New York state officials who had built a smaller version of this proposed data center. The atmosphere of consternation had a heavily libertarian bent: George Orwell's *1984* and references to police states featured repeatedly, and the record contains an excerpt from John Stuart Mills's "On Liberty." One computer scientist claimed the development of data centers would be as "potentially dangerous and powerful as a nuclear explosive device";[56] another expert warned that at the rate of technology's development, there would not be much left for taxpayers to celebrate by the time the United States reached its bicentennial. Despite this rhetorical posturing, the hearing was remarkably ahead of its time. It referenced strategies that closely resemble today's headlines about data privacy: "information relational retrieval" techniques that infer relationships between people using metadata; automated data mining that would reduce the "cost per unit of dirt mining by unautomated human garbage collectors," and thus smear reputations for pennies on the dollar; even speculation of a data-personhood determined by a computer trawling through records as diverse as "book clubs [and] magazine subscriptions."[57]

This hearing indexed a moment of transition from user as programmer in a computer lab to user as part of a population. While these data banks and "computer utilities" anticipated the data centers and the always-on utility of today's cloud, they were still inchoate in form. What the future might look like would still be very much up for grabs. Advocates therefore sought explanatory parallels for its risks in previous public infrastructures. Testimony from the congressional hearing compared it to other "natural monopolies," such as the nineteenth-century infrastructures of the railroad and the telegraph; earlier, Greenberger had also drawn a parallel between the new computer utility and the electrification of cities by describing the gradual replacement of gas lamps with Edison electric streetlights in the early 1900s.[58] Two analogies emerge from this hearing, however, that are of particular interest to our story: the telephone line and the plumbing system. These analogies offer a way to understand veiled cultural attitudes toward computing that may not emerge from a more direct look, and I consider them in sequence below.

Of the two analogies, the telephone line is perhaps the most obvious precedent: wire taps on a telephone line (even when there is no physical line any more) continue to be the legal standard by which US courts consider digital eavesdropping cases. But one twist emerges in the context of time-sharing. One legal scholar compared the privacy concerns of sharing a computer with sharing conversations on a party line.[59] The unwritten subtext to his example is a generally forgotten cultural shift in the way that telephone lines were imagined. Eavesdropping on party lines did not used to be considered an invasion of privacy, historian Ronald Kline tells us; indeed, eavesdropping was a widely accepted practice in rural communities that often formed that community's "social network." It was for economic reasons—eavesdropping drained the batteries in their equipment—that telephone companies developed public awareness campaigns to teach their users not to eavesdrop. These campaigns described the social strife that resulted from eavesdropping and shamed the men who listened nevertheless by likening them to thieves—or gossiping women.[60] Taking the form of poems, films, and comic strips, these lessons in party line etiquette served to recast social behavior as antisocial behavior, as in *Bobby Gets Hep,* which describes a teenage boy, Bobby, whose penchant for tying up the party line leads to a barely avoided disaster (figure 2.3).

Now we consider eavesdropping on a telephone an antisocial act, a violation of privacy, but what has actually changed is the conception of the *user.* Similarly, what is considered digital privacy is formed less by the technology itself than the social codes or norms around the user that produce its individuality. This section explores the progressive development of these codes in time-sharing systems that made the user seem individual—and, reciprocally, made computing an individual matter. There is no single defining moment or cultural artifact that can encapsulate this development; IBM ran public awareness campaigns in the 1980s that bore some resemblance to AT&T's campaign, but a variety of technologies and strategies have also shaped this discourse. The specific threats to computer privacy—wiretapping, computer viruses, and, now, the bulk leaking of data repositories, whether by state or nonstate actors—have varied over the last fifty years, and the strategies have changed in response. But by the end of this section, we shall see that these strategies, considered in aggregate, grow out of the intersection of political and economic discourses about the proper role of a state to its subjects.

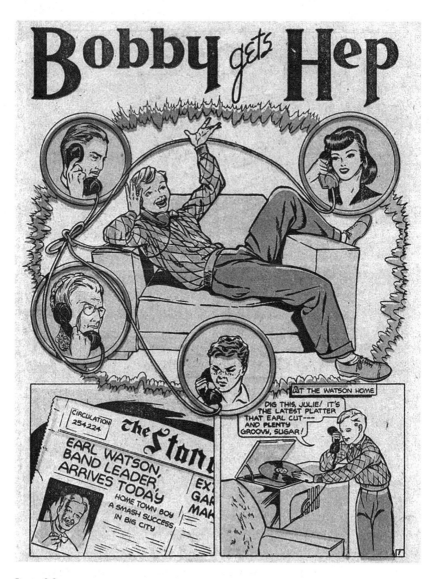

Figure 2.3
Bobby Gets Hep, Bell System comic for teaching party line etiquette, 1946. Scan courtesy Ethan Persoff, http://www.ep.tc.

In this light, it is worthwhile to note that strategies for imagining (and producing) a private user at the 1966 hearings resembled the governmental process of urban planning. Because of the number of municipalities considering data banks at the time, urban planners were an integral part of the hearing's audience, and, reciprocally, they invited computer scientists working on time-sharing to urban planning conferences.[61] Comments media archeologist Jussi Parikka: "[The] concern was how to fit dozens of people within this electronic 'space'—a problem that was analogous to the general problem of modernity in cities: how to deal with the issue raised by a huge number of people living in condensed urban spaces? . . . what is overgrowth, waste or a social problem"?[62]

It is in this context that we find our second analogy for understanding computer privacy. Testifying at the hearings, Baran inadvertently stumbles on a potent metaphor: the sewer. The safeguards required to protect privacy, he argues, may only come to be built during a moment of crisis: "We have, for example, been practicing [safeguards] in the design of sewerage systems and in electrical distribution systems for some time. But, historically, it usually has taken an epidemic to build a local sewerage disposal system."[63] Baran's description was quite prescient: waste—and specifically, the risk of contamination, uncleanliness, or infection—becomes a recurring leitmotif in discussions about privacy and time-shared computers. Legal scholar Arthur R. Miller singled out time-sharing in a section of "Personal Privacy in the Computer Age," writing about the damaging possibility of a "residuum of one customer's information accessible to the next user who is placed in control of the heart of the machine."[64] And citing Baran's example of automated dirt collection, a second legal scholar, Kenneth Karst, anticipated today's parlance on data leakage as he writes: "The risks of leakage in a shared-time system are obvious."[65]

Waste is particularly apt because it allows us to understand the effect of what Parikka terms "digital hygiene" in today's digital culture: the idea that a user is responsible for keeping her data from mixing with others, for avoiding infection with computer viruses, and so forth. Hygiene, of course, is not only produced by infrastructure, such as sewers, but is also a historically specific practice for the exercise of power. If we now think we have a direct and unmediated relationship to our own hygiene (making, for example, the privy inextricable from privacy), this is the distant legacy of a process of modernization. As Dominique Laporte tells us in his *History of Shit*, the individualization of hygiene may be traced to the modern state enjoining its subjects to keep (and bury) their own shit within the bounds of their homes.[66] Rather than dumping one's waste into the streets for all to see, the state interpellated the household as a private unit for managing one's own domestic life.

Baran's own reference to the sewer is fleeting; a year later, he will normalize it by comparing the computer utility to something that can "pipe computer power into homes," a metaphor that continues to be used to this day.[67] Yet it is through this lens of waste management that we can excavate a buried history of managerial control within the cloud. If, as Laporte puts it, "Surely, the State is the Sewer," we can discover how the state exercises power over its users—and how the individual user was produced—by revisiting computer history through the lens of waste management. How, then, should computer users be kept private; how should they be managed as a population? To answer this question, I offer two case studies of social "risks" that, at various moments of time-sharing, seemed to threaten the well-being of users as a whole: programming errors and computer viruses.

Case 1: Programming Error

Earlier, we saw that time-sharing systems developed as a response to programming errors and wasted time debugging. In a follow-up to "Man-Computer Symbiosis," J. C. R. Licklider and Robert Taylor offer a tongue-in-cheek vision of a future where there are so many programming bugs that "unemployment would disappear from the face of the earth forever" as everyone turns into a programmer: "the entire population of the world is caught up in an infinite crescendo of on-line interactive debugging."[68] As the number of users sharing each system multiplied, each program's errors could cascade onto those of other users, slowing down their programs and causing the system itself to crash. Errors, in short, could grow to the point where they would affect more than the initial user; they could form a kind of epidemic. And initially, the solutions were not subtle; the 1968 study that tested the effectiveness of programmers concludes: "validated techniques to detect and weed out these poor performers could result in vast savings in time, effort, and cost."[69]

These "poor performers" may well have been culled, but most operators found gentler ways of disciplining wayward programmers. Programmers were trained to follow what one scientist termed "defensive programming techniques."[70] Additionally, an automatic routine—termed the system monitor, supervisor, or executive—kept track of the hardware resources used by each user, audited their program executions, and kept a user's program from erroneously writing over or otherwise interfering with other users' programs. Writes Licklider: "There are even arrangements to keep users from 'clobbering' anything but their own personal programs."[71] The predecessor to a modern-day operating system, the monitor was also the only program empowered to perform certain actions, such as writing to output.

The monitor's protections acted as a sort of privacy barrier between each program, and, consequently, between each user. But a draconian system monitor was the subject of protest by one programmer, who likened these behaviors to governmental overreach: "This is bureaucracy run rampant and a protest is in order . . . May I lodge a violent and heartfelt protest against this unwanted and unfair interference by the monitor with my rights as a programmer!"[72] His editorial was published in *Communications of the ACM* under the title "Ye Indiscreet Monitor," a clear evocation of the way that the monitor seemed to "peep" in on each program as it was running.

Inside the metaphorical city of electronic space, the monitor was a draconian system of governance—one more benevolent than culling individual users, perhaps, but nevertheless felt as a violation of privacy. Moreover, the "indiscreet monitor" was not always effective in reducing error rates and wasted resources, leading computer scientists to look for other techniques. In 1959, the year that John McCarthy proposed the time-sharing modifications discussed earlier, McCarthy also described the idea of "garbage collection," in which so-called dead objects (memory that is no longer in use or "live") would be automatically culled.[73] Garbage collection served as a safety measure that could reduce programming errors and memory leakage between different programs. It improved the system's overall performance, because it would not be slowed down and choked by too many dead objects. Programmers would, ideally, not even notice when the garbage collector came by (though, in practice, one felt a several-second delay as the entire system paused); ideally, one would program without noticing the garbage that one produced or the resources one used.

Working in the background, garbage collection was a more "discreet" method of managing users than the monitor—even if it attempted to subtly redirect and change their very approach to programming. It was a positive, behavioral measure that did not punish or restrict a specific user, but sought to target users as a whole. In terms of the metaphor of urban planning we saw earlier, garbage collection was not unlike a public health measure that targeted the entire city's population. By sequentially walking through computer memory to "free" those dead objects, it recalled the Victorian emphasis on hygiene and cleanliness, which social theorist Thomas Osborne describes as seeking to "free the city [by] exclud[ing] all dead matter from the space of the city."[74]

Garbage collection is now a standard feature of many contemporary programming languages that power Web 2.0. (This is not to say that garbage collection has been universally embraced: it removes a programmer's ability to decide for themselves how to allocate memory.[75]) From a cultural perspective, garbage collection represents a shift from punishment to barely detectible methods of modifying behavior, a shift that would repeat in another realm: computer viruses.

Case 2: Viruses

Though rogue programs such as "The Unknown Glitch" had been in existence since the early days of time-sharing, viruses became a widespread problem in the 1980s. Computer scientists now explicitly invoked a metaphor of public health to manage this waste and ensure a user's "digital hygiene." After quarantining infected users, scientists tried to develop monitor programs as a first line of defense. A program "constantly runs in the background checking for modification to system initialization files and asks the user if these are desired," yet this monitor "introduces substantial overhead for the user who has to answer technical questions about operational procedures in order to be able to use the system and may interfere with other programs."[76] Once again, however, scientists found a monitor solution too intrusive and turned to epidemiological techniques. As computer virus researcher Fred Cohen writes:

> A small number of users appear to account for the vast majority of sharing, and a virus could be greatly slowed by protecting them. The protection of a few "social" individuals might also slow biological diseases . . . As a result of the instrumentation of these systems, a set of "social" users were identified. Several of these surprised the main systems administrator. The number of systems administrators was quite high, and if any of them were infected, the entire system would likely fall within the hour.[77]

While the 1968 study identified problematic users and fired them, here Cohen identifies "social" users and then experiments with a technique—a self-encrypting program—that he dubs vaccination. This technique was a laissez-faire approach to managing social risks in a time-shared environment; merely "protecting" a few key users could stop diseases and neutralize the threat of contagion.

How did the "social" user, once a potential threat to privacy, become a celebrated and valued user in today's sharing economy? How did "going viral" on social media come to signify marketing opportunity? A full answer is complex, and outside the scope of this study. Nevertheless, a marked change in the role of the user was in the air at the time of Cohen's study. For Cohen, the gravest threat to computer privacy was not from viruses themselves, but in the "social issues implied by viruses and the ramifications of our present social policies,"[78] specifically legal restrictions on copyright and source code that would prevent researchers from sharing information. Ironically, widespread hysteria about privacy and computer viruses could cause a "rapid movement towards isolationist systems . . . we may see a return to the 'dark ages' of computing where everyone is on his/her own and cooperation wanes."[79]

Cohen's prediction of a "dark age" of computing did not come to pass; the advance of open source, social media, and so on means that there is likely more cooperation now than ever. Yet he was correct about one thing: the "isolationist system" is now the default mechanism for ensuring privacy in the cloud—and arguably, the preexisting infrastructure for any sort of Web 2.0-style cooperation. Both a set of technological practices applied en masse to the cloud, and also a generalized ideology, this idea has turned what was once envisioned as a public utility or a community resource into a set of private utilities, and has fragmented a "global city" into a set of gated communities. This technology is known as virtualization.

Virtualization is a way of constructing a simulated environment that both allows a user unprecedented freedom (it seems as if she has control over an entire virtual environment) and restricts that user from "leaking" or contaminating the data of other users. An extension of the way that time-sharing allowed many users to share a computer, virtualization has allowed for thousands if not millions of users to share a data center in the cloud: whether a "virtual drive" of 10 or 100 GB that maps onto thousands of real hard drives; a "virtual machine" that gives the user the appearance of his own server in the cloud that can be instantly created on demand; or even a "virtual (private) network" that appears as if she has her own private channel inside the public Internet.

By separating one user from another, virtualization systematically manages social risk even as it vanishes into the background of the cloud. In today's cloud, these virtual walls and gates (sometimes called "jails," "sandboxes," and so on) are now so refined that it is almost impossible to sense the presence of other users on the same storage device, server, or network. As the culmination of the process of making control less and less explicit and less intrusive, a process we saw in our study of programming error and computer viruses, virtualization is now all but invisible: "As is true of the plumbing beneath the city streets, it takes an effort of will to bring software to conscious attention," Campbell-Kelly comments.[80]

But virtualization is far more than the technology itself, which had been in existence since the earliest time-sharing systems. Interest in virtualization coincided with the moment that the "user" was recognized as a private economic subject, enjoined, as we saw in the last section, to mind his or her own "business," to become productive, to work in "real time," and therefore to avoid wasting time. It is for reasons of productivity that the cloud is designed to remove infrastructure from sight, so that its users can focus on higher-level applications—namely, more "useful" jobs that lift users from the factory floor and toward the noble air of the knowledge economy.

Consequently, virtualization software is best understood in the terms that Baran briefly mentioned in the 1966 hearing: both as a utility that "pipe[s] computer power into homes" and as a sewer. Acting as a sanitary partition between users, virtualization ensures user productivity by removing the "wasted resources" of computing from the equation. These previously illiquid expenditures of capital include the physical hardware of disk drives and servers, but also the labor involved in assembling them, the labor of maintaining and removing unsanitary elements (malware, trash, spam, even the occasional worm or virus) from the servers, and the physical stream of waste that those computers ultimately produce. Waste, after all, is the residuum of consumption and productivity, the inevitable by-product of the circulatory networks valued by capitalism. In an economic system that values sharing, exchangeability, and movement above all else, waste is stoppage, the constipation of a continually moving system. Virtualization allows fixed units of labor and hardware to become mobile again.

As Osborne explains, the rise of this circulatory system of capital produces a specific formation of power. He observes that the Victorian infrastructures of sanitation in London

> function as the material embodiments of an essentially political division between public and private spheres; pipes, drains and sewers functioned to establish the sanitary integrity of the private home, yet without recourse to direct intervention . . . pipes are literally neutral and anonymous; they supply the home as a private space, and although by their presence they clearly have a certain moralizing impact upon conduct, this is achieved essentially through non-disciplinary means and not by imposing rules of conduct on the occupants but only by leaving the home and the family to itself.[81]

Osborne's point is that pipe building is a governmental measure that enacts a philosophy of political liberalism. Previously, the British state had tried to extend its reach into the home—physicians were to burst in on households of the sick and burn their clothes—with mixed results. The parallel is to the supervisory techniques of the "indiscreet monitor": in both cases, the extension of the state into the private sphere was too visible, and thus, it appeared, too intrusive. In contrast, pipe building targeted a population rather than specific individuals, and became consonant with keeping "private" life private, while delegating responsibility over individual health to the private household. It is consonant with the gradual shift in the topology of power away from the disciplinary state (one that "peeps" from a Panopticon, for example) toward a state that is concerned with regulating and optimizing its population even as it leaves the population to itself.

Virtualization is an even further application of a political principle that "leav[es] the home and the family to itself." As I have argued, virtualization results not just from better technical solutions for managing privacy in shared computers, but also a changing conception of the user that requires, as Osborne puts it, the "sanitary integrity of the private home." But there is a small but crucial difference in political ideology between Victorian pipes and the data pipes of the cloud. Whereas liberalism would establish a boundary between public and private spaces, the economic system at work in the cloud, neoliberalism, seeks to subordinate the public sphere to the logic of the marketplace.

Virtualization creates the idea of a private user out of what was, in the mid-1960s, originally envisioned as a public utility. Built by private companies, rather than public government, this private infrastructure is doubly removed from sight; it is impossible to determine the reach or extent of cloud providers, because the pipes are now trade secrets. While data pipes may seem inherently neutral, witness the "net neutrality" debates that seek to establish whether certain kinds of Internet traffic can charge more for transport than others. As of the time of this writing, the implications of the FCC's proposed "net neutrality" rules—drafted after years of heavy lobbying by both sides of the industry whose business would be materially affected—are still unclear. But the decision nonetheless provides concrete evidence that even the very idea of neutrality is contested terrain. "Neutrality," Osborne reminds us, is often the neutrality of laissez-faire economics; it is a political ideology.

Promising to allow a more efficient use of capital, virtualization is an "isolationist system"—one that both literally isolates users from each other and also makes manifest an economic system of individual agency. In the logic of the cloud, a user chooses "freely" which pipes to allow into the home. Users may decide for themselves, for example, which economic incentives to take on (50 GB of free storage, for example) in exchange for choosing which cloud-providing companies to allow onto their mobile devices. This economic ideology also means that most of the gates and walls in the cloud are not limited to those found in virtualization, but tend to be constructed by users. Each time we mute an irrelevant post, dismiss an ad, or mark an e-mail "spam," we exclude what is wasteful from our digital environment—and, in the process, also contribute to the statistical filters that decide whether a message is a waste of our time. Conversely, we tag photographs on social networks, identify friends, and "like" allied events, organizations, and corporations, indicating the data that should be included, productive, and worthwhile. The net result is that we have become willing partners with the algorithms that channel our online experience. Interpellated as "users," we identify with use and use value, and therefore mend and build the gates that keep us within a zone of productivity online. It is, in a twist of Stewart Brand's complaint about the "passive consumerism" of noninteractive computing, a kind of active consumerism.

What sort of sociality results from this kind of imagination of community? "A fully realized neoliberal citizenry," political theorist Wendy Brown writes, "would be the opposite of public-minded; indeed, it would barely exist as a public. The body politic ceases to be a body but is rather a group of individual entrepreneurs and consumers."[82] As is well known, online communities that evolve out of algorithmic modes of connection often reify marketing ideals of like-mindedness and demographic behavior by eliminating time-wasting or unprofitable results. Search Google two times for the exact same keywords and you might expect the same results. But if you are logged in as one user, the word "nature" might return results related to fishing and hunting, while a second user might receive results related to environmental justice. Algorithmic filters cause search engines to return different search results, depending on your imputed gender, demographic, and social class.

The Victorians may have meant to open the city by purging it of waste—sewage, abattoirs, fevers, zones of infection, cemeteries. But an entirely unintended consequence may have been the establishment of communities planned by the desire to manage risk. In sociologist Ulrich Beck's description of a "risk society," a society contains invisible contagions that are virtually impossible to conceive of, even as they continually threaten economic catastrophe. It is no coincidence that computer viruses of the 1980s were one of the threats cited by Beck in his account of risk, and though the viruses have generally been tamed since then, the consequence is somewhat unexpected; it once again involves the idea of city planning. Beck observes that city spaces have increasingly been designed to minimize the statistical chance of violence, traffic, and contingency. The result is a city of gated communities that, he argues, optimizes productive activity and safety by sealing off encounters between those at different ends of the socioeconomic curve.[83]

The cloud now resembles this city of gated communities. The long-term consequence of privacy concerns is the infrastructure of virtualization that allegedly protects us from viruses, cascading error, and waste, even as it produces "users" that are part and parcel of a structure of neoliberal power. But the very same errors that once served as the rationale for these isolationist systems can also be useful for uncovering this implicit system of control. As Finn Brunton writes: "'Community' online is free of accidents of proximity and geography . . . what spammers make maddeningly clear is that it is constructed from time, our human time—our attention."[84] Following Brunton's lead, the next section takes up another risk that can disrupt the carefully constructed facades of community: the data leak.

Cloud Cartography

Victorian drains, as with the cloud, performed a second sleight of hand: they transmuted waste into its etymological twin, vastness. Both waste and vastness derive from the Latin *vastus*—desolate, but also empty, expansive. The drains cleansed the waste from each household and also provided a never-ending supply of fast-running water, turning water into a (seemingly) unlimited resource that could be summoned on command. This, after all, is the meaning of piping in computer power; to turn time-sharing into a utility is to call forth as much computer power as one needs from a vast set of central servers that have access to virtually unlimited computer resources.

Thus, the term *cloud* refers to the same cultural fantasy of its analog namesake—what cultural historian Steven Connor calls the "belief in the air as the abode of the endless": inexhaustible, limitless, invisible.[85] Connor argues that this seeming inexhaustibility is what has allowed humans to treat the air as an infinite receptacle for pollution. The digital cloud's manufactured sense of limitlessness is the reason that the cloud is perhaps the premier receptacle for backup "dumps," so that archaic, forgotten, or obsolete data—the reverse side of real time's constant demand for newness—can be dumped en masse into the cloud and kept in its undead space, excluded from the vitality of what is designated as "live."

While we think of the cloud as an infinite expanse, the fact is that cloud users often share the same rights-of-way and physical spaces from 100 to 150 years ago. It is true that computer scientists are constantly working to remove some of these limitations. IP addresses, something like a phone number for your computer, were once thought to be inexhaustible, but have come close to exhaustion in the last few years, just as phone numbers in popular area codes, such as Manhattan's 212, have all but run out; now, IP addresses are to be replaced by a longer number, called IPv6. But the point is not how much the cloud's virtual space needs to grow in order to accommodate all its users; the point is that our imagination of this limitlessness allows us to forget the cloud's limitations.

In "The Question Concerning Technology," Martin Heidegger tells us about a dam on the Rhine in which water becomes a type of "standing-reserve."[86] Access to the seeming plenitude of the countryside transforms the rivers that feed it into a resource that can presumably be summoned on command. This vision of the world is perhaps an explanation for why we only see underlying infrastructure when it breaks. In the era of the computer utility, we are unable to see anything outside of that utility, which bears ethical consequences that are complex and interrelated. Most obviously, to lose sight of the cloud's infrastructure is to forget about the literal stream of waste that the cloud produces: the pollution from coal-fired power plants used to feed the data centers; the stream of electronic waste that accompanies cloud providers' need to constantly upgrade computers. But the same could be said about the many other infrastructures that we choose to ignore (highways, meat processing plants, shipping lines), whether because of disinterest, politics, or social disgust.[87] Merely obtaining more knowledge about digital culture's materiality may not address the root problem.

That problem, as I see it, has to do with our mental map of cloud computing, the heuristic that we use to imagine how information is organized, whether in physical space or in digital space. Recall that cloud-computing software maps a common infrastructure into individual users. A single cloud provider normally hosts tens of thousands of clients, known as "virtual machines," on the same physical machines, and relies on virtualization software to isolate each client from the others. Virtualization is itself a logical map, a topography that results from creating a set of personal channels that isolate us into individual users (and therefore seems to give us as much data, storage, computing power, etc., as we personally want). At the same time, these channels also promise to connect us and help us share more than ever.

Thus the mental map that best describes this contradictory topography is the one that the cloud itself offers for mapping and traversing it—the "network aesthetic" of isolated nodes representing each user, linked to others by graphs to represent the logic of social connection (figure 2.4). These graphs are the visual complement to virtualization software; they help us transform the seemingly unrepresentable world of limitless data into its virtual representation, into virtual "communities." Seemingly dispassionate and uniquely suited for visualizing today's network culture, these diagrams of the virtual, as Anna Munster, Alexander Galloway, and Tiziana Terranova have demonstrated, are in fact deeply integrated in the mechanism of power. "The network intervenes in this calculation as a productive machine and as a predictive/preemptive mode of simulation,"[88] simultaneously helping to predict social connections (offering other users you might enjoy meeting) and also helping to produce and even police these connections. (Network analysis

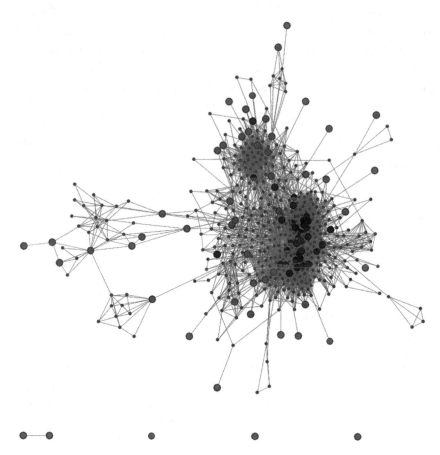

Figure 2.4

Map of a user's Facebook social network, graph generated by Wolfram|Alpha, Wolfram Alpha LLC, 2014.

gained popularity both as a way for businesses to track marketing prospects, and for police to track and target associates of criminals—revealing a subtle affinity between marketing and security that chapter 4 explores.)

What is needed is therefore less to "see" the cloud through the channels that it makes available to us than to develop a different map entirely. We need, instead, a mental imagination of data that takes into account the moments when they go stagnant, when they mingle with data from neighboring users as sewer-like pipes collect and filter them into the dark pools of the cloud.

It is here that we might turn to today's resurgence of data leaks. It is a cruel irony that the cloud—sold as a more secure way of protecting us from

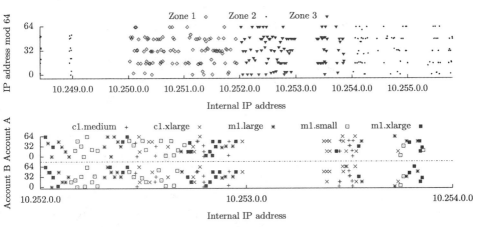

Figure 2.5

Statistical mapping attack on cloud servers. Figure from Thomas Ristenpart, Eran Tromer, Hovav Shacham, Stefan Savage, "Hey, You, Get Off of My Cloud: Exploring Information Leakage in Third-Party Compute Clouds." Reprinted with permission of Thomas Ristenpart.

vulnerabilities—has introduced an entirely parallel set of vulnerabilities. Edward Snowden's leaks have shown that that the National Security Agency (NSA) PRISM surveillance system functions almost entirely due to cloud technologies; the centralization of data in the cloud enables the NSA to install optical splitters inside data centers. (These splitters allow the NSA to automatically copy virtually all traffic sent over fiber-optic cables.) And consider that WikiLeaks' original purpose was to serve as a cloud drive for uploading and sharing secure data—offsite archives that would back up data and secure them from threats, not unlike the way that files may be backed up in Google Drive. I am not claiming that the cloud has invented leaking; a historian of the Pentagon Papers would surely find the photocopier as potent a tool as, say, a system for anonymizing web surfing. But I do think that the data leak offers a different way of mapping a public.

Since the early days of time-sharing, virtualization software has prevented data leaks by using a map. This map translates physical infrastructure into logical (or virtual) locations, but the software must keep that map secret from its users if it is to serve as an effective security barrier. In 2009, computer scientists at UC San Diego and MIT developed a technique for unmasking part of this map and forcing data to leak from one partition to another (figure 2.5). With enough data and some knowledge of statistics, the scientists were able to reverse-engineer the internal structure of a provider's cloud. They dubbed this technique "cloud cartography."[89]

Cloud cartography is a powerful way of attacking the cloud's weaknesses. If you know how the cloud works on the inside, then you can often get information from a specific client to "leak" to another client, because they share the same physical base. In other words, a hacker with a good map can illicitly access data from an adjacent virtual machine; it is a little like a burglar renting the apartment next door to the jewelry shop. If you consider the amount of confidential information stored in the cloud—the scientists give the example of medical records—then the stakes for preventing data leaks are very high. As they conclude, in language that is entirely familiar to us, "fundamental risks arise from sharing physical infrastructure between mutually distrustful users, even when their actions are isolated through machine virtualization as within a third-party cloud compute service."[90]

Once again, we see the cultural fantasy of "mutually distrustful users," who are always isolated first as atomistic nodes before they can be reconnected through social media or network graphs. This is the meaning of algorithms that determine our social networks, who we trust, do business with, and have shared interests with; this is why the cloud resembles a city of gated communities, optimized for productivity and yet "private" at the same time. Rob Horning incisively comments: this is "how Facebook addresses its users, a bunch of isolated nodes connected by its graces and its software, all competing for one another's attention and approval, urged perpetually to up the stakes of their sharing by Facebook's algorithms, which determine whether their content will surface widely and reap the sought-after recognition."[91]

But I believe that this model can be read against the grain. For the data leak that the cloud cartographers identify offers a different map than the default map presented by the cloud. It is like a core sample through a row of computers stacked in a data center: one user, in a crowd, connected only by proximity to the stranger immediately next to him or her. In the cloud, the supposed threats to privacy—constituted as the contagions known as data leaks, viruses, spammers, denial-of-service attacks, and the like—no longer follow the logic of "community." As they propagate down through each server behind the scenes, following only the logic of proximity, they remind us that privacy is not the only way of understanding a user.

Consider the analogous scenario of a fire drill in a Manhattan skyscraper, in which a thousand workers who would rarely ever cross paths—parceled out as they normally are into cubicles or retail or maintenance—congregate in the streets, if only for an hour. Such a crowd gathering in a public space is an experience of heterogeneity. The people don't know each other and have no productive reason to be out in the street together; they're joined only by the sound of an alarm bell. The crowd gathers people who happen to be adjacent, even as they are paradoxically disconnected from each other in their everyday lives. Similarly, inside a data center, data are connected only paratactically to each other, porn next to military documents next to banking records next to your e-mail. In that model of physical proximity, we might see an alternate map of community.

In the next chapter, we will continue our story by venturing inside some of these data centers. These locations, which aggregate exabytes of data, are everywhere and nowhere at the same time: everywhere, because they are an essential part of today's digital economy; nowhere, because they are such an ordinary part of the landscape that they are almost always overlooked.

INTERLUDE: LEARNING FROM SANTA CLARA

There is nothing special about a data center. Typically squat and windowless, they are part of the typology of warehouses and office parks that make up today's postindustrial landscape. For how generic their architectural forms are, data centers might as well be water towers in Germany, or gas stations in Texas—and perhaps they ought to be photographed that way.

Forget the images of blinking lights on computer servers that make the Internet look more sci-fi than it actually is. What data center managers pay attention to is not this spectacle, but the temperature. Row after row of standardized nineteen-inch telco racks alternate between "hot" and "cool" aisles, so named because the exhaust fans from thousands of servers send temperatures skyrocketing.

When I was taking pictures of one data center in a historically African American neighborhood of San Francisco, a security guard came outside and asked me what I was doing there. Learning of my interest in the building's history, he showed me an old wooden shack in the back of the building that they were about to demolish. The shack was a last remnant of the site's origins from the 1920s: first a Planters Peanuts factory, then a warehouse for Macy's, before it was repurposed as a telecommunications facility. He was an amateur photographer himself. With a wry look, he offered me a parting bit of advice: "If a guard comes out and asks to inspect your camera, run!"

Space Park

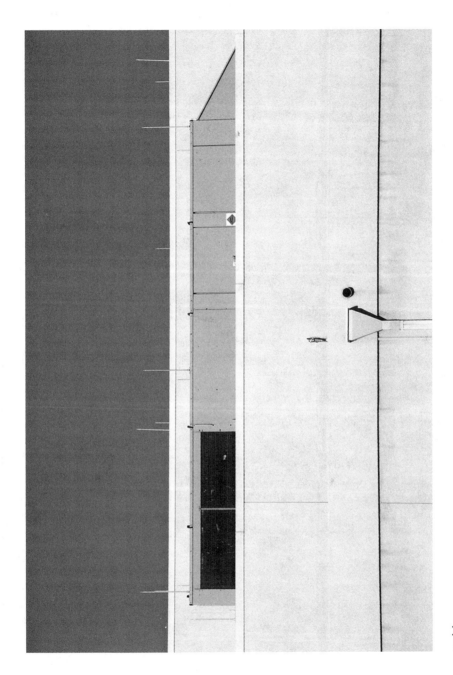

Walsh

Market

Alfred

"The Internet Must Be Defended!"

In the town of Bluffdale, Utah, about twenty-five miles south of Salt Lake City, a group of commercial data centers for Twitter, eBay, and Oracle, among others, cluster on Pony Express Avenue.[1] Like waystations along the original Pony Express, data centers on Pony Express Avenue are there to take advantage of a relatively sheltered climate; an untrafficked and unobstructed route for transmitting information quickly from coast to coast; and cheap water to cool off the machines: computers, like horses, overheat when worked hard, and most of the operating cost is in cooling systems. Data centers— miniature cities of computer servers and hard disks that enable data to be stored and concentrated "in the cloud"—are sized by their energy capacity. Recent constructions range up to 100 megawatts, equivalent to the power consumption of eighty thousand homes. Invisible and out of sight, data storage in the cloud may appear to be the ultimate technology for reducing paper waste and increasing efficiency, but as Greenpeace tells us, "Apple, Amazon, and Microsoft are powering their twenty-first-century clouds with dirty, nineteenth-century coal energy."[2] Indeed, if all the data centers constituted a country of their own, Greenpeace calculated, it would be the fifth most power-hungry country in the world. Such is the role of data centers, which can resemble a sleight-of-hand trick: for data to be placeless and borderless, data must first be displaced; for the cloud to appear decentralized, its data must first be centralized.

This insatiable demand for water and power explains why many data centers are built in out-of-the-way locations at a remove from major population centers: the desert border or the exurb, close enough to the urban core to benefit from fiber routes but far away enough for utility bills and land to be cheap. Power consumption and cooling capacity are thus practical considerations that determine a data center's placement, but security also plays a role. In a report trumpeting the state's data center industry, Utah's Economic Development Corporation cites FEMA statistics showing that over the last fifty-eight years, Utah logged the fewest federal disaster declarations—tornadoes, earthquakes, and so on—out of any state. However, the scope of disaster quickly slips between natural and man-caused disaster: the same report also touts Utah's geographic isolation as a way of reducing "vulnerability to attacks." If cloud storage sells itself as the ultimate place for files to survive coffee spilled on your laptop, or a lost phone, Utah's report reveals how this vision of personal security can quickly bleed into the idea of national security.

Indeed, down the street from the data centers on Pony Express Road in Bluffdale is a data center much like the commercial ones I just described. This facility, however, is surrounded by barbed wire and armed guards, and houses the National Security Agency. Completed in late 2013, the NSA's new data center funnels data from the agency's many eavesdropping sources planted inside the public Internet so they can be scanned for hostile threats.[3] What is most interesting about the Bluffdale site is not only what happens within it, but the simple fact of its location. The center is housed at Camp Williams, a training camp belonging to the Utah National Guard. It was here that a major in the Utah militia once took charge of the Pony Express during its short-lived service from 1860 to 1861.[4] In fact, the Pony Express was only possible because the protean state used Utah militiamen to forcibly carve out channels of safety through Paiute land. Now, 150 years later, the US government is still trying to secure messages and transmissions against potential enemies, but the enemies—cybercriminals, terrorists, and so forth—are different this time around.

Even as the NSA facility's militarized exterior may differ from the commercial ones that I described, both types of data centers look increasingly similar on the inside. With the threat of hackers, spammers, viruses, and natural disasters, civilian data centers now resemble highly secured checkpoints, employing a phalanx of post-9/11 technologies—bollards to prevent car bombs, "man traps," and iris and hand recognition systems. (Not that any of these are foolproof: a data center manager once told me, only half-jokingly, that a hacker who wanted to bypass a hand recognition system could always cut off someone's hand to get in.) One data center, named The Bunker, is based in a former Royal Air Force radar bunker in Kent, and describes its 3.5-meter thick blast walls as part of a heritage of security: "Security is our way of thinking . . . We consider everything outside the client firewall as hostile."[5] By fashioning themselves as *data bunkers*—fortified locations in the cloud for data storage—data centers carve out private pathways across an unsafe, public Internet, not unlike the guarded camps of the Pony Express, in which messengers retreated for the night from the unsafe territory outside. Data centers are only one part of the new regime of security, but as the most visible component of this infrastructure, they serve as metonyms for the trust we place in corporations such as Amazon and Apple to provide for our security in the cloud.[6]

Why do we consent to transferring our personal data to private companies' data centers? The simplest answer is because it is mostly "free," and because the free cost of storage is "freeing": as the previous chapter showed, we are induced to become users in the cloud through a number of economic incentives experienced as enabling, even liberatory. We acquiesce to what Deleuze called a "control society," a form of power that offers its subjects unprecedented flexibility through positive inducements and other mechanisms of self-regulation. But as this chapter demonstrates, we also give our consent because digital culture continually invokes the idea of a potential threat to our data. While securing data in the cloud typically works through the gentle structures of control—for instance, antivirus programs invisibly scan downloads for their users—the military camp-like structures that have reappeared in the form of data centers suggest a largely unseen yet militarized aspect of data security that cannot be described by regulatory power alone. The second half of this book is intended to serve as a corrective to the typical direction of new media studies, to both acknowledge the use of "control" as an explanatory rubric and also to redirect the conversation to a latent violence standing in front of us all along.

The data center remains among the least studied areas of digital culture, with cloud computing producing a layer of abstraction that masks the physical infrastructure of data storage. Paradoxically, then, data centers exist at the border between the dematerialized space of data and the resolutely physical buildings they occupy. Like architecture, data bunkers—and, metonymically, the cloud security apparatus of which they are a part—delimit the boundaries between inside and outside.

As I show in the first section of this chapter, the data bunker is, fundamentally, an architecture that excludes "unfree" Internet practices, of which spammers and hackers are only the most obvious targets. However necessary and proper it may be to root out hackers, the very idea of turning the cloud into an exclusion zone raises the specter of an internal but unnameable enemy—often an enemy, as I show, with the taint of foreignness. Yet to see the Internet as a space that must be defended from an invisible enemy may actually end up creating external divisions rooted in physical space. For example, a number of entrepreneurs have set up extraterritorial "data havens" said to lie outside the reach of sovereign states. For this reason, I suggest that the data bunker embodies a return to what is known as sovereign power, a kind of explicit power rooted in territory rather than in more implicit methods of regulating a population.

We are constantly asked to internalize a "bunker mentality" through our daily use of cloud computing technologies, and the second and third sections of the chapter investigate the consequences of this mentality for our perceptions of and interactions with digital culture. Extending architectural theorist Paul Virilio's meditation on the ruins of World War II bunkers, I contend that bunkers are a way of invoking the specter of a future disaster, a disaster that the cloud both generates and protects us from. I end by considering a European library consortium's attempts to entomb digital media in a former Swiss Air Force bunker. This project, intended to protect our cultural inheritance from decay, is an example of how the cloud is increasingly used for the "cold storage" of data. These attempts to shield our data from the flow of time, however, place us in a melancholic relationship to the present, leaving us forever fixated on a loss that is always about to come. To forestall this melancholy, let's go back in time and examine where this imagination of disaster originates.

In an online game called Invasion of the Wireless Hackers, kids can learn how to defeat hackers trying to break into a wireless network. Each time a player clicks on an icon of a winged invader, "Invasion" responds with a question about wireless network safety; the game ends when the player answers all the questions (figure 3.1a, b). This game is available at OnGuardOnline.gov, a platform developed by the US National Initiative for Cybersecurity Education and the Department Homeland Security to help users take ownership over their online security practices. The initiative's stated goal is to convince

a

b

Figure 3.1a, b
Invasion of the Wireless Hackers, flash game, www.onguardonline.gov.

the American public of their "shared responsibility" in cybersecurity by coding individual online security practices as a kind of civic good: "Americans can . . . make choices that contribute to our overall security."[7] But who are we really defending our data networks against?

The game ends with an admonition: "Remember: awareness and vigilance are the key to safer wireless networking!" As with other games at OnGuardOnline.gov, the title riffs on a classic TV show or movie, in this case the 1956 Cold War film *Invasion of the Body Snatchers*.[8] This slippage between wireless hackers and body snatchers recalls Cold War-era exhortations of "awareness and vigilance," which directed American citizens to be on the lookout for subversives hiding within their own population. "Invasion" thus portrays hackers as animated creatures "closing in on your computer" from the outside, while also suggesting that they may be lurking in one's very own neighborhood. Whether bodies resembling pods or hackers disguised as users on an invisible wireless network, the game's implication is that enemies are difficult to distinguish; an enemy invasion may be an invasion from within.

Further, if we examine other parts of the government's education project, we can infer the real message: the enemy is not just within our ranks but may actually *be* us. OnGuardOnline's sister website—Stop. Think. Connect.—also warns about hackers, but its main goal is to "help Americans understand the importance of practicing safe online behavior."[9] Its tips for Internet security caution college students to avoid peer-to-peer sites for music downloads—a clear signal that browsing illegal music download sites is a "risky" form of behavior. Each tip sheet concludes with the admonition to be a "good online citizen"; bad behavior, it suggests, affects us all. Thus the educational campaign is a way of prodding us to internalize these lessons of good behavior. As we saw in chapter 1, the networks of power that govern us always seem to contain or even produce the fantasy of another network: the deviant network. The subject formed by this structure of power is one engaged in a process of self-surveillance, constantly alert and on guard against improper behaviors, such as the spread of viruses through promiscuous computer networks.

Michel Foucault observed that modern societies have typically used the threat of an external enemy that has made its way inside as a way of exerting power on the individual subject through disciplinary measures, and, as power becomes less obtrusive, self-monitoring and self-governance. Indeed, if we attend to government statements about network security, the threat of an external enemy has never been sharper: in 2007, the Department of Defense's Defense Science Board published an alarming report on the threat of "foreign influence" within commercial software, blaming the irreversible trend toward globalized labor pools—a multinational software company employing "foreign nationals working in the United States," for example.[10] This "foreign influence" would, in the Defense Science Board's view, plant malware or backdoors within software used by US companies and government agencies for the purposes of industrial and state sabotage. In an October 11, 2012, speech, US Secretary of Defense Leon Panetta went one step further, explicitly warning of foreign agents who may perpetrate a "cyber Pearl Harbor" by targeting America's physical infrastructure, such as its power plants.[11]

The DoD's invocation of dangerous software from foreign agents as indistinguishable from software produced by American nationals—a kind of body snatching in code form—transfers the threat from an external enemy onto a potential domestic enemy. This transference employs the same reasoning that justifies the NSA's surveillance of the Internet: the agency's target is nominally foreign users suspected of terrorism, but because the global Internet is, by its nature, enmeshed in US network infrastructure, and because it is frequently difficult to distinguish whether a communication is domestic or foreign in nature, every US-based communication is part of its dragnet. The idea of the foreign enemy, in other words, is what justifies the state's targeting of domestic Internet users. But this enemy is a bit of a phantom; it appears at times to be a sophisticated, state-based hacker, as in Panetta's speech, and at times a petty cybercriminal that runs a foreign file-sharing site or sends an e-mail scam, as in the Department of Homeland Security's website.

We can find a partial explanation for the enemy's many-faced identity by examining a moment of slippage in the Stop. Think. Connect. website: it describes itself as a "global cybersecurity awareness campaign to help all digital citizens stay safer," but later lists its goal as outreach to the "American public." This double address to both American citizen and global digital citizen reveals the US government's goal of linking the supposedly universal values of digital citizenry with American values. In 2010, the then US Secretary of State Hillary Clinton declared Internet freedom a "pillar" of America's foreign policy, shrewdly positioning the United States as the primary defender of the Internet: "On their own, new technologies do not take sides in the struggle for freedom and progress, but the United States does. We stand for a single internet where all of humanity has equal access to knowledge and ideas."[12] In Clinton's speech, she names the usual threats—hackers, predators, cybercriminals—but then turns, more sweepingly, to target those countries whose censorship over the Internet fragments this vision of a "single internet," such as China, Russia, Syria, Iran, and the former Libyan government. In a later speech on Internet freedom in the Netherlands, Clinton expanded on this point by singling out a third set of potential enemies: uncooperative countries that want to create their own set of regulations for their country's Internet, rather than subscribing to the regulatory framework of a single, global Internet.[13] These countries distrust the current US leadership of the Internet oversight organization ICANN; former president Bill Clinton has also equated giving up US control of ICANN with an erosion of Internet freedom.[14] In this logic, the enemy is not just a rogue state or an individual hacker, but anyone who challenges the idea of a unitary, global Internet, and the freedom represented therein.

We should take Bill Clinton's assertions at face value, as many dissenters claim that the United States is the enemy undermining Internet freedom because of its surveillance practices. But regardless of who is right, both sides would agree that the threat extends beyond individual hackers to encompass those who would curtail Internet freedom as such. Indeed, Internet freedom results from the political philosophy of liberalism—a "relational and contextual practice," in the words of Wendy Brown, "that takes shape in opposition to whatever is locally and ideologically conceived as unfreedom."[15] Within this ideal, the Internet claims a universalism that resembles the universalist assumptions of liberalism itself; it promises that data are the same everywhere, regardless of how or by whom they are accessed. Not Chinese data, then, or American data, but just the data of a "global . . . digital citizen." Freedom thus stands as a kind of universal value that must be defended against practitioners of unfreedom; these "unfree" persons and countries are marked as dangerous aberrations. And yet, it's worth noting, the notion of freedom as a universal value comes out of a specific philosophical tradition in Western humanist thought.

It is this shape-shifting, contextual practice that explains why both the US government and activists who work against that government warn of an unfreedom that threatens the Internet. The enemy may be different, but the threat of its unfreedom is virtually identical. Consider this observation by surveillance studies scholar David Murakami Wood, who wrote, in a series of blog articles published in 2010–2011, that "because so much that is social [is] vested in these electronic chains of connection and communication, we must now argue clearly and forcefully that, nation-states and what they want be damned, 'The Internet Must Be Defended!'"[16] In Murakami Wood's scenario, the role of the villain is played by a nebulous group of state and non-state actors. Tying a series of disparate causes together—including explicit state censorship, as in the case of the Chinese Internet nicknamed the "Great Firewall of China"; intellectual property laws that allow individuals and corporations, such as the record industry, to overzealously enforce copyright claims; corporate ownership of the Web's infrastructure; and direct surveillance of the Internet by state agencies, such as the NSA—Murakami Wood argues that the Internet's commons are increasingly coming under attack, even if the various transgressors can only be identified by their opposition to the concept of "Internet freedom."

Yet in making this argument, Murakami Wood, we might observe, employs the same fundamental faith in liberalism mobilized by those aiming to protect the Internet from the contamination of the Other. For Murakami Wood's posts, rousingly titled "'The Internet Must Be Defended,'" make a somewhat ambiguous reference to Foucault's 1975–1976 lectures, published in English under the title "'Society Must Be Defended.'" In these lectures, Foucault argued that in the early nineteenth century, nation-states began to move away from explicit, racialized war to a form of politics that, through more indirect means, promoted the idea of society under threat. This threat depicted a racialized Other and also its correlate, foreign behaviors that had made their way "inside" to undermine liberal civil society. For Foucault, the modern state moves away from waging war against an external enemy to exercising power over its citizenry. This form of power works institutionally through the policing of aberrant behaviors and eventually shifts into the hands of the population itself, as they are educated or induced to practice self-monitoring. ("Remember: awareness and vigilance are the key to safer wireless networking!," warns OnGuardOnline.gov.)

It may seem surprising to link Internet freedom to race (or even its specter)—it is almost certainly not Murakami Wood's intention to do so—and the technocratic realm of encryption protocols and Internet governance may appear to be an unlikely breeding ground for racism. But as I aim to show, the shadow of the racialized Other still resurfaces in calls for Internet freedom—albeit in the form of what theorist Leerom Medovoi has termed a "race war without race," a struggle between a "tolerant and right-honoring zone of liberal civil society's 'inside' and the intolerant, right-violating 'outside.'"[17] For Medovoi, the legacy of Foucault's "society that must be defended" is a global conflict that no longer manifests as race itself, but is displaced onto other contests between values, as in the seeming choice, during the Cold War, between democracy and totalitarianism, or in the present-day project of globalization: you are either with the free market or against it. Clintonian logic perfectly situates Internet freedom within the latter project; you are either with or against what she calls the "defenders of the internet," a global coalition of persons and states that support a specific kind of regulatory framework, free-market solutions to technological problems, and the political values of liberalism.

This contest between values is only part of the story, however; and to tell the rest of it, we might turn to the xenophobic component that occasionally *does* erupt within the explicit naming of the Internet enemy as Other. These eruptions both affirm and complicate the aforementioned description of power. Online vigilantes, for example, claim to defend Internet users from harm by invoking a trope of (white) "little old ladies" victimized by Nigerian fraudsters. But as Lisa Nakamura has shown, their attempts to turn the tables on the spammers often operate through the visual tropes of race baiting.[18] Asking their Nigerian targets to prove they are for real, the vigilantes request photographs of men wearing bras, inserting phallus-like cucumbers in their mouths, holding up signs saying "I take it up the ass," or performing other sexually degrading acts. Such shameful or emasculating poses, Nakamura shows, bear the legacy of colonialism's visual culture. By spectacularizing their bodies, these photographs supposedly serve to out enemies seen as hiding or posing as "normal" Internet users, and in turn, to reinforce the division between the supposedly free Internet practices of the West and the unfree practices of the Other.[19] The underlying irony is that, even though in digital culture, a (black) Nigerian has come to epitomize the image of a spammer, the overwhelming majority of spam actually flows out of the United States.[20] Digital vigilantes not only turn the focus of their attention to the wrong place, but by producing a spectacle of abnormality, they also reinforce a narrative of Nigerian Internet practices *as* abnormal.

In his history of spam, Brunton argues that 419 ("Nigerian") scams really offer "an enormous narrative about the failures of globalization, from which you, the reader, can profit."[21] Brunton means, of course, the narrative of Western exploitation in Nigeria, which has ironically produced the mise-en-scène of embezzled oil contracts, dictators bearing Swiss bank accounts, and so forth. But his point about the unevenness of globalization also applies to cloud storage. Consider, after all, that the rationale for storing e-mail in the cloud is to let a central automated system, such as Gmail or Outlook.com, filter out from one's inbox 419 messages deemed fraudulent and marketing pitches deemed spam. In a more general sense, cloud storage is meant to protect users from a myriad of other attacks on Internet freedom: cyberattacks, hackers, and even state surveillance (if we believe Google and Microsoft's recent claims about beefing up their data center security).[22] Though we still use the public part of the Internet for everyday browsing, we increasingly rely on moving messages and files to and from the cloud's highly secured data centers. Cloud storage and cloud-based applications smooth out the chaos of the internets and produce a singular Internet, a global vision that only offers a glimpse of what lies underneath when an anomalous message slips, against odds, through the filter.

Yet this vision of a single, global Internet is grafted onto a labor pool that is by definition built out of the "foreign influence" the Department of Defense warns against: factory laborers in Zhuhai, China, who manufacture electronic components while being unable to freely access the digital networks that those components enable; the teams of Russian programmers who rent for a thousand dollars a website on "cloud labor" companies such as Elance-oDesk (now Upwork), or, on the opposite end of the spectrum, Moroccan freelancers, also hired through oDesk, who earn $1 per hour to screen content from Facebook. The main task of these freelancers is to decide whether pictures of disturbing content—such as "'deep flesh wounds,' 'excessive blood,' and 'crushed heads, limbs,'" to take an example from the manual Facebook issues to freelancers—conform to its community standards policy.[23] All of these examples come from Internet workers in countries that Hillary Clinton identified as aberrant or unfree, who have unequal access to the very digital infrastructures that they help build and maintain. To defend against messages, attacks, and images that do not meet Western community standards, the cloud relies on foreign labor, even as it excludes those laborers from sight. The logic of outsourcing data to data centers, in other words, relies on a practice of outsourcing labor—even as that very practice of outsourcing is cloaked underneath the rhetoric of a universal Internet.

Today, this rhetoric refers to a global Internet that connects multiple cultures and transcends national borders, but it is in fact an evolution of an imperial vision from the nineteenth century. We can see this in the immediate predecessor for the cloud's global fiber-optic backbone: submarine cables. As Nicole Starosielski has shown, submarine cables designed to bind together British territories in the Pacific with England hopscotched across its island dominions, such as Fiji, the Fanning Island, and the Midway Islands, avoiding landings on rival empires. Cable stations served as spaces where British-trained overseers supervised pools of native labor and converted them into a resource that supported the connectivity of the British empire as a whole. Thus, Starosielski argues, the cable station also served as "part of the colonial project—to civilize and tame the natives . . . in proper British behavior and self-presentation."[24] Describing illustrations from the Eastern Telegraph Company's newsletter *The Zodiac* that depict seminude Gilbertese natives with exaggerated racial features as the British cablemen's bumbling assistants, Starosielski demonstrates that racial difference served to underscore the precarious position of an empire reliant on native labor yet keen on enforcing those laborers' otherness. The British depended on the cablemen to perform repetitive tasks that we might see as analogous to the work of present-day Facebook image moderators: the cablemen spent day after day watching for signals in a dark, airless room. The irony of these island waystations was that their cablemen were not there primarily to serve their particular locations—the Midway Islands, say, or Fanning Island—but rather to connect Australia and New Zealand and Canada and Great Britain; they were inside the network but not necessarily part of it, their unreliable bodies and allegiances containing the potential to form what I earlier termed a deviant network within the network. As Starosielski reveals, cablemen's bodies were "the place where the border between the network's inside and outside was enforced."[25]

Starosielski's examination of "in-between" spaces, such as the cable station, allows her to unearth a hidden history of cable routes; this same approach will also help us complete the story on cloud security. For the cloud's physicality and its virtuality likewise meet at the data center, the modern-day descendents of Starosielski's cable stations. (In many cases, as in the Palo Alto Internet Exchange, they are the same place: old telecommunications buildings that continue, for historical reasons, to have a certain density of fiber-optic lines.) These data centers produce a cloud that transcends national borders, but they are also rooted in specific geographies; they produce a set of secure pathways through an otherwise "unsafe" Internet, but because they concentrate so much data, they also are among the most exposed sites for attack. For this reason, data centers are built according to the arcane arts of network security. Network diagrams resemble board games mapping the overlapping geography of hostile empires: there are tunnels, firewalls, checkpoints, trusted ("home") and untrusted ("foreign") zones, enclaves isolated by virtualization technology—and, at the border between the public Internet and a corporation or user's private data, the DMZ, or demilitarized zone. It is in the DMZ that data centers typically sit.

In attending to the data center as an interface between a network's physical outside and its virtual inside, we witness a surprising consequence. Typically, scholars of communication tend to understand digital networks as enabling moves away from specific physical spaces. By this reasoning, it is unimportant where a data center is situated, as long as it meets a set of technical requirements (power and cooling; fiber-optic cables). And, in large part, this is the case; data centers are no longer confined to tech centers in major urban areas, such as Silicon Valley or New York, as they used to be in the 1990s, but are now sprouting up in rural sites in Iowa and North Carolina, even near the Arctic Circle at Luleå, Sweden. But as if the ghosts from an earlier moment in history were returning, many highly publicized data centers, such as the Pionen nuclear bunker underneath Stockholm that housed WikiLeaks, have located themselves in former military installations. These spaces were once left for dead, but now, inside formerly shuttered blast doors meant for nuclear war, inside Cold War structures once fallen into disuse and still overgrown with vines on their five-foot-thick concrete sides, and inside gigantic caverns that once served as vaults for storing bars of gold, we see the familiar nineteen-inch racks appear, bearing servers and hard drives by the thousands. If digital networks no longer require such dramatic protective measures, why are so many data centers housed inside militarized structures built to defend physical territory?

Let me outline the stakes of this question by first retracing the path we have traveled thus far. I have argued that cloud computing companies induce users to place their data in the cloud through the promise of security. This notion of security, however, is actually a widespread discourse not authored by any single company, state, or agent, but by a myriad of often antagonistic stakeholders that nevertheless share a seemingly common value ("freedom"). They produce this idea of security by conjuring the image of an external, unfree enemy, an outsider to network sociality; it is from this alleged enemy that the Internet must be defended. The idea of security thus works on the level of user behavior, turning security into a "shared responsibility," as individual users are asked to be on the lookout for unfree activities. This vigilance and self-vigilance is a mode of power that Foucault and Medovoi identify as a distant outgrowth of the tactics of a racist state, which linked the external enemy to culturally aberrant behaviors within liberal civil society. Foucault and Medovoi argue that this way of exerting power over a subject signals a gradual shift in the locus of power away from external rivalries (one territory at war with another) and toward internal monitoring. But strangely enough, the reverse may also be true: the very specter of an internal but unnameable enemy in the cloud may actually end up creating external divisions rooted in physical territory.

Put another way, the reason data centers have reappeared as bunkers commanding a specific territory rests on the supposed need to "protect" the Internet from the Other. Yet these criminals are typically spammers or cyberthieves, and there is no technical basis for using buildings that were originally built to defend against chemical weapons or an invasion by Soviet tanks to defend against cyberattacks; a few dollars invested in faster encryption technology would be far more effective. The cause for this paradox, as I will show below, is the reanimation of what is known as sovereign power within the cloud, power as dependent on or coterminous with a specific territory. Consider one such manifestation that occurred in response to WikiLeaks' ejection from Amazon's cloud service, the incident that prompted Murakami Wood to post that "The Internet Must Be Defended!" Outraged over the arrest of WikiLeaks founder Julian Assange, one security specialist wrote that pro-Wikileaks hackers were "grouping together on a specific cluster of Internet Relay Chat (IRC) servers . . . to send a message that the Internet is a sovereign territory."[26]

What does it mean to consider the Internet a sovereign territory? For hackers, the question of sovereignty is more than a metaphorical one; the registrar for the Internet's top-level domain names, such as .com and .org, is a Virginia-based company called Verisign, and in one prominent case, the Department of Justice seized a foreign domain name, demonstrating what Canadian law professor Michael Geist terms the United States' "super-jurisdiction" over the Internet.[27] At the time of this writing, an agency reporting to the US Department of Commerce still exercises ultimate control over the Internet's "DNS root," the service that translates names, such as google.com, into IP addresses, numbers readable by computers such as 74.125.232.65. The United States similarly taps into network traffic passing through backbones and data centers run by US companies, which, given the historical geography of the Internet, is still much of it. In response to this situation, John Perry Barlow, cofounder of the Electronic Freedom Foundation, commented: "I felt like the answer to sovereignty was sovereignty. To fight them [the US government] on their own terms."[28]

Barlow's comment refers to pending legislation in Iceland to protect electronic privacy rights, and an eventual goal of establishing "data havens" in Iceland free from the "'intolerant outside'" of US law. But in some cases, data bunkers have skipped the step of lobbying to change a country's laws, and declared political sovereignty outright. Pirate radio broadcaster Paddy Roy Bates, for example, occupied a World War II-era structure floating in the North Sea in 1967; citing treaties on international waters, he pronounced his domain the sovereign "Principality of SeaLand," and himself "Prince Roy of SeaLand." Besides selling fake passports and titles, SeaLand's main business after 2000 was HavenCo, a "data haven" that claimed—by virtue of the so-called principality's independence—to be neutral to commercial or political interests, and thus to be the best place to store data. Since HavenCo's financial collapse in 2008, SeaLand has remained mostly silent. It has variously been linked to an online casino; a file-sharing site called The Pirate Bay; and another organization that has attempted to reassert its sovereignty in the cloud: WikiLeaks.

For HavenCo, the territory occupied by the data bunker is synonymous with the data's ability to exist outside a state's territorial claims. But there is a darker side to asserting that the Internet is "sovereign territory." In Foucault's study of sovereign power, we first see the most familiar meaning: power as dependent on or coterminous with a specific territory; the size of a kingdom, he writes, translates to how great the king is.[29] But this idea of sovereignty is closely linked to a second conception of sovereignty couched in the king's ability to supersede the law and to wage war. In its extreme form, this means taking a subject's life—that is, sovereignty as the power to kill.

This second meaning of sovereignty, the right to kill, is the ugly side of hacker attempts to seek their own exception to the rule of law. Around 1996, crypto-anarchist Jim Bell, an associate of Julian Assange from the

Cypherpunks mailing list, realized that combining anonymous digital currency and encryption schemes could be a potent combination. (Cypherpunks are hackers who believe in the power of cryptography to bring about social and political change.) The following year, he published a manifesto titled "Assassination Politics" to the Cypherpunks list, which called for the eradication of politicians (and other crooks) through the establishment of a cryptographic "dead pool."[30] Any user could donate money to an account that would pay out only when someone—presumably the assassin himself—knew the exact time, date, and circumstance of a target's death. In Bell's mind, by allowing users to kill off any "unwanted politician," he had invented a system for preventing tyranny and restoring individual liberty.

This was not the first design for a cryptographically supported killing system; as reporter Andy Greenberg notes, another cryptographer had previously mused online about "liquidation markets" (motto: "You slay, we pay") three years earlier. But Bell's "assassination politics" ignited a firestorm, and many hackers felt forced to tangle with or disavow his method, if not the sentiment behind it. If Greenberg is correct, even Assange may have felt the need to distance himself from "assassination politics" in his subsequent manifesto: "The act of assassination—the targeting of visible individuals, is the result of mental inclinations honed for the preliterate societies in which our species evolved."[31]

However, at the margins, the twin ideas of territoriality and "the right to kill" exist as an unassimilated layer within contemporary digital culture, evidence that some version or mutation of sovereign power is present in the cloud. For most scholars of digital culture, sovereignty takes the form of a fiction produced by computer code. As Wendy Chun explains, computer programs and networks effectively produce a sense of an all-powerful "'You' as the sovereign subject, 'you' as the decider."[32] Of course, "you" are not really in control; the program or protocol is, and it is merely asking a user to choose from among a set of preprogrammed paths.[33] In this line of thought, the idea of actual sovereignty—of a central decider, of borders and territory—all but disappears with the advent of borderless and decentralized computer networks that confound a sovereign's ability to rule over subjects within his or her borders.[34] But the headlines about sovereign challenges to US jurisdiction, the racial violence of "defending" the Internet from Nigerian spammers, and the real assassinations resulting from NSA tracking, all add up to the cold fact that the metaphorical violence of new media may be actualized as literal violence.[35] Sovereignty, in other words, may be much more than a mere fantasy or residue of a long-forgotten past; it may have found new life in the data bunker.

The field of new media studies has typically posited a broader shift away from sovereign power and toward newer forms of power. This theory, initially proposed by Foucault and reinterpreted by Deleuze (among many others), claims that traditional institutions for exerting power—the executioner, the military bunker, the hospital ward, the school—have given way to more subtle forms of regulation or control. In Deleuze's reading, sovereign power shifted in the Napoleonic era to disciplinary power, with prisoners encouraged to reform inside a prison, rather than merely being punished or executed for their crimes. Finally, Deleuze contends, power shifted a second time toward a control society via the post–World War II financial system.[36] In this model, American counterterrorism operates less through brute force than through detecting and flagging financial transactions (abnormal dollar/euro amounts wired through foreign banks, for example); should a criminal eventually be found, he is either made to pay a heavy fine, or fitted with an electronic device that allows him freedom of movement, at the price of being tracked.

There is abundant evidence that this shift away from cruder methods of exerting power has taken place; I myself presented evidence earlier that the attempt to manage time-shared users gradually moved from explicit modes of exercising power (terminating or disciplining wayward programmers) to implicit ones of management (economic incentives that manage and even produce user activity). And this shift is certainly not all-encompassing; prisons, of course, still exist, as do executioners. Yet in the rush to declare every new form of digital technology a means of controlling or optimizing life, scholars have all but ignored the question of sovereignty. Sovereignty, in short, feels antiquated; it seems to belong to the era of kings, and not digital protocols. Yet Foucault himself stated that "the problem of sovereignty [is] never more sharply posed than at th[e] moment" it becomes necessary to redefine its role within today's regulatory structures.[37]

Thus when discussions of sovereignty come up in new media studies, they inevitably turn away from actual bodily death and toward a metaphorical form of sovereignty-in-quotes. But the cultural fantasy of networks as sovereign is precisely what gives rise to manifestoes—and actions—in the same genre as Bell's "assassination politics." Digital scholars risk committing an error of omission if the conversation turns continuously to control or bio-politics at the expense of the less mediated and less technological methods of exerting power. It bears repeating that power is always hybrid; the very infrastructures that enable the deterritorialized networks of the cloud also enable the sovereign violence within.

The data bunkers I have considered serve as gateways for this reanimation of actual violence. As Judith Butler writes in her study of sovereign power: "*The historical time that we thought was past turns out to structure the contemporary field with a persistence that gives lie to history as chronology.*"[38] What is at stake in this study, then, is a different way of imagining not just the contemporary moment, but also how we approach history and futurity. The history that we might imagine as moving in one direction because of technological progress, shifting away from physical to electronic space, is filled with dislocations and anachronisms, even reversals. These complex temporalities will occupy us for the remainder of this chapter.

Bunker Archaeology

In a modern-day update of what critic Susan Sontag termed the "imagination of disaster," a data management company named Iron Mountain defines disaster recovery as a way of "counteract[ing] . . . the consequences of hardware malfunctions, human errors, software corruption and man-made or natural disasters."[39] Iron Mountain has made its business out of securing bank deposit records, medical and legal records, and sensitive corporate information inside its data centers. In this it extends its original mission: the company was originally named Iron Mountain Atomic Storage, Inc., and began by operating vaults embedded in a mineshaft deep inside a mountain in upstate New York—vaults designed to survive war or an atomic explosion.[40]

The cloud may not prevent disaster, but it may help its users recover from it. If it is the threat of hackers or fire that convinces individual users to back up their files to the cloud, it is disaster recovery (DR) that sells cloud computing to corporate customers. DR can mirror or replicate a company's entire computing environment—often not just files, but also entire operating systems—to the cloud; when a disaster strikes, a virtual machine in the cloud simulates a failed computer's setup. If the virtual machine does this fast enough, clients may not notice the failure at all; the server is said to "fail over to the cloud." Disaster recovery also works in a second way: so-called cold storage services in the cloud, such as Amazon Glacier or Iron Mountain's Virtual File Storage, allow users to back up and archive exabytes of infrequently used data, data that does not need to be 'live,' or immediately accessible. In archives meant to freeze and preserve data for several decades or more, we see an echo of Iron Mountain Atomic Storage, Inc.'s original business case, which guaranteed that bank records would be available after a nuclear war ended.

Disaster recovery is twinned with the idea of Internet security: the former occurs after the disaster, and the latter attempts to preempt it. Both aspects of cloud computing motivate our participation within the cloud by continually prompting us to imagine a threat to our data. But, reciprocally, how we imagine a threat also shapes the cloud. The previous section described how the specter of a hidden, unfree enemy has prompted some companies to repurpose military bunkers as so-called data havens, a hint that the cloud is not just built to solve specific technological problems but is built around the shape of our imagined vulnerabilities. Because of this, what "the cloud" refers to is as much a cultural fantasy as a technological specification: in some sense, the cloud *is* its fevers.

What are the affective and phenomenological ways in which the data bunker works in the cloud of our imagination? The idea of a nebulous network that is always about to unravel because it contains a break somewhere within is, in its extreme form, a feverish condition that chapter 1 likened to paranoia. While paranoia seeks to preempt the enemy, a second impulse seeks to survive it. This impulse is behind the desire to secrete and hoard exabytes of data inside a bunker for a disaster that is always about to come, and it manifests itself in architectural forms that evoke fixity and endurance. Indeed, the brand name "Iron Mountain" suggests solidity over time by invoking the image of its namesake, and the limestone mines beneath.

This idea of survivability, as we will see, is at the heart of an affective, even libidinal, stance toward disaster that I describe as "bunker mentality." This phrase borrows from scholar David F. Bell's description of a political climate obsessed with imagining disaster after 9/11.[41] The phrase—originally used by journalists in reference to George W. Bush's presidency—refers, in Bell's view, to the Bush administration's growing obsession with secrecy and "shadow governance."[42] This regime both hides its actions from the public and hides, literally, underground. Think, for example, of the undisclosed locations where former vice president Dick Cheney waited out the tense days after 9/11, understood to be a combination of Cold War bunkers underneath

Raven Rock, Pennsylvania, and Mount Weather, Virginia, both locations hidden from the public.[43]

As I incorporate it, the defensive response of "bunker mentality" may apply more generally to the realm of data. Consider the Mount Weather bunker, for example: it was originally used to allow electronic financial transactions to continue should the Federal Reserve banking system ever be attacked by a nuclear strike, and it is now not just a place for the government to evacuate in case of a terrorist attack, but also the location of the National Audio-Visual Conservation Center, where the Library of Congress's entire videotape and sound collection is currently being digitized. Because these digital data are themselves vulnerable to disaster, cloud technologies replicate the data to "a remote and secure disaster recovery facility" called the Legislative Branch Alternate Computing Facility, used in case Congress is attacked: a bunker behind a bunker.[44] Disaster reaches across many levels; national emergency is a short step from the mundane decay of videotape or floppy disks. The Library of Congress links its archival work to a bunker designed to withstand the government's imagined destruction.

The establishment of one data bunker produces an imagination of disaster that replicates, endlessly, as more data bunkers. This pattern of "bunker mentality" reduplicating itself is most visible in in the cloud, where disaster recovery is a palliative for technological failure in an age of networks. Iron Mountain's disaster recovery mechanisms, we recall, offer protection against "hardware malfunctions . . . software corruption," a reminder that cascading computer failures from a botched update or a rogue software program have become commonplace. Many of these contagions that haunt the cloud result from the overconnectivity of one network with others: one cloud server fails to sync with another, or one network's router misfires, causing a chain of errors that ripple through all other interconnected networks. Thus disaster recovery in the cloud often protects us against the disaster of the cloud itself; it is as if the cloud were an autoimmune response that inadvertently produces the very systemic failures that it claims to defend us against.

However contemporary its technology, the cloud's "bunker mentality" actually describes a retreat from technological progress. This response can be traced back to the history of its namesake, the military bunker. As Bell shows, the bunker became obsolete during World War II, but it reemerged after 9/11 as a shelter from an increasingly technologized form of war. In contrast to the "new type of warfare based on speed and on real-time surveillance, the military bunker reappeared as a challenge," Bell claims: the primitive hole cut into the earth allows its occupant to hide from US satellites sweeping the earth's surface.[45] (Perhaps the contemporary bunker's most visible user was Saddam Hussein, who managed to evade capture for several months after the fall of Baghdad.) If modern warfare is predicated on fiber optics, digital networks, and real-time surveillance, the bunker "calls into question that vision"; if the West's military might is predicated on technology, the bunker makes its occupants invisible, and that power void.[46]

In a brief but tantalizing aside, Bell likens the bunker's tactics to those of a sleeper cell. The sleeper cell hides within a population, biding time until sleeper agents can emerge in the future, and causing the specter of race war, a society penetrated by foreign powers, to resurface. Like the sleeper agent, the bunker's temporality is also predicated not just on hiding but also on waiting: waiting out the conflict until foreign powers withdraw, for instance. If the bunker plays obsolescent counterpoint to modern warfare's technology, it also inverts modern war's real-time qualities. The opposite of quickness and virtuality, the bunker posits endurance, the *longue durée* of the wait. The bunker waits, as if asleep, for an attack or a disaster that may never come.

It is this temporal aspect that I wish to dwell on. The bunker's reemergence in the cloud has made disaster recovery readily available, in part by making disaster constantly imaginable. By guaranteeing that a corporation's servers will, virtually instantaneously, fail over to servers in the cloud, the cloud pairs two very different speeds: disaster recovery mechanisms measured in milliseconds with the almost indefinite period of time within which the disaster will arrive, during which time files are kept in deep storage.[47] While the usual symbol of the cloud is the fiber-optic cable, which transmits data at the speed of light, the bunker complicates this by introducing a second element: wait time. The cloud takes on the temporal attributes of both real-time networks and sleeper-like bunkers that await the system's inevitable failure.

Counterintuitively, the faster the technologically mediated disaster arrives, the more central these slow places for the storage and protection of data become. As data storage becomes virtualized, the data bunkers increasingly resemble monuments—not just in size, but also in terms of the promise they represent for long-term survivability. Indeed, by squirreling data inside data bunkers for the indefinite future, the cloud is even being used as a supercharged version of an analog archive. Iron Mountain's limestone caves for cold storage, for instance, hold the original negatives and glass plates comprising the Bettman Archive—over eleven million photographs from the nineteenth and twentieth centuries—as well as the equipment for digitizing these images. This equipment may seem to presage the Bettman Archive's inevitable conversion from analog to digital, but in fact scientists believe the analog negatives may survive for thousands of years. We can extrapolate from this example a larger principle: just as it represents a digital architecture that mediates between the real physical environment and the virtual cloud, a data bunker also operates at the interface between the analog and digital media stored within. Neither analog nor digital format is necessarily "better"; rather, they both share an imagination of future loss.

To understand the temporal and phenomenological aspects of "bunker mentality," I turn back forty years, as Bell does, to a moment when bunkers themselves became obsolete. My source is architectural theorist Paul Virilio's seminal text *Bunker Archaeology*. Originally written by Virilio to accompany a 1975 exhibition of his photographs at the Musée des Arts décoratifs, *Bunker Archaeology* contains a series of essays and photographs that reflect on his decades-long encounter with abandoned bunkers on the Atlantic coast of France that were part of the Atlantic Wall; built by Germany during World War II, this network of bunkers consisted of fifteen thousand shoreline fortifications stretching from Norway to the Spanish border. In the book, Virilio laces his analysis of war with lyrical moments spent clambering inside bunkers after they have begun to fall apart, walking past a landscape dotted with bunkers, even remembering the sight of the ocean nearby. He uses these vignettes to offer a speculative history of these bunkers, which were militarily outdated as soon as they were built because of the arrival of aerial-based warfare. Yet as I read Virilio, the bunker's military obsolescence is largely irrelevant, for in waiting for the threat to pass, the bunker makes outdatedness a virtue; it helps its occupants survive one moment in history by envisioning a different historical moment. Thus, if a data bunker represents the simultaneous cohabitation of real time and wait time, this is perhaps a feature of bunkers in general: as Virilio suggests, they are not just buildings, but also a type of temporal architecture.

Introducing his subject, Virilio observes that the Atlantic Wall is located at the extreme limit of the shore—at the end of land, looking over an ocean where a theoretical attack might arrive. But the wall also occupies another kind of liminal space: the wall, Virilio writes, had been built "at the precise moment of the sky's arrival in war," where the plane becomes the ultimate weapon for raining down bombs, discharging poisonous clouds from chemical weapons, or even delivering the mushroom clouds of nuclear attacks.[48] These attacks transform the whole earth for a potential theater of annihilation; if all of space was now a potential zone for death, it metaphorically prefigured the planet's "return to a gaseous state."[49] In the face of this transformation, the Atlantic Wall is, of course, useless; the architecture of a threat tied to the land's two-dimensional surface—namely, armies dug into their trenches—it can do little in the face of three-dimensional warfare.

Retreating deeper into the earth, the bunkers are the visible scars of a forcible transition between two modes of warfare. The bunkers, for Virilio, thus become a metonym for media change: in the book's afterword, penned in 1991, he uses them to discuss a larger shift in power from real space to "data in real time"—and, in turn, wars that rely on ever more instantaneous data transmission and the twenty-four-hour news cycle of information.[50] Of course, history may not flow in a single direction, as Virilio implies; Bell demonstrates that the underground bunker has increasingly *reappeared* as an effective, if low-fidelity, response to aerial and satellite-based war. *Bunker Archeology* is therefore most useful as an account of how these larger transformations in media affect us. The work stages a subject caught between two ways of seeing—the land-based, territorial vision of a defensive bunker and the atmospheric vision of aerial warfare—embedding what Virilio will later call the "logistics of perception" inside daily life.

By exploring the act of looking at and through the bunkers' forms, Virilio examines the bunker as a media object in its own right. In a richly phenomenological account of the beach at Saint-Guénolé where he spent his childhood, Virilio begins by guiding his reader frame by frame through his memory. As his eyes pan across the water's expanse, he suddenly discovers the presence of his own body, the sensation of warmth transmitted by the bunker's concrete shell. He is immediately struck by the contrast between the qualities of light inside and outside the bunker, the open field of light over the sea juxtaposed with the darkness of the bunker's closed environment. "So I turned around for an instant to look at what my field of vision onto the sea had not offered up ... between the protective screen, looking out onto the Breton port, aiming today at inoffensive bathers, its rear defense: with a staggered entrance and its dark interior in the blinding light of the guns' opening towards the sea."[51]

This key moment sees Virilio recognizing the bunker as a technology of vision, much like a periscope or cinema. By referring to the bunker's "protective screen," he means the literal embrasure, the sheet of concrete meant to protect the person peering out of the bunker, but he also means that a bunker is a machine for viewing images, as is the screen of a movie theater. The vision through the bunker's narrow gun port is locked to a specific target: one can see only the port, or, now, the bathers on the beach. In contrast, Virilio describes the way he looks at the ocean as "scanning" the space of the horizon "with nothing interrupting my gaze."[52] Scanning is the opposite of fixing one's gaze at a specific target, and so Virilio's experience at Saint-Guénolé offers a sort of parable for aesthetics: the eye may be structured by the militarization of our perceptual apparatus, but it can look in two different ways. The surveillant eye of an airplane searches for the anomaly in an open environment, categorizing potential threats as hostile or foreign. In contrast, the protective screen of the bunker both enables and closes off the field of vision; it frames the outside, making the infinite expanse viewable as a landscape.

To expand on Virilio's thinking, each type of view is a response to threat. From above, the vision of infinite space subordinates the human body to the scale of the sky: the optics of a plane's gunner or a missile's camera. Virilio links this vantage point to the incessant increase in war's tempo in the quest for a never-ending "reduction in the 'time of war.'"[53] Looking outward from the bunker, however, is an almost infinitely slow process. The bunker waits for its target to come into view; it is less a process of active seeking than a process of waiting. The verb "to wait" is derived from the Old French *waiter*, meaning to watch with hostile intent, to guard. And to watch in this way, Virilio implies, is to place oneself in a suspended time that exists outside the time of everyday life. "Why this analogy between the funeral archetype and military architecture? Why this insane situation looking out over the ocean? This waiting before the infinite oceanic expanse?"[54] This tercet of questions, in a sense, answers its last question with its first. Waiting is a funereal process, a form of death; the bunker is not just a watchtower, but also a coffin.

The monumental shape of the bunker reminds Virilio of a monument's original typology: the sepulchre. Its form evokes the same funereal dread of "the Egyptian mastabas, the Etruscan tombs, the Aztec structures . . . [forms that] shed new light on what 'contemporary' has come to mean."[55] These tombs are not just markers of the past; as religious monuments, they persist past the builder's death and even keep alive the fantasy of their dwellers' return. This is what leads Virilio to conclude that the bunker is "a place where he buries himself to subsist . . . the crypt that prefigures the resurrection."[56]

Waiting for life to resume, the bunkers transport Virilio into a temporal limbo; they conjure a "different historical time than the moment of my trip," and hold the rules of chronology in suspension.[57] The result is a curious temporality rooted in the death of the present. Activated by the imagination of disaster or war, Virilio's bunker sits, "anachronistic during normal periods, in peacetime."[58] Even the bunker's passing resemblance to a spacecraft strikes him as belonging to an anachronistic vision of a future from a past era. Like cryopreservation, the bunker is fundamentally a *temporal* architecture; the spectral image of the Other that is excluded and reanimated by the bunker is now the "other in time." The bunker's heterochronic architecture produces the imagination of a future looking backward on the current moment and, as such, incorporates a phantasmatic time outside the boundaries of lived time. It inhabits, one might say, the tense of the future perfect: "Despite my current death, my voice will have been heard."

And this lesson is well suited to other types of bunkers, even digital ones. Though the sentries that defend and guard us against threat are no longer soldiers manning bunkers, but rather computer programs that go by names such as Microsoft Defender, it is clear that the cloud constantly exhorts us to be watchful and vigilant. This "bunker mentality" causes us to watch our data even when there is no actual enemy out there, when the disaster is not so much unnameable as nameless. But because such programs do this work behind the scenes, ours is a passive watchfulness that reacts to threats that come into view and imagines how we might recover from disaster. As Virilio describes, this atmosphere of perpetual watchfulness comes with the sense of endless waiting. Indeed, digital culture seems to have evolved hundreds of words to describe waiting, many of them drawn from communications theory: lag, latency, slowdown, buffer, throttle, hold, downtime, interruption, freeze, congestion, chop, blockage, traffic, delay. Yet the overwhelming emphasis on "real time," namely, what is (just) about to come—the next refresh of a web page or the next phone notification—subordinates and even voids the phenomenological *now* in favor of the future perfect. We look retroactively from the perspective of a future that always seems to be only a fraction of a second away.[59]

But Virilio's subtler conclusion has to do with the data bunker's connection with death. "Death," too, pervades our language for the digital: there is the "dead link," "dead hard drive," "killing the program"; the "time to live" counter stamped onto all data packets sent across the Internet to mark their inevitable expiry, lest they multiply like cancerous cells. And while these banal, everyday deaths shift our attention away from the larger deaths of, say, terrorism or war, this sort of death is nevertheless latent inside the structure of disaster that the cloud is designed to mitigate. The cloud encourages us to wait in fear of things going terribly wrong. Designed around this fear, the cloud allows us to lock files in the seemingly limitless storage of a data bunker for safekeeping, a keep in which to keep files for perpetuity. As our very own "survival machine," it ostensibly allows us to manage the disaster. Yet the survival machine is often a sepulchre that contains an almost unbearable psychic burden or weight. Gripped with the beckoning maw of the bunker's entrance at Saint-Guénolé, Virilio eventually clambers inside: "the visitor . . . is beset with a singular heaviness; in fact he is already in the grips of that cadaveric rigidity from which the shelter was designed to protect him."[60]

This idea of shelter is what leads Virilio to explore the wider consequences of security and territory in his later work. On his way, he will pen an essay that the 1965 issue of *Architecture Principe* published immediately adjacent to his bunker photographs. This essay is titled "Architecture Cryptique," cryptic architecture; it is a later iteration of his thoughts on bunkers. A difficult essay, it imagines cryptic energy, "the energy of everything that hides itself," not just as a single line of bunkers, but as a network of survival networks.[61] Infrastructure designed as a survival machine, as a crypt. Virilio may have been thinking of physical structures, but his words also speak to the digital infrastructures that increasingly lock our data away.

So let us climb inside a few of these digital crypts; seen correctly, these structures are less technologies from the future than ruins in disguise.

The Melancholy of New Media

In May 2010, a consortium of European libraries and research institutions entombed a metal box containing our collective "digital genome" in a former Swiss Air Force bunker beneath the Alps, taking inspiration from seed banks and animal genome projects (figure 3.2). Though the act was in part

Figure 3.2
At the Swiss Fort Knox in Saanen, Switzerland. Photograph: Information & Software
Engineering Group, Technische Universität Wien. Courtesy of Andreas Rauber.

a publicity stunt, the box also bore deadly serious news: digital media,
the supposedly immortal replacement for analog media, is itself subject
to decay, even death. Rather than a perfect replacement for the organic
(and thus impermanent) mediums of paper or microfilm, they explain,
digital media is in fact "brittle and short-lived."[62] Part of this reflects the
physical substrate on which digital media is kept: a recordable DVD lasts
perhaps fifteen years before the dye fades, with some brands showing

ill effects in as soon as 1.9 years;[63] magnetic hard drives fare worse. A bigger problem is the rapidly changing nature of file formats and decoding systems, which produce a condition in which a user can rarely open a file created a decade ago without significant difficulty. In one famous example, the BBC's 1986 "Domesday Project" was conceived nine hundred years after the original Domesday Book and intended to be read nine hundred years into the future. But programmed in the obsolete BCPL language, stored on an equally obsolete laser disc, and requiring a modified Acorn BBC Master computer to view, it was essentially unusable a mere sixteen years later.[64] There is, as the consortium's project dramatized, no such thing as pure information; digital media is always tied to the systems of encoding that make it understandable.

Addressed to the data archeologist of the future who might decipher its contents, the "digital genome" box included five digital files—a sample JPEG image, an HTML webpage, a QuickTime movie, a PDF document, and a Java program—along with the 6,085 associated other files required to decode, convert, or view those file formats, stored on mediums from punch cards to DVDs. But the box is not accessible to any user in the current moment; instead, the box is a time capsule to dramatize the problem of digital preservation. The primary purpose of sealing the box inside a data bunker named "Swiss Fort Knox"—located somewhere near Saanen, Switzerland, though the exact location is a closely guarded secret—ensures that the box is hidden from view. Sent into a quiet and undisturbed limbo, it now waits for a future moment when these "digital genomes" may be reanimated and resurrected, like new plants grown from the seeds of extinct plants.

The consortium's project, named Planets, presents a common narrative from the field of digital preservation. The consortium's brochure opens with an illustration graphing the declining lifespan of each successive media: clay tablet, papyrus, vellum, and so forth, finishing with magnetic tape, disk, and optical media.[65] And the burial project itself states the case for a digital genome by describing the inevitable changeover from analog to digital: "We do not write documents, we word-process. We do not have cameras and photo albums, we have digital cameras and Photoshop. We do not listen to radios and cassette."[66] The implication, the consortium makes clear, is that each medium has a certain lifespan, after which it becomes replaced by the next one. Yet what is most interesting about this narrative is how it frames media as either living or dead by contrasting the "live" updates of an

Internet-connected database with a "dead" one: "The term *database* suggests a living entity; is a dead or decommissioned database still a database?"[67]

By doing so, the Planets project picks up on a widespread rhetoric of media as dying or dead, with each "death" and "birth" of a medium said to signify a historical rupture or break. In a historiographic model Paul Duguid termed "supersession," each successive medium is said to kill off the previous one. Duguid illustrates supersession by quoting Victor Hugo's archdeacon: "This will kill that. The book will kill the building . . . The press will kill the church . . . printing will kill architecture."[68] At roughly the same time as the publication of Duguid's historiography, Bruce Sterling put the phrase "dead media" into circulation with his 1995 "Dead Media Manifesto," which called for a community of "communications paleontologists" to track down obsolete and completely forgotten medias—everything from Incan quipus, a counting system using knots on string, to Victorian phenakistoscopes, a pre-cinematic moving image technology.[69] More recently, a number of media scholars have expanded the field of media archeology to include objects that are marginal or obsolete, but not entirely gone, such as vinyl records, Polaroids, and typewriters: these are termed media that are "living dead" or, alternately, "zombie media."[70] While this list of dead or about-to-die media focuses largely on analog or physical medias, the consortium's project suggests that even today's newest *digital* media are types of "living dead," in mortal danger of perishing.[71] A PDF file, for example, is already on its deathbed because it is in a proprietary format, while many contemporary messages are encrypted, making a single-sentence e-mail message unreadable in the future without a massive pool of supercomputing power.

I do not write to challenge this narrative of dying and resurrection; instead, I argue that this fantasy allows us to understand a hitherto invisible aspect of the relationship between old and new media. For there is something excessive, even extravagant, at the heart of these fantasies. Though the digital genome project was assembled by a sober-minded consortium keenly concerned about the future of preservation—including the British, Austrian, Dutch, and Danish national library systems, the state archives of Switzerland, and a number of European universities—they chose to bury their box inside a former Swiss Air Force data bunker guarded by bulletproof checkpoints and twenty-four-hour surveillance systems, electromagnetic pulse protection, negative pressure systems to flush out chemical weapon attacks, and "hermetically sealed" air gaps. But as data security scholar Steven Murdoch comments on the Swiss bunker project, "The threat of a rogue system administrator deleting all the data because they know they are about to be fired is orders of magnitude more likely than an EMP [electromagnetic pulse] or invasion. The fact that the hosting centre is under a mountain doesn't stop the system administrator corrupting the backup files stored there."[72]

Why a physical bunker, then, which always seems to exceed the technical requirements for storing data in the long term? This excess provides us with a clue. The consortium and similar digital preservation projects talk about media in terms of their death, then respond to this "living death" by sealing the media inside a crypt for an indefinite period of time. They hope to one day recover these memories by decrypting the data or words hidden inside of them. But there is a better term to describe this phenomenon: *melancholia*. As psychoanalysis tells us, melancholy is a result of a loss, whether the actual death of a loved one, or a more metaphorical loss, such as the loss of an ideal.[73] Though related to mourning, melancholy is unlike it on one crucial point: the loss is so painful that the melancholic disavows that loss, internalizing and burying an identification with the lost object within him- or herself. While a rejected lover may mourn the person who has spurned him or her and then move on, an individual who is gripped by melancholy is unaware of the full extent of this loss. Yet inside his or her psyche, analysts Nicolas Abraham and Maria Torok explain, that phantom-like "shadow of the [lost] object" endures indefinitely, secretly hoping for its resurrection or reincarnation.[74]

Melancholy, in short, is something of a preservative. A crypt is created within the psyche that conceals a trace of the lost object, a libidinal space that simultaneously sets the object apart—marks it as belonging to the realm of the dead or gone—but also keeps a version of it alive. Lodged like a parasite inside the subject, the phantom remains inaccessible and encoded as it waits for its eventual reincarnation (or, at least, its decryption). The melancholic's response thus fits the fantasy produced by a bunker: as Virilio writes, the bunker is another name for "the crypt that prefigures the resurrection."[75]

Melancholy describes an increasingly important aspect of our relationship with the cloud. In chapter 1, I argued that the vision of a cloud as a network connecting everything is a feverish vision, one that, in the extreme, manifests itself as paranoia. Analogously, the fever around data bunkers, manifested in the desire to secure or defend data, is in fact a melancholic attachment to the data. Just as the melancholic creates a psychic architecture to hold and preserve its lost object, the data bunker closes off the "outside" in order to secure data from external threats. Because a data bunker is in effect a crypt for our data, the data bunker is not just a symptom of a melancholic's desire, but the very architecture of that melancholy.

Data bunkers allow the death inherent in disaster to be contained by transmuting it into something like limbo: waiting, suspension, a "living dead." In Derrida's explanation of melancholy, the melancholic's crypt always contains "a living dead, a dead entity we are perfectly willing to keep alive, but as dead."[76] In the name of preserving its contents, a data bunker is a phantasmatic structure that excludes media that are "dying" from the time of everyday life, and excludes "dead" media from living media. Data inside the cloud—namely, digital data—are marked off from outside data—namely, analog data. The result is an agonistic dynamic which portrays older media as dying or dead. The bunker user sees the digital in opposition to analog, or new media in opposition to old media (as with the time capsule project). In certain cases, analog data may be converted, transferred, and thus admitted into the cloud, but in the process, these data are marked as somehow different, as not "natively" digital. (The digitized book is never the book; it is the formerly analog book, the book that is viewed as a foreign object.[77])

To bring this discussion to a head, the idea of loss may seem like a purely theoretical or technical concern that belongs to the realm of data preservation. And yet, as I have tried to show, it is activated by a larger imagination of disaster produced by the cloud, one that can easily slide between mundane concerns about formatting errors and concerns about national security. This imagination produces two impulses, which coalesce in the data bunker: first, a paranoid desire to preempt the enemy by maintaining vigilance in the face of constant threat, and second, a melancholic fantasy of surviving the eventual disaster by entombing data inside highly secured data vaults. Comments one electronic records archivist on the Swiss Fort Knox project, "We need more projects of this nature: time capsules containing other types of digital objects, storage media, software, hardware, and documentation should be placed in Iron Mountain and other undeground storage facilities . . . statistically speaking, we are really overdue for a deadly pandemic, and the next global war will likely have a nuclear component."[78] The archivist's melancholic reflection on the loss of digital media redoubles back onto a paranoid imagination of a nuclear war that is to come. One bunker does not assuage the problem, but only multiplies the crypt-like structures deemed necessary to house our data.

In *Bunker Archaeology*, Virilio laid out this paradox: even as possibilities of an imagined time "after the resurrection" fill the melancholic with a sense of expansiveness, the immobility and weight of the bunker itself transfers onto his or her body. In a sense, the thingness of the defensive structure built around a melancholic's data has come to possess its owner. As Virilio describes, a visitor to a bunker is "beset with a singular heaviness; in fact he is already in the grips of that cadaveric rigidity from which the shelter was designed to protect him."[79] That shelter weighs on the visitor, "grips" the visitor, to the point where he even empathizes with and internalizes its objecthood. It is perhaps for this reason that we seem to take comfort in the militarized presence of the bunker's building itself—the blastproof walls, the armed security guards—as a defense from these imagined threats, whether the threats are cyberwarfare brigades, hackers, or even the gentler "death" of digital media itself.

We have so far considered the idea of threat primarily as a metaphor, whether the kind of theoretical killing that comes from a cypherpunk's "assassination politics," or from one media killing off another. Yet the militarized architectures within the cloud are, I argue, physical manifestations of a resurgence of sovereign power within the realm of data. The next chapter returns to the actual violence produced by this structure of power.

4   SEEING THE CLOUD OF DATA

War as Big Data

What does it mean to see and be seen within a cloud of data? With the mean North American user consuming over 45 GB of Internet data each month,[1] the marvel of the cloud may be less its vastness than the software tools that manage, simplify, and make it intelligible: the indexers, the recommendation and visualization algorithms that offer users a sense of control over these data. Yet the same algorithms that make the cloud usable are the ones that define a "user" as that ever-growing stream of data to be analyzed and targeted. To use the cloud is to willingly put on an electronic collar; it is to fuse our hunt for data with our identities as marketing prospects. In short, in an environment where all data are needles in petabyte-sized haystacks, we are both the targets of others and targeters ourselves.

By examining the target/targeter dynamic, this chapter moves from the cloud itself (networks, virtualization, data centers) to the ways that the idea of the cloud disperses itself in contemporary life. Targeting can take many forms, and while it typically manifests itself in the cloud as a marketing campaign, Caren Kaplan has argued that "the 'targets' of two seemingly distinct contexts and practices—the target of a weapon and the target of a marketing campaign"—are anything but distinct.[2] Though we tend to think of security and marketing as separate ideas, government agencies openly purchase information from private-sector marketing databases, such as flight records and credit data, in order to track dissidents, criminals, and provocateurs online and then arrest, deport, or torture them. Indeed, as Kaplan demonstrates, targeted marketing came out of the Eisenhower-era science of geodemography, the practice of integrating demographic information into geographic locations, such as a zip-coded neighborhood, and GIS (geographic information systems) databases jointly developed by scientists and military researchers to acquire precision targets during the Cold War.[3] These technologies did more than just map populations onto specific geographic locations: they quickly became mechanisms for sorting, monitoring, filtering, and ultimately producing consumer identities.

From the beginning, GIS marketing was a by-product of a military's need to convert populations into targetable spaces, and there continues to be considerable crossover between military practices and marketing practices to this day. While scholars such as Greg Elmer, Joseph Turrow, and John Cheney-Lippold have studied the ways that online search and advertising algorithms shape and define users' imputed race, gender, and marketability online,[4] a fuller picture of digital culture would also investigate the ways that marketing crosses over into the realm of security. These various targeting strategies hint at a deeper structure of power that produces them, and this chapter is intended to complement existing research by describing the violence latent in an otherwise bloodless idea of targeting data. To do so, I start with an insight of Foucault, which holds that power does not necessarily come from a single source or event ("the US government") but rather exists continuously through everyday interactions with institutions, knowledge structures, pleasures, and even patterns of culture. In turn, these discourses produce subject positions that may appear natural but are in fact an effect of power. As previous chapters have shown, the cloud uses economic and affective incentives—fulfillment, safety, or even intimacy—to produce the subject position of the "user." Users work hand in hand with digital algorithms, serving as active partners in the cloud's mechanism of control.

Military targeting may seem to produce a different subject position than marketing campaigns. In his 1984 study *War and Cinema*, Virilio understands this subject in terms of spectatorship by quoting former US Secretary of Defense William Perry: "Once you see a target, you can expect to destroy it."[5] For Perry, optical technologies such as surveillance cameras, aerial photography, and satellites turn the things and bodies that they gaze at into potential targets. Calling the 1990–1991 Gulf War a "television war" suggests that remotely "seeing" a target is a way of exercising power at a *distance*: looking, then projecting the power to kill back into the world through cruise missiles, snipers, and aerial bombardments. Images of missile-mounted cameras routinely appeared on national TV in the 1990s, while the US military's National Training Center in Mojave, California, which contains a simulated

Middle Eastern village named Medina Wasl, hired a full-time film crew and a cast of Arabic-speaking actors trained to portray civilians. Even videogames of the time, which offered consumers the ability to "play" war, by and large framed war as a set of images and representations for visual consumption—in other words, generally as a simulated, remote, or fictional event.[6] Together, these visual technologies form what James Der Derian called the "military-industrial-media-entertainment complex."[7]

After September 11, 2001, the US government moved away from the episodic production of televised spectacles and toward the incorporation of security into everyday life. This marked a historical return of sorts to the Cold War, when Congress, suspicious of deviant networks within the state, drafted a national security law based on a paranoid, cloudlike imagination of the telecommunications system as a potential source of conspiracy. In a parallel response to the current threat, the Bush and Obama administrations have deployed a literal cloud of security by bringing together security networks previously isolated across different branches of government. After 2001, agencies traditionally devoted to prosecuting foreign wars (e.g., the CIA) or terror (e.g., the Department of Homeland Security) began to connect their networks to those agencies working on domestic crime (e.g., the FBI).[8] This has led to a number of legal controversies, such as the NSA's use of phone metadata, but also vaunted successes, such as the capture of several al-Qaeda operatives. Indeed, sociologist David Knoke argues that network analysis was directly responsible for the raid on Osama bin Laden's compound in Abbotabad, Pakistan, by unmasking the identity of bin Laden's courier Abu Ahmed al-Kuwaiti.[9] The overall effect of this shift is to turn remote seeing into cloud seeing, and to turn "war at a distance" into something that might be better described as "war as big data."

The visual culture of "war as big data" is less cinema or television than the computer interfaces that help identify and locate data patterns: visualization tools that identify abnormal behaviors or organizational structures; the link-and-node charts that locate a suspect's associates (figure 2.4); automatic facial recognition software that runs on public images or videos; filters for aggregated information; and so forth. Further, if "war at a distance" produced a subject position of a viewer, "war as big data" produces the subject position of a user, that is, a subject that actively participates in securing the system as a whole.[10] A cloud user is constantly enjoined to perform digital "hygiene"; in other words, to keep their private data private. Likewise, the cloud's disaster recovery functions make disasters and security threats continuously imaginable. When users are responsible for selecting privacy settings, making disaster recovery backups, and even flagging suspicious behavior online, security becomes an everyday responsibility.

One of the most unique aspects of digital culture is therefore a user's ability not just to become a target, but also to defend him- or herself, "target back," and participate in a shared project of security with the state (even, as we shall soon see, in war itself). Software tools for launching denial-of-service attacks, for sending anonymous payments, and for targeting other users through social network analysis are all readily available to the general public;[11] even many sensitive location databases, such as the Space Track database for satellites and FAA flight record data for airplanes, are accessible to interested users online. As Kaplan suggests, we should consider an expanded sense of militarization that "move[s] beyond the model of consumers as feminized, passive targets of unscrupulous advertisers in order to see the ways in which people participate in their construction by 'volunteering,' if you will, to engage in the products generated by technoscience . . . Residents of the United States are mobilized into militarized ways of being."[12]

To explore this expanded sense of militarization, the first two sections of this chapter take up two case studies. First, I consider Dutch radio frequency hackers in the 2011 NATO bombing campaign in Libya, and the ways they blur the lines between observers and actors within the theater of war; second, I turn to artist Trevor Paglen's data-gathering methods for documenting the CIA's "shadow state" of surveillance. Both Paglen and the RF hackers use sophisticated technological tools to look back at the presumptive cases of control, seemingly to expose or even undermine a regime in which surveillance and dataveillance have become routine practices. Despite their technological savvy, both parties invite the audience to adopt their tools and methods, in effect asking viewers to become active participants.

Though these practitioners of countersurveillance (or "sousveillance") may appear to disrupt these regimes of surveillance, the actual story is more complex. Sousveillers typically assume that data can reveal a hidden truth normally covered up by mass media. But a paranoid approach to knowledge, Eve Kosofsky Sedgwick has argued, typically duplicates and reproduces the methods of a paranoid subject's nominal enemy.[13] For this reason, the sousveillers and the regime they seem to oppose share a set of tactics as well as a common belief: namely, that in order to effect change one must actively engage as a user. Using the example of the RF hackers, I show that the discourse of a "user" as an active participant or freelancer comes out of a neoliberal ideology of economic efficiency. Hence, even attempts at counter-surveillance reinforce this subject position. Despite their oppositional goals, the practices of sousveillers may ultimately serve to invite others inside the state's apparatus of security. By extending Paglen's work, I argue that the element of desire that connects surveiller and sousveiller can help us move away from this counterproductive binary.

In the chapter's conclusion, I contend that user engagement with security has disturbing consequences: when users are invited to perform or play at the sovereign's role as a "decider" (and, ultimately, the sovereign's right to kill), security and participation fuse into what I term the *sovereignty of data*. In the regime of "war at a distance," Virilio showed that war and cinema share a common apparatus of image production, representation, and circulation that makes war as much an exercise in visibility as a cinema set. Similarly, the structure of militarization within the "war as big data" means that the cloud places users uncomfortably close to the mechanism of state violence. The sovereignty of data may manifest itself primarily through targeted advertisements, and through the bloodless forms of control and governmentality typically described by new media scholars, but occasionally appears as a targeted killing.[14] Rather than imagining ourselves as victims of a surveillance state, we are in fact partially complicit with a violence that fails to respect the boundaries between real and virtual space. To effectively challenge this system of power, we cannot merely consider one form of targeting in isolation from the other; conjoined in the sovereignty of data, they call on us to understand power in the age of the cloud differently.

In the run-up to NATO's 2011 intervention in Libya, a Dutch radio hacker named Huub (@fmcnl) tweeted to the US military that one of their F-16 fighter jets was mistakenly broadcasting its identity in the clear due to a misconfigured Mode S transponder. When a second fighter plane made the same mistake later that day, Huub joked that Muammar Gaddafi's radar installations must be down for the US Air Force to be so cavalier with its security protocols: "Hmmm, second fighter showing his ID, a USAF F-15E from 494FS Lakenheath UK, I presume Gadhafis radar equipment has destroyed :o)." Huub was not working alone; he was part of a network of amateurs who were tracking and narrating the chess match in which NATO planes and Libyan units jockeyed for position before the commencement of hostilities. The previous day, Huub had released audio of a US EC-130J psychological warfare plane broadcasting a warning to the Libyan navy ("If you attempt to leave port, you will be attacked and destroyed immediately.") Other volunteers used off-the-shelf websites, such as flightradar24.com and commercial satellite images tagged on Google Earth, to track the movements of military jets, ships, and other potential targets for bombing.

In contrast to the 1990–1991 Gulf War, seemingly a spectacle that the public assimilated passively, the 2011 Libyan war offered a massive dataset for the public to actively sift through on the Internet.[15] As a result, it gave us arguably the first cloud-enabled war. NATO spokesman Mike Bracken described a NATO "fusion centre" that data-mined Twitter feeds and open source databases on the Internet to glean potential targets, battlefield conditions, and other tactical information: "'Snippets of information' . . . could then be tested, corroborated or not, by NATO's own sources, including imagery and eavesdropping from Nimrod spy planes."[16] At the same time, in an interview with the Dutch public broadcaster NOS, the hacker Dirk de Jager also called on listeners to participate in mining these data. Begin with data collection, he said, then sort and analyze the input, and finally the "data puzzle pieces" would fall into place.[17] One might listen, as Huub did, to live air traffic control streams from Malta via liveatc.net and attempt to identify a mysterious plane communicating with the controller—possibly a getaway plane for Gaddafi's relatives—and correlate that with another stream from Twitter, or to geotag the data's location in what is known as KML format[18] (figure 4.1). And when the conflict started, the Malta feed even let users anticipate drone strikes by listening for the code "MQ-1," the designation for Predator drones.

By disrupting the secrecy of NATO's operations, Huub and de Jager also seemed to counter the regime of state secrecy represented in that respect. Huub's goal, he wrote, was "to listen to 'the truth,' without any military or political propaganda,"[19] and de Jager similarly argued that because of the availability of real-time data, state "censorship is no longer possible."[20] Unsurprisingly, their tweets received a fair degree of criticism for their presumptive interference. One user, @Joe_Taxi, tweeted back to Huub: "If you are not delaying your tweets by a WIDE margin, you are putting the pilots in harms way!!!! . . . When the sounds of the #operationoddesydawn aircraft are heard in #Libya it should be a complete surprise." *The Guardian* helpfully suggested that Gaddafi should start following Huub's Twitter feed to gain

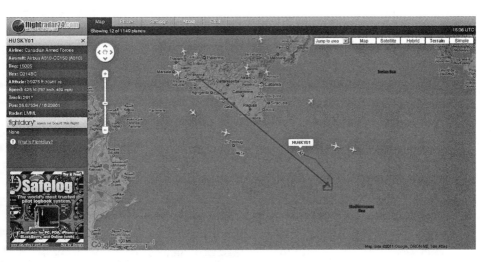

Figure 4.1
Flight track of Canadian Air Force plane "HUSKY01." Screenshot courtesy of www.flightradar24.com.

advance warning of each attack. Reflecting back on Huub's tweets, USAF Captain Jeff Gilmore wrote in the *Small Wars Journal*: "Accurate tail numbers, routings, home bases for fighters and intercepted propaganda messages by C-130 Commando Solo aircraft are still available on the web for all to hear. It is downright scary to think of our nation's vulnerabilities from just one overzealous aviation fan."[21]

While Huub and his fellow hacktivists seemed to suggest a new avenue for countering state "propaganda," the results were far murkier. After all, Huub's leak of the audio from NATO psychological operations was itself a way of disseminating NATO propaganda. And a casual observer might have interpreted a tweet from @hms_cumberland linking to Huub's clip as a statement of direct support by NATO.[22] This was not a statement from the British warship *HMS Cumberland*, as might have been assumed; @hms_cumberland was, in fact, an unofficial account. Though this tweet was merely an act of a military enthusiast, the confusion inadvertently revealed a cozy relationship between several hacktivists and NATO forces. (The press assumed several of these 'unofficial' accounts were fronts for NATO, and at least one French naval officer had indeed set up an unofficial Twitter account for gathering tactical information.[23]) And Huub's tweet, for its part, gathered as much praise as criticism from the military community. As military blogger David Cenciotti commented approvingly, Huub's tweets exposing the NATO planes' security flaws exemplified "what can be done with off-the-shelf products and a bit of knowledge . . . skilled enthusiasts following air operations can help the coalition to improve self-protection and safety of some of its High Value assets."[24]

The relationship between an avowedly pro-NATO blogger, such as Cenciotti, and the enthusiasts that he cites with approval is complex. As the war progressed, some enthusiasts began to explicitly feed targets to NATO: *The Guardian* profiled the contributions of one such hacktivist, "a 48-year-old shift supervisor at Dairy Queen ice cream parlour in Tucson, Arizona," who sifted through satellite photography to tweet coordinates of a suspected Gaddafi communication headquarters to @Nato and @NatoPress; ten hours after that tweet, he noted proudly, NATO had bombed those exact coordinates.[25] Other hackers may be apolitical or passionately opposed to military action, and may look upon such amateur targeters with abhorrence.[26] But regardless of what any particular hacker group supported or opposed, the very framing of the Libyan war as a big data problem was itself laden with ideology. My goal here is not to judge the effectiveness of hacktivism, but rather to understand why hacktivism in the cloud may manifest itself in the same forms as the sovereign states that they claim to oppose.

Some of the more evident reasons that hacktivists and government spies have more in common than they would admit lie in the practices shared by both. State and nonstate actors alike use open source tools for a variety of goals, undermining any claim that certain technologies are inherently liberatory or destructive. For example, cypherpunks typically promote the TOR system to counter NSA surveillance. But TOR, a system for accessing the Internet anonymously through encryption and "onion routing," was originally funded and designed by another branch of the US military, the Naval Research Laboratory (NRL). And as Mike Reed, one of TOR's original programmers at the NRL, relates, TOR was developed to anonymize the government's own secret communications and intelligence gathering operations by hiding it within the flow of civilian TOR traffic: the more hacktivist traffic, the better for the government's intelligence agencies.[27] Reasoning that an anonymous backchannel such as TOR has a higher rate of illicit traffic than public Internet browsing, the NSA has even used searches for TOR as a way of targeting potential suspects, and embedded a security hole in TOR browser plug-ins to track users accessing child pornography, leading many cypherpunks to describe TOR as a "NSA honeypot" (i.e., trap). Using TOR may successfully encrypt an individual user's network traffic, but it does little to solve the larger political problem of state surveillance.

If hacktivist techniques are all too often co-opted, what, then, do acts of hacktivism accomplish? Geert Lovink and Ned Rossiter sum up the difficulty inherent in electronic resistance movements: "They point out the problem, and then run away. Capital is delighted, and thanks the tactical media outfit or nerd-modder for the home improvement."[28] Responding to this critique, Rita Raley argues that we might judge hacktivists less by what they accomplish than by their performative qualities—namely, by the vision of potential change that they may offer their audience, however temporary that vision may be. As I will suggest, Lovink and Rossiter's point may still be valid, but not for the reasons they claim. The risks are subtler; the cloud embodies a mechanism of power that welcomes such performances of resistance or virtuosity, because it asks and even compels users to express themselves through the digital tools the cloud offers them.

To understand this point, consider that Huub and de Jager's methods turn the collection of military information into something like an interactive game. De Jager offer a certain sequence of steps for making the "digital puzzle pieces" fall into place:

1. *Data collection:* Build a list of terms from news sources, Wikipedia, etc. (e.g., names of airports, aircraft types, names of ships and fleet relationships).
2. *Listen:* Look for these terms in Twitter or listen directly to the data streams, producing "a message that at time Y jets take off and land from base A, or that there are X Canadian soldiers billeted in the local hotel."
3. *Sort and combine:* "In this phase, you should think logically. An aircraft carrier off the coast of Alaska will not be involved in an attack on Libya."
4. *Annotate:* Tag and add your information to aggregators such as Google Maps and Google Earth.

In this context, war becomes a sort of massive reality game built on individual participation. Yet by "raising his or her status as an active participant," in Eugene Thacker and Alexander Galloway's words, these war games proposed by de Jager "enfold the player into codified and routinized models of behavior": deciphering, decoding, logical thinking, and so forth.[29] What is often overlooked in analyses of these activities is that these modes of behavior—deciphering, decoding, etc.—are precisely those sought after by the new information economy, "where flexibility, systematic problem solving, quick reflexes, and indeed play itself are as highly valued as sitting still and hushing up were for the disciplinary societies of modernity."[30] Indeed, in a very practical sense, hacktivism may function as much as a way of furthering putative political causes as vocational training for information workers in a network society. And the military community itself recognizes this: in 2012, for example, NSA director General Keith Alexander recruited hackers at the DEF CON hacker conference by delivering a keynote on the "shared values" held by the intelligence and the hacker community.[31]

While Alexander focused his remarks on the shared value of security—appealing to the hacker community to "help secure cyberspace" and "protect networks"—we might observe other, less obvious values undergirding calls for hacker participation in a war of big data. For example, the hacker community's relationship to gender is both obvious—there are many more male hackers than female hackers—and insidiously complex. In valorizing the "active user" over the presumably "passive consumers" of mass media, hacktivist ideology reifies an assumption about gender that has run throughout media history. As William Boddy has argued, "100 years of historical experience of electronic communications in the home repeatedly rehearse a series of gendered and normative oppositions between the active and passive audience, from the male wireless amateur versus the distracted housewife in the 1920s, to the degraded 'couch potato' versus the heroic internet surfer of the 1990s."[32] Thus the myth of the truth-seeking hacktivist versus the naive consumer of propaganda recreates a fictitious binary between participatory media practices that "fight back" and gullible, femininized media consumption. While some scholars claim that hacker culture's machismo is changing for the better as it incorporates more women hacktivists motivated by social causes, this view only perpetuates this binary by suggesting that women are more "socially minded" than men.[33] More research is urgently needed to expand the discussion, even as a problematic association between masculinity and activist users continues to undergird the case studies I consider in this chapter.

But the central claim I am making is that invitations for hacktivist participation are inextricable from the ideology of the marketplace. *Wired*, for example, cites Huub's radio scanner, which "retail[s] for a little more than $500," as proof that the hobby is affordable for "average folk."[34] Cenciotti's call for more amateur hackers to join the war effort frames hacking as a hobby that is "simple and cheap," yet one that protects the military's "high value assets." Thus, in this logic, a hobbyist's $500 is an investment that pays off immensely: if it can keep a plane from being shot down by revealing security errors, it can potentially save the military the $45 million cost of a "high value" F-16. Similarly, NSA director Keith Alexander concluded his DEF CON speech on "shared values" by arguing that hacker participation in Internet security "would help us with our economic growth. This would be huge for our country. And this area that we're talking about [the technology industry] is the fastest growing area for our nation for the past three decades. Look at what makes up the Dow Industrial, the NASDAQ . . . That's what fuels our economy."[35] (Given how closely enmeshed security is with the marketplace, it is little surprise that former US intelligence analysts have ported their software for mapping communications networks to a new but closely-related field: mapping wealthy investor portfolios.[36])

Some hackers may object that the freedom they espouse is not an economic one, but a libertarian ideal; as hacker Richard Stallman put it, "You should think of free as in free speech, not free beer." That Stallman was compelled to distinguish between the two suggests, however, that the twinned definitions of "free" are fundamentally difficult to separate. Anthropologist Gabriella Coleman has shown that this distinction did not even appear in the free/open source software community until the mid-1990s. Many hackers Coleman interviewed for her 2013 study *Coding Freedom* commented on the considerable slippage between these two terms: one hacker, for example, exclaimed, "The first draw was, I don't have to pay for this—awesome!" In Coleman's words, even in saying "free as in speech . . . there is some sort of free beer always available, too."[37] The neoliberal framework of the cloud purposely confuses economic intimacy with personal intimacy, making free speech resemble free beer. In doing so, the cloud monetizes users through implicit incentives to "use." Through this system, users are continually asked to engage in ever more online activity; to participate in constructing themselves as autonomous subjects; and even to misread economic incentives (such as free disk space) as personal freedoms.

While free speech may be a hacktivist goal, online expression of any sort is nevertheless constrained by this implicit injunction to continually "use more"—and the profits of active use typically accrue to the companies who own online platforms for expression. (Investment banks charged with Twitter's public offering arrived at its multi-billion-dollar valuation in part by estimating how much each of its 230 million MAUs, or "monthly active users," was worth. The answer: around $78.[38]) Power in the age of postindustrial capitalism, political theorist Maurizio Lazzarato reminds us, is "a technology for creating and controlling the 'subjective processes' . . . one *has to* express oneself, one *has to* speak."[39] Seen correctly, a hacktivist's freedom most closely resembles that of a free laborer who contributes online reviews, forum moderation, and source code. Free laborers volunteer their services out of their love for the game, even as they are aware that their labor generates value for others. Judged in terms of the cost savings they can provide to NATO, then, the RF hackers working in Libya are difficult to separate from the neoliberal consensus that turns to the marketplace for solutions, and continually seeks lower-cost or even "free" alternatives. Yet to volunteer as a hacker—whether indulging in a "simple and cheap" hobby, or using open source software as "free beer"—is to work within a neoliberal system of free labor.

Hacktivism is a narrow case, and the reader may be wondering: how does this invitation to participate manifest in digital culture more generally? As the remainder of this section shows, the invitation is inherent in the visual culture of the cloud, which offers a specific way of seeing and interacting with big data that presumes to connect all pieces of information to others. A system of knowledge in which everything seems to be connected—a system I previously identified as "network fever"—is a paranoid epistemology that offers to reveal meaning buried beneath the surface, but also serves to lubricate the market mechanisms by which that meaning was created.

To illustrate this way of seeing, consider the case of *Washington Post* investigative reporters Dana Priest and William Arkin, who created the Top Secret America website in 2010. Like other websites that visualize data in the cloud, Top Secret America aggregated massive amounts of data about which private contractors worked for the CIA or NSA, including expenditures and geographical locations. By overlaying a visual interface onto a "Top Secret" world, Top Secret America purported to use appropriations data to understand and even expose a hitherto unrepresentable world. Users could sort by specific weapons technologies (counter-IED explosives operations, for example), search a geocoded map by zip code to find "counterterrorism organizations near you," and so on, creating a visual interface resembling the hacktivists' geocoded maps of military units in Libya.

Once again, Top Secret America sparked a debate over secrecy similar to that of Huub's tweets. Commentators attacked Priest and Arkin's project as a national security risk, faulting them for disclosing too much information about America's covert operations.[40] Priest was eventually asked about her motivations: did she belong to the radical transparency movement, which attempted to subvert NSA surveillance by exposing its secrets? No, she responded; that wasn't her intention: "The goal is to figure out if the system is working as well as it should and to make it better."[41] Indeed, the then US Secretary of Defense Robert Gates even praised Top Secret America as a valuable service that could help eliminate redundancies and over-priced contracts from a bloated intelligence budget. Motivated by the same market ideologies—the idea of efficient markets and economic, rather than legal, rules—that undergird the mechanism of security in the contemporary West, the do-it-yourself tactics of participatory media are a perfect match for the surveillance state: any citizen, it says, can engage with his or her security regime by exercising surveillance over budgets and other tasks of management.

What is most interesting here is the critics' confusion: a project that attempts to *aid* the government in its secret program of surveillance is indistinguishable from projects that aim to *undermine* the government's surveillance programs. Confusing the two types of projects is, however, an easy mistake to make: Top Secret America's interface visually resembles those of oppositional websites, such as *The Guardian*'s map of Iraq war casualties. Indeed, the link-node interface, the graphs, and the toolbars to filter and sort data are so common that they have become naturalized in an age of big data; these interfaces are as inseparable from large datasets as Renaissance perspective is from photographic images. These data interfaces came out of a distrust for normative media representations (talking heads on TV, the "NATO propaganda" at press conferences, potentially Photoshopped satellite images of Iraq, and so on). When the hacker collective Anonymous retweeted an article about Huub's link, asking: "Want unfiltered information (aka the truth) on the bombings in Libya? Read http://bit.ly/ftZpWx and follow @FMCNL #libya #UN," we recognize the implication that big data gives citizens unmediated access to "the truth." Portraying themselves as iconoclasts—literally, destroyers of icons or images—hacktivists seek to establish a parallel and alternate ecology of media that is supposedly less prone to manipulation or censorship. If any given image can be duplicitous, the only way to find the truth—so goes de Jager's claim—is to correlate and situate that image within a network of other images, to look through its duplicitous surface and decode and decrypt the hidden network within the network.

As transparent and useful as these cheerful, rainbow-colored graphs may be in a world of big data, these interfaces are nevertheless visual fictions, ways of simplifying a hopelessly complex totality. In doing so, they represent a specific epistemology: the "interpretive project," as Sedgwick puts it, "of knowledge in the form of exposure . . . of *unveiling hidden violence.*"[42] As Sedgwick describes it, the impulse to expose seemingly hidden knowledge is a signature of a paranoid structure of thought. To be clear, Sedgwick does not mean that the users of these graphs are pathologically paranoid (in any case, any person who maps a surveillance state has good reason to be paranoid); she is describing a type of knowledge production that is uniquely applicable to digital culture. After all, what does it mean for Top Secret America to offer a representation of something that is "top secret" and therefore unrepresentable?

Top Secret America is keenly aware of its inability to see; icons of question marks underscore the "secretness" of its subject, the data that it was unable to include. Top Secret America's graphs therefore reiterate the problematic of the cloud itself, which attempts to map an infinitely complex system of servers, networks, users, and applications into a simplified interface. An icon of a cloud, the reader will recall, originally stood for any unrepresentable network on network maps, such as the Internet; in today's computer and mobile operating systems, this cloud icon now represents a reserve of seemingly unlimited computer power, or storage space; it has become, simply, a representation of the unknown. Thus the logic of the cloud entails a paranoid worldview in which everything is hopelessly complex but, with the right (data) tools, can be made deceptively simple and explainable: a master key or representation that explains everything. "Conspiracy, one is tempted to say, is the poor person's cognitive mapping in the postmodern age," writes Frederic Jameson; "it is the degraded figure of the total logic of late capital, a desperate attempt to represent the latter's system."[43]

By understanding visualization projects as realizations of paranoid knowledge, we can understand how this epistemology disseminates itself through digital culture. We have already observed the visual similarity among many websites that might normally oppose one another: a hacktivist project to undermine the government looks like a security project meant to bolster the government. As Sedgwick explains, "Paranoia seems to require being imitated to be understood, and it, in turn, seems to understand only by . . . imitating and embodying" its target.[44] This accounts for not only the visual resemblance between disparate websites, but also the mimetic relationship between surveillance and countersurveillance operations. Huub's attempt to counter the "propaganda" of the state simultaneously provides the state with feedback on how its operations are functioning. Huub's attempts are not necessarily co-opted by the state, but both parties do share the same structure of paranoid knowledge. The effect is to produce something of a *mise en abyme* mechanism of duplication, where sousveillance—tactics for watching the watchers—mimics surveillance, and surveillance mirrors sousveillance.

The duplicative logic of paranoia explains why the think tank the RAND Corporation argued that we must "fight networks with networks";[45] or in the almost identical words of General Stanley McChrystal, commander of US forces in Iraq and Afghanistan, "to defeat a networked enemy we had to become a network ourselves."[46] Though McChrystal and RAND are discussing the organizational structures of modern war as a big data problem, the same dictum applies to the larger culture through which we interact with the cloud. It is as if the only way to "look" at a duplicitous network is to imitate its structure or interface; cloud seeing continually produces more cloud seeing. And yet such visual interfaces are themselves methods of obfuscation that veil the mechanism of power "behind candy-colored lines and nodes," to quote Galloway.[47] "The point of unrepresentability is the point of power. And the point of power today is not in the image. The point of power resides in networks, computers, algorithms."[48]

Thus the attempts to expose or unmask the mechanism of power in fact only succeed in preserving its underlying logic. In some cases, these attempts can even be a form of cynicism that performs the gestures of political action but actually ends up preserving the status quo (for instance, the regime of surveillance in Top Secret America). But are such sousveillance projects doomed to failure, and if so, why do we persist in attempting to unmask the source of surveillance? The next section continues this discussion by considering a second case study, the photographs of geographer and artist Trevor Paglen, who acknowledges the embeddedness of an activist with his or her target and therefore offers a very different take on how to look at the surveillance state.

"The Other Night Sky": Seeing and Counterseeing

One summer in 2008, Trevor Paglen and an amateur satellite watcher named Ted Molczan led viewers in a Toronto gallery outside and directed them to look skyward. But their gaze was not aimed at stars, or at least not natural stars; instead, they were trying to locate a classified American reconnaissance satellite, Keyhole-11. Paglen and Molczan have obsessively tracked what they call the "other night sky," the sky filled with debris from failed space missions and reconnaissance satellites that go all but unnoticed save for a small cadre of skilled amateurs. Ironically, though the US military finds these unwanted observers irritating, the observers were in a sense replicating a military-funded program during the Cold War for spotting Soviet satellites. Termed "Operation Moonwatch," it anticipated the network of Internet-savvy data collectors that Paglen and Molczan would use to find Keyhole-11.[49]

From their data, star charts, and computer models, Paglen and Molczan predicted that Keyhole-11 (abbreviated KH-11) would pass over Toronto at exactly 10:13 p.m., and so the group waited to see its trail cut across the night sky. There was a chance, however, that KH-11 would not be visible. This is because the Keyhole satellites can "cloak" themselves by using a mirrored structure to reflect the nothingness of space back to certain cities. The satellite normally appears as a brief streak of light in the sky, but after the mirror mechanism is activated, it will blink out of sight. One can easily imagine the initial goals of this technology—to keep the satellite invisible to enemy nations. But today, satellite watchers believe that the National Reconnaissance Office cloaks the satellites over Toronto precisely because it is worried about KH-11 being spotted by Molczan, an amateur astronomer. If Molczan has indeed caused the satellite to be cloaked, then he and other satellite watchers have reached a level of technological sophistication that can approach that of sovereign governments, such as China and Russia. John Pike, director of GlobalSecurity.org, explained it thus: "If Ted [Molczan] can track all these satellites, so can the Chinese."[50]

As Pike described the phenomenon of satellite cloaking to Paglen, he punctuated his explanations by imagining how a sovereign government might locate US spy satellites: "If I had a gigantic bank of computers, I could run my data on all this space debris . . . It would seem to me that if the Red Chinese did this . . . they'd conclude that these were the American stealth satellites."[51] To counter the state with statelike tactics is not only to flatten the distinction between an individual activist and state surveillor, it is to create a set of agonistic binaries between us and them, civilian and military worlds, self and other. For Paglen, such photographs of the government's surveillance apparatus are his way of "developing a lexicon of the other night sky . . . toward reclaiming the violence flowing through it. But this is not a passive exercise. As I photograph the other night sky, the other night sky photographs back" (figure 4.2).[52] In his statement, Paglen's call to action both tweaks those who might prefer more "passive exercise[s]" and offers a political philosophy that is unique. Far more than "passively" watching, the method Paglen epouses often requires a certain performative imagination. By putting him- or herself into the minds of a sovereign Chinese government and by adopting its tools—that is, "a gigantic bank of computers"—a potential activist puts into the practice the words enunciated by cypherpunk John Perry Barlow: "The answer to sovereignty was sovereignty."

But can sovereignty ever be effectively answered with sovereignty? In Toronto, the satellite briefly became visible to observers; then it disappeared, as if it were winking at the watchers down below. "To the group's delight," an observer wrote, "as the star party looked on, KH-11 looked back."[53] Why did the group delight in being watched by a spy satellite? The satellite's "wink" signals a kind of complicity: we are intertwined with and even participate in the mechanisms of power. An undercurrent of desire connects the watched with the watcher, and suggests that there can never be a clear separation between the two parties. As this section shows, the apparatus of perception that I have called "cloud seeing" ultimately puts us in a position of tacit support for the state that surveils us, complicating efforts to draw clear lines of, say, us versus them. But this complicit relationship is not a dead end; the undercurrent of desire that makes us complicit can also provide a way out of the paranoid logic of countersurveillance.

To return to the sky above Toronto, Keyhole-11 is an unusual satellite by design; it is named Keyhole because it "looks back down to earth rather than out into space."[54] Initial versions of the Keyhole satellites used superthin, high-resolution Kodak films; periodically, the film canisters were ejected in capsules that would be dramatically scooped up in midair by a hooked length of nylon rope winched from specially equipped air force planes. Later, undoubtedly to the relief of their operators, "improved" Keyhole satellites incorporated digital CCD sensors (the same sensors we now find in our digital cameras) rather than film. In addition to the CCD sensors, the Keyhole

Figure 4.2

Trevor Paglen, *KEYHOLE/ADVANCED CRYSTAL in Hercules (Optical Reconnaissance Satellite; USA 116)*, 2008, C-print, 60 × 48 in. Courtesy of the artist and Metro Pictures.

satellite has inspired another technological system of representing information in physical space that is more widespread than one might realize. On a literal level, many online location-based applications, such as Google Earth, HERE maps, Google Maps, Google Mobile, and so on, use a file format called KML, Keyhole Markup Language; this language, and its associated cartographic technologies, was developed by the geospatial mapping company Keyhole, Inc.[55] Rescued from bankruptcy by the CIA's venture capital arm In-Q-Tel and the National Geospatial-Intelligence Agency, the agency responsible for data analysis on Keyhole satellite images, Keyhole, Inc.'s customers consisted solely of US government defense agencies until it was acquired by Google in 2004. The practice of orienting oneself and targeting a business by location, as well as the practice of marketing to potential customers online, activate a cartographic imagination that is technoscientific at its heart. Users of location-aware websites and technologies implicitly share (or are induced to share) a desire with marketers and states to make the world as visible and targetable as a KML map. It is not just that Keyhole satellites look down on us; users of locative media continuously engage with Keyhole-derived technologies to look back across the physical world around them.

But there is another reason why the satellite's name is fitting. In *Being and Nothingness*, Jean-Paul Sartre tells the story of a man gazing through a keyhole.[56] Absorbed by the scene, the voyeur is unaware of anything but the pleasure of looking. All of the sudden, he is startled by a sound: a noise in the hallway, perhaps, or just the rustle of leaves. The sound makes him realize he has been caught gazing. And it is precisely this realization—that someone else has been looking at him—which allows him to enter into Being. In the Toronto example, it is the clandestine pleasure of being watched that confirms our status as "being-for-others," as Sartre puts it. We look at the sky not simply to find something out there, but also to confirm our own existence among others, albeit an existence embedded inside a matrix of surveillance.

Echoing hacktivist proclamations about truth, Paglen has suggested that the discovery of the Keyhole satellite means that "truth is sometimes like a point of light reflected in the evening sky, able to be seen by anyone who bothers looking through a telescope."[57] (To be clear, one must first know *where* to look in the infinite expanse of the sky; this is where Paglen and Molczan's process of data-mining satellite coordinates comes into play.) But what sort of truth is this? Merely the existence of a satellite in the sky, hiding in plain sight; we have, after all, no interpretive framework for knowing the kind of satellite or star we are looking at, much less what Keyhole sees through its lenses. Thomas Keenan comments on an unexpected use of Paglen's images in Guantanamo detainee Majid Khan's court trial: "The evidence was not about what was exposed in the images, but about the mere existence of such images."[58]

The key to Keenan's comment is the phrase "mere existence." To discover the satellite brings us no closer to the truth; instead, it operates on an onto-logical level, on the level of "mere existence." Satellites exist; stars exist; the black world exists, as do the trees and the bridges outside, and, and because everything is a sort of "point of light" reflected back to us, we exist as visible beings to be looked at by others. Yet existence is firmly intertwined with recognition and relationality. Paglen acknowledges this dynamic when he writes that he is "interested [in] something I call 'entangled photography' or 'relational photography' . . . Sometimes the 'entangledness' of the photo-graph can arise from these complex relations of seeing and counter-seeing in my work (i.e. photographing spy satellites or Predator drones photograph-ing me)."[59]

My colleague offers an anecdote: her students have redefined "being watched" as "becoming visible." For them, actions on the Internet that might traditionally be interpreted as risks to one's privacy, such as having digital images of oneself uploaded by others, are ways of being recognized. Without these images, her students are invisible on the Internet—nobodies. Indeed, self-surveillance has become something of a common practice: think of the increasingly normal routine of Googling oneself to see who "the Internet" thinks you are. Or the feature on Facebook that allows one to see one's profile as seen by others—a bit like looking through a digital mirror, and identify-ing with that digital image. Though each user's participation is by necessity intertwined with the algorithms that produce the very idea of a personal, autonomous "user," an odd intimacy results from the dynamic in which a user never knows exactly what the (essentially) invisible algorithms know about him or her.

To be sure, military surveillance through a Keyhole satellite is not the same as Googling oneself. But there is nonetheless a thread of intimacy that runs through both the satellite trackers looking for recognition from their satellites, and a user looking for recognition online. This intimacy comes, in part, from the sense of familiarity we have with using algorithmically enhanced ways of seeing and targeting physical space, such as Keyhole

Markup Language, to look back on the spaces in which we live and work, even as this gaze converts populations into targetable spaces for both mar- keters and security agencies alike. But it also results from the undercurrent of desire that runs throughout any gaze that can never be fully reciprocated. The "hole" of the Keyhole denotes an absence that will not entirely reveal itself to us, and yet that absence is the very reason we so fervently desire to know what it sees.

Paglen's artworks in "The Other Night Sky" establish an agonistic dynamic between seeing and counterseeing, move and countermove, normal world and black world, open and secret, night sky and other night sky. But Paglen exaggerates the difference between the two sides for effect. After all, as Karen Beckman has noted, with an "investigative method [that] mirrors the cur- rent administration's obsession with tracking and archiving airport activity," Paglen "works in an uncomfortable proximity to the realm of paranoia."[60] To uncover the deviant network within the network, he uses tools similar to those of the CIA: geographic information systems software and location feeds, such as the US Space Surveillance Network and FAA flight record data. This identification with the military frequently crosses over into camarade- rie, if not outright nostalgia: in a typical scene from his nonfiction book *Blank Spots on the Map*, Paglen describes drinking Coronas in the bullet-splattered Mustafa Hotel in Kabul with other Americans, all military contractors named Bob. A military brat himself who grew up on air force installations, Paglen allows that "coming to Kabul was, in this small way, like coming home."[61]

Though Paglen takes care to distinguish himself from the Bobs in his narrative, this is not always easy to do in Paglen's artwork—and this is part of their force. In *The Workers/Las Vegas, NV* (2006), an eight-minute video loop depicting CIA workers on their way to the office, the moving portraits are firmly situated within the realm of the ordinary. The apparel of these CIA workers—fanny packs, a Raiders jersey, and duffel bags—is unremark- able, as the title of a related photograph, "Morning Commute (Gold Coast Terminal)/Las Vegas, NV/Distance ~1 mile/6:26 am" (2005), indicates. *The Workers* is installed as a video screen in a gallery, but in a smaller format, likening it to surveillance video. Boring stuff, that; by watching *The Work- ers*, we agree to perform the same visual labor as security guards watching a CCTV screen. So if, as Paglen claims, covert operations employ even more workers than legitimate government workers—if the "shadow government" is many times larger than the open government—then the people involved

Figure 4.3
Trevor Paglen, *Drone Vision* (2010), looped DVD video, 5 minutes. Courtesy of the artist.

in surveillance operations are not fundamentally different creatures from, say, academic employees of state universities (as Paglen and I are). Although Paglen describes his goal as mapping the "otherness" of the "other night sky," his video loop is even more complex than he claims: it reveals no otherness, just us looking at a picture of ourselves.

What would it be like if we moved away from the move/countermove dynamic and acknowledged the user's complicity in (and desire for) the mechanism of surveillance? One of Paglen's works, *Drone Vision* (2010), takes on this challenge. *Drone Vision* presents video originally recorded from the cockpit of a Predator drone, given to Paglen by a hacker who intercepted the feed from the drone's satellite uplink. Paglen then edited the hacked footage into a video loop, making a piece of art from this raw data (figure 4.3). The loop consists primarily of landscape images—real clouds, and occasionally a black-and-white landscape somewhere over Eastern Europe—and the drone's visual responses to an operator who is, it seems, trying to see something, anything at all, of interest. At times, the drone operator scrolls a text menu to select a target altitude, the blinking cursor moving or directing our eyes as the operator considers his or her options. At other times, the operator causes the camera to jerk back to an object of interest, seemingly fighting the forward drift of the airplane's motion. Aside from one zoom on a truck carrying what appear to be suspicious-looking vegetables, much of the time, what one senses is the operator's boredom.

However distantiating, the piece has a quality of *almost*—we almost have control over the piece; we almost make the menu selections; we almost see the target; it is almost a video game. The gaps in the drone's control system seduce by almost creating a space for a user to enter. It is fascinating to watch from the position of the drone, to look out from midair and imagine the target, and this creates a partial sort of identification with the human operators. Much like video shot from Tomahawk missiles landing in Iraq and rebroadcast to American taxpayers, we are rewarded for our desire to see by being allowed to peer through the surveillance apparatus itself.

The way *Drone Vision* works thus raises a number of troubling questions. One might wonder, for example, if this piece somehow makes us militarized simply by placing us in that visual position; alternately, one might wonder if it makes the military's aesthetic qualities seductive. However, what is perhaps the most interesting question lies in its implicit claim to oppose the surveillance state. The piece's context directs the viewer to the fact that the footage was not meant for public viewing. Reveling in the backstory, as it were, Altman Siegel Gallery's press release gleefully states that the video's downloading was possible because the satellite uplink was unsecured, a mistake we presume militaries would not make.[62] (How ironic the label "secure" in the upper left of the frame!) And the viewer's pleasure in *Drone Vision* lies in knowing that the video came from a hacked satellite uplink, mimicking the process that government agencies use to duplicate our own data feeds in the cloud.

Equating a "hacked" means of production with a political claim, as Altman Siegel Gallery does, makes the piece troubling: it allows us to play at being a drone operator while we also, supposedly, critique the militarized visual culture exemplified by a drone strike. Yet as artist Walead Beshty writes, "To take the dominant symbolic order and undermine it, thereby rejecting certain kinds of meaning through pure negativity . . . [is to] re-animate all sorts of problematic constructions simply in order to knock them down provisionally."[63] Such artworks depend on the dominant symbolic order for legibility and visibility—in other words, in order to "get" *Drone Vision*, you have to be in on the joke; you have to see and interpret it through its militarized lens. To classify *Drone Vision* as an oppositional artwork—as Paglen's gallerist misreads it—is myopic: the work's supposed moment of resistance to an "other" night sky simply reifies the categories that it ostensibly resists.

On closer inspection, however, *Drone Vision* offers a way out of the entanglement between hacker and military, seeing and counterseeing. In the fantasy of the hacktivist, to play out this entanglement is ultimately to level the distinction between activist and state surveillor, surveillor and sousveillor: for Molczan to become "like the Chinese government" in their ability to counter the US military; for Paglen to imitate the military contractors he is reporting on. But a different approach might be to note the voyeuristic relationship the viewer enacts with the image at hand, the *almost—but not quite* quality remaining. This distance between viewer and drone operator is animated by an undercurrent of desire, as if the viewer were looking at the operator through a keyhole. The operator does not look back; the drone does not respond to our commands. To maintain the voyeuristic distance between watcher and watched is instead to acknowledge the lack of reciprocity in the gaze, and the unevenness in their relationality. The video stages a kind of nonrelational aesthetics that better describes our desires in the cloud: a desire to be recognized online; a desire to have the satellite wink back, even when, most of the time, it does not.

Paglen's method for finding satellites came out of an earlier project, in which he mapped the network of extraordinary rendition flights—CIA-sponsored flights that delivered detainees to secret airbases around the world for the purposes of torture. For that project, he turned to a network of amateur plane spotters, who obsessively track and upload coordinates and images of planes that they spot to websites such as airliners.net. He then cross-referenced these coordinates with government documents and victims' accounts of the extraordinary rendition process in order to find the actual locations of the torture sites.[64]

Paglen's use of public databases takes advantage of the increased flattening of the difference between public and secret data. Because the CIA disguises itself in civilian holding companies whose existence is purely legal, not physical, it is, in some ways, an agency made up mainly of paperwork. (For this reason, the CIA is a curiously "public" agency.) In response, Paglen filed several Freedom of Information Act requests to locate the persons registered as corporate directors of CIA airplane leasing companies, asking government clerks to photocopy relevant records for him. They complied, and Paglen was able to gain access to the passport photographs of these so-called directors.

In describing these CIA operations, Paglen has written that "state secrecy is a form of executive power. It is the power to unilaterally and legitimately conceal events, actions, budgets, programs, and plans . . . a form of monarchical power that contemporary states have inherited from the kingdoms of yesteryear."[65] This idea of secrecy as the sovereign's power to violate the law—an idea voiced by political theorist Carl Schmitt—is, in Paglen's view, continually at odds with the "normal" functioning of the democratic state, one that operates on the principles of "equal rights, transparent government, and informed consent."[66]

Paglen's narrative is a powerful one, but it could be extended even further. For to ascribe sovereign power merely to a secret state is true on a literal level, but as Foucault reminds us, power is always relational; power is not wielded by a single institution ("the state"), but is dispersed throughout individual subjects, knowledge structures, and other practices. As a result, we are alternately interpellated by and induced to participate in this system of power. This explains why the form of sovereign power has attached itself to places far outside of the realm of covert operations or military detention camps. Specifically, we have seen hacktivists attempt to use computer algorithms to counter sovereignty with sovereignty, enacting a fantasy that computer code can trump state surveillance or propaganda. The idea that code is a higher power—"code is law"—forms the basis for this fantasy: as an inflexible system of protocols that all parties must follow—whether government or hacker or user—code will create the exception that bypasses a (corrupt) legal system; code itself is sovereign. And yet, this fantasy of sovereignty is not just confined to hacktivists alone; as I will argue below, the sovereignty of data is what enables any user to use the cloud.

Necropolitics

I have so far claimed that the sovereignty of data is primarily a fantasy produced by the cloud's ideology, but cultural fictions and cultural "realities" are often intimately intertwined. In the course of this book, we have seen the sovereign's "right to kill" displaced onto banal orders of everyday digital culture: the "dead link," "dead media," "time to live," "killing the process," and so forth. Readers literate in UNIX will recognize, for example, the program "kill," which is used to terminate other programs in a myriad of ways (abort, hang up, interrupt, quit, alarm, terminate). As I contend, the metaphor of a user as a sovereign "decider," able to kill off programs at will, hints at a submerged structure of actual violence beneath everyday practices. To investigate this further, I revisit a case we first encountered in chapter 1: the "Internet kill switch."

The kill switch is almost always offered as a joke, as, for instance, a widely circulated meme of a big red button in a central control room that says Press Here to Stop the Internet. In several of these cartoons the red button is inside a military control room, next to the red "hotline" telephone used for US-to-Soviet Union telephone calls in emergencies during the Cold War, implying that the kill switch is the cybernetic equivalent of launching a nuclear strike. As the *MIT Technology Review* sums up the meme: "What if the president of [the US] could pick up a cold war-era style phone . . . and order that it be shut down?"[67] This cartoon is funny because the red button, and the central control room depicted within, flies in the face of everything we want to believe about the Internet's architecture—that it is decentralized and therefore has no central points of control; that the rerouting process is automated and labor-free; that it is too complex to be simply switched off; and that it cannot be shut down by any single person. This cartoon typically circulates within a relatively sophisticated group of US Internet users, typically to satirize proposed legislation that would give the US president the power to flip the kill switch, or to express alarm that the US may censor its citizens as Libya, Egypt, and Syria have done (whose regimes have all used the "kill switch").[68] To joke about the kill switch is, on the surface, to make a political point about Internet freedom and how it must be defended against inept politicians. But what the joke really does is signal technological savvy: the person who "gets" the joke understands that a kill switch is a metaphor, not an actual weapon for killing.

To imagine the kill switch as a Cold War-style weapon, then, is to misread the nature of the Internet as a medium for the circulation of information, commerce, and free speech. And yet the Syrian government began to deploy its Internet kill switch several times starting in 2011, almost always in connection with military operations. On November 29, 2012, for example, the regime cut Internet connectivity and simultaneously launched a counteroffensive against insurgents near the Damascus airport, in what journalists now understand to be a military trap to lure rebel fighters away from their supply routes. Why the regime cut Internet connectivity has been the subject of wide speculation; theories offered tended to fall along two major lines. The most widely circulated hypothesis has been that the network blackouts work as propaganda, helping the government cover up or censor atrocities from civilian observers; a second and less widely held theory is that blackouts allow the Syrian government to effectively press military offensives.

In 2014, Anita Gohdes, an empirical researcher of conflict violence at the University of Mannheim, decided to find out whether the "propaganda" or the "military strategy" theory was more likely correct. Using a time-series model to analyze Syrian casualty data, she discovered that violence spiked significantly during Internet blackouts, but there was no statistical correlation between blackouts and the underreporting of violence.[69] In cases such as the Hama blackout in 2011, and in Damascus blackout in July 2012, she observed that the network blackouts were responsible for an increase of thirty mean killings over the norm. Gohdes concluded that the "cutting of all connections . . . ha[s] the potential of constituting a tactic within larger military offensives. . . Regimes implement large-scale disruptions selectively and purposely in conjunction with launching larger battles."[70] The Internet kill switch, in other words, was not primarily a media effect for disrupting the flow of news and free speech, but was instead a new weapon in its own right.

The kill switch, then, is and isn't a weapon; in the case of Syria, the metaphor of the kill switch becomes actualized as a killing machine. The larger problem embodied by the kill switch is that sovereign power in the cloud, almost always assumed to be a metaphor for the feeling of user mastery, may manifest itself as actual violence more often than we think— six times alone in Syria, as of the publication of Gohdes's study. This problem has been undertheorized within the field of new media studies, which looks for implicit forms of control within civilian technologies such as the Internet. Precisely because these two kinds of targeting are related, however, current research on societies of control may help us understand these new forms of violence.

Put another way, how can we use the theories built around new media to productively discuss real conflicts in physical space? Leerom Medovoi has offered a way forward by asking: "What if we approach war, not as an exception to or the opposite of regulation, but rather as continuous with it,

as the point when regulation's militarism has surged into the open?"[71] In
this provocative comment, Medovoi points to a way to understand a violence
that is innate within—rather than as an exception to—the control or regulatory structure of the cloud. War and regulation, in Medovoi's schema, both
grow out of liberalism's need to establish a line between internal and external enemies. While a state normally declares war against an external enemy,
the war on terror comes out of imagining that external enemy as part of
the inside: "Terrorism becomes, like murder or rape, the naming of a deviant type against which society must be defended."[72] That is to say, in this
logic, terrorists are branded "abnormal" Islamists who "hate our freedoms,"
and whose very political beliefs are merely aberrations from a "normal," tolerant (and tolerated) Islam. Similarly, the project of globalization seeks to
define the free market in opposition to the ideologies of unfree countries;
and though it nominally does so by promising peace and an orderly set of
regulations for free trade, its core logic, for Medovoi, remains the same: an
abhorrence of cultural abnormalities that "threaten or resist its Jupiterian
vision of incorporation into a global liberal society."[73] These unfree countries
may be induced to open up their markets by incentives or by force; after all,
the gambit of the post–Cold War era has been to assume that free trade will
lead, eventually, to a free people (and vice versa). Thus, Medovoi concludes,
globalization merely adds a single word to the old rallying cry of a racist
state: now it is "global society that must be defended."

If both the war on terror and the global marketplace resemble each other
in this way, then it follows that war is less the exception to regulation than
part of a continuum of power that continually fluctuates between its explicit
(war) and implicit (regulatory) manifestations. Can this idea apply to the
cloud? The ideal of a global, singular "cloud" may locate itself in the desire
for all data to become incorporated in the cloud's networks, whether the
geotagging of all physical data into Google Earth, or, more metaphorically,
the value of "Internet freedom" that is said to apply equally to all countries.
But this vision of a global "Internet that must be defended" is, as the phrase
implies, perpetually shadowed by the threat of deviance, and the specter that
threatens to undo this vision has taken many forms. Brazil, for instance, is
trying to build its own public Internet that would bypass US surveillance over
the "global" Internet. Meanwhile, the US Department of Defense's warning
of "foreign influence" within software products restages an invisible threat
of foreign values that supposedly subverts liberal civil society from the

inside. The cloud, I have argued, manages this deviance by constructing a soft architecture of exclusion embodied by data bunkers, virtualization software, Internet firewalls, and most subtly of all, the idea of the private user. The teeming online population is thus regulated and kept in check by isolating and turning each subject into a user.

In certain moments, however, when "regulation's militarism has surged into the open" (Medovoi), we can glimpse the symbolic violence embedded in the cloud's architecture erupt into actual violence.[74] In chapter 3, we saw the idea of protecting the Internet from unfree practices, such as spam, manifest itself as racial violence against Nigerian fraudsters. We also have seen the kill switch, severe cousin of Internet protocols for regulating and controlling networks, used as an actual military weapon. In the remainder of this chapter, I turn to a final case study, examining how the CIA's acts of extraordinary rendition reveal a porous interface between targeted marketing and extrajudicial targeting. I have termed this hybrid form of power, which blurs the distinction between the regulatory protocols of data networks and the sovereign's right to kill, the *sovereignty of data*.[75]

Extraordinary rendition—the extrajudicial delivery of US suspects to other countries to be tortured—may seem to be best explained in terms of sovereign power; torture, after all, originally grew out of the power of a sovereign to compel a prisoner's body to speak. And the state secrecy involved in masking the suspects' eventual destination, as Paglen put it, is likewise "a form of monarchical power that contemporary states have inherited from the kingdoms of yesteryear."[76] But extraordinary rendition also partakes of an impulse found primarily in global markets, as Slavoj Žižek writes: "The exemplary economic strategy of today's capitalism is outsourcing . . . Is torture also not being 'outsourced,' left to the Third World allies of the US which can do it without worrying about legal problems or public protest?"[77]

As Žižek explains, capital by nature seeks the most efficient place to operate, the cheapest way to do something. This logic extends throughout the American political economy and even reaches the power to kill, which capital efficiently displaces onto other regimes and spaces. Under this carceral system, the prisoner's body becomes borderless and exchangeable, as inert as a financial transaction. This signals a new twist on the usual reasons for imprisonment. Earlier, a captive's body—trapped and immobile in its prison cell—exemplified a society decided and ruled by a single sovereign. Indeed, historian Paul Halliday has shown that the writ of *habeas corpus*, typically assumed to be a way of preventing wrongful imprisonment, was originally designed as a legal tool to even out the reach of a sovereign's power, ensuring "that no jurisdiction, whether normal or novel, was beyond . . . oversight."[78] Translating literally as "deliver the [prisoner's] body," *habeas corpus* standardizes all of the prisons and courts within a legal system so that a captive can be transferred within its judicial network. But in looking for the most efficient way for a prisoner to be rendered or processed, extraordinary rendition seeks to make the captive fungible across multiple sovereign networks of imprisonment. Just as Amazon Web Services makes it more efficient to process a computer transaction in the cloud than to process it in-house, even including the time and cost it takes to first transmit the data to an Irish EC2 server farm, it is more "efficient" to render a prisoner in Poland, even counting the time it takes to extract and transfer the prisoner to a torture center in Stare Kiejkuty. The extraordinary rendition system is a global network of networks, in which the prisoner's body is the packet switched from one judicial network to another; in doing so, extraordinary rendition applies the network architecture of the cloud to torture.

Perhaps the most compelling theorization of sovereign violence's stamp on contemporary detainees comes from Judith Butler. After the US government captures a prisoner in the war on terror, Butler argues, it "temporarily" places that body within a detention camp, Camp Delta, which is exempt from the rule of law. By deferring the application of law, a camp declares that prisoner to be a detainee, who is not yet able to receive a trial. Since sovereign power is founded on the suspension of law—to paraphrase political theorist Carl Schmitt, the sovereign is a sovereign because he or she may decide when law no longer applies—this state of law-in-suspension enables the "petty sovereign" to decide whether the prisoner should live or die. These petty sovereigns are prison guards, bureaucrats in military tribunals, middle managers in intelligence, drone supervisors, and so on. Able to add a name onto a kill list or a capture list as well as revoke citizenship from a potential target, they wield the power to kill without any juridical oversight. As Butler describes it, this process engenders "a ghostly and forceful resurgence of sovereignty in the midst of governmentality."[79]

To extend this analysis, we might observe how governmentality's new data-centric methods themselves gave rise to a new strain of torture. In extraordinary rendition, the body is less important for its physicality or material being than its potential value as targetable or actionable intelligence. Within this changing understanding of a subject (an understanding grounded in what I have described as "war as big data") "individuals," in Deleuze's words, "have become 'dividuals,' and masses [have become] samples, data, markets . . .":[80] the body remade in the image of data. The extraction of information from captives thus performs another version of marketing, which mines data, in aggregate, from a population so that it can anticipate a targeted population's purchasing behavior. The captive's body becomes one node in a larger set of data, valuable for its ability to preempt a terror network's future behavior rather than for its individual actions in the past. As General David Petraeus's guidelines for counterinsurgency in Afghanistan read: "Target the whole network, not just individuals."[81]

Torturing a captive to extract information therefore represents the forcible conversion of the body into a network. The individual's claim to his or her own body is overwritten with multiplicity; the need for data that are only useful in relationship to data from other individuals forces the stamp of the multitude upon the individual. Within this context, a torturer understands a victim's body as an unreliable source that must be pre-processed and understood in the context of other data. Traditionally, to "render" something is to turn it into its representation: rendering engines for video games, for example, turn raw data into 3-D representations. Though we tend to use the word "render" differently when we discuss moving prisoners, in fact the same logic applies: the victim's body is delivered, as bare life, to the engine of data extraction.

This ideology carries over to more mundane realms. The US Department of Homeland Security's practice of collecting biometric data from foreign travelers in order to enter the United States—another method of turning bodies into users—is not as new as it seems, as philosopher Giorgio Agamben shows: "I want to call to memory that the practice of tattooing the inmates in Auschwitz was possibly regarded as a 'normal' and economical form of regulating the incorporation of the deported ones into the camp. The biopolitical tattoo imposed upon us today when we want to travel into the United States is the baton of what we might accept tomorrow as the normal way of registering into the mechanism and the transmission of the state if we want to be identified as good citizens."[82]

Technological actions such as biometrics may appear to resonate most strongly with Foucauldian investigations of how society optimizes life—through genetic and medical testing, or through the codedness of DNA and the code of new media. This is why most new media scholars have read bio-politics as synonymous with a control society.[83] Yet to turn a body into usable data, as Agamben shows us, is also to unconsciously invoke the ugliest of spaces—the Nazi extermination camps—exceptional spaces that, he argues, are nevertheless foundational to Western democracy.[84]

Yet the idea of the biological tattoo is not just "imposed upon us today"; it is part of the way that security interfaces with participation inside the cloud. The cloud continually encourages each of us to don a "tattoo" of sorts in order to become fully realized users: tagging photographs of our friends on Facebook with their name or location may seem to be an enjoyable form of affective labor, yet we are simultaneously producing the world's largest database for facial recognition. This tagging thus takes place within, and serves to reinforce, an ideological framework that defines the subject as a user.

The cloud is a subtle weapon that translates the body into usable information. Despite this violence, it functions primarily as a banal ideology that convinces us that usability is, in Agamben's words, "'normal' and economical," or that identifying ourselves is the "normal way of registering into the mechanism and transmission of the state." Yet maintaining this framework requires our continual participation. While this participation is primarily reinforced through the carrot of market mechanisms—free storage, free downloads, cheap computing, social connections, and so forth—the stick behind it comes from the evocation of disaster: foreign hackers, spammers, and terrorists. The nameless but continual threat of unfreedom makes each user responsible for his or her own online security. In this way, users participate in the same security framework that animates the war on terror.

The mistake is to believe that warlike acts are temporary exceptions to the normal operations of the cloud. In what former Transportation Security Administration director Kip Hawley has called a time of "permanent emergency," violent practices such as extraordinary rendition become part of daily life.[85] To explain away the brutality of militarized spaces as black sites outside the rule of law—to understand them as exceptions within an economy primarily interested in selling and buying information—is to miss a crucial point. The information economy traffics in bare life, and indeed is only possible through it.

In this chapter, I have argued that the cloud constructs a way of perceiving the world that fundamentally constrains our range of actions by co-opting the very idea of action itself. By default, this leaves us a limited set of choices, which typically manifests itself as a walled garden of ideology for scholars to debunk, or a set of moves for hacktivists to laugh at and call into question. Constrained in this way, it is no wonder that so often critical or oppositional responses take the form of dark humor: the kill switch, the sovereign user.

The longer-term effects of cloud seeing are to deaden our ability to see people as anything but users, and ultimately, to become complicit in the actions of the regime itself as it maps our patterns of use and activity and triangulates our associates. The typical response to revelations about the cloud's tracking software is to fight back, typically by looking for a hidden "truth" beneath a deceptive surface. But this is to put one's faith in a paranoid form of knowledge that merely replicates the subject position and knowledge structures already inherent in the cloud. The problem, as I see it, is this: a gaze often confirms and reciprocates. When we gaze at a control society in the hopes of exposing its structure, our gaze ends up acknowledging its right to power.

If we must exist within a connected world, where it is extraordinarily difficult to opt out, it may be more productive to acknowledge the structural inequality of this relationship, the distance we have to travel before we reach anything called the truth. Maintaining the voyeuristic distance between watcher and watched is to acknowledge the lack of reciprocity in the gaze, and that, more generally, there is a void in the apparatus of representation that cannot be filled by software tools, more data, or better algorithms.

Hacktivists typically use the cloud to tear down and destroy images that they see as propaganda. Yet a more effective avenue for political change may be to reinvest the image itself with credulity. In a world where each user is an iconoclast, perhaps the bravest thing of all is to become—to resurrect a very old word—an *iconodule*: someone who has faith in images. Images do not necessarily function by making the invisible visible or a hidden truth tangible, as an epistemology of exposure assumes, but rather mediate between an abstract totality and the frame of human experience. To offer just a few illustrative examples, while the cloud normally collapses global networks into a series of narrow, seemingly personal channels, images such as Jenny Odell's cut out photographs of digital infrastructure can help mediate between the scale of the global and the intimate, the macro and the micro. Images, too, can help us expand the temporal frame of inquiry outside the narrow parameters of real-time data; works such as Rebecca Baron's documentary film *How Little We Know of Our Neighbors* (2005) and Andrew Norman Wilson's video *Workers Leaving the Googleplex* (2009–2011) can help us think historically about the desire for surveillance and the technology industry's labor practices, respectively; they can help open a critical history of the present.

To capture our own sensuous investment in digital culture—where, I have argued, the digital cloud properly lies—we might begin by mapping the images we see in it. A history of the virtual, then, as a form of paying attention to this imaginary, much like a summer afternoon spent recording shapes in the sky: a flock of geese; a series of tubes; perhaps a railroad rumbling by.

CONCLUSION

Like a muzzled creature, the cloud strains to be more than it is. No longer content with virtualizing hardware and other infrastructure (in engineering terms, Infrastructure as a Service, abbreviated IaaS) or software applications (Software as a Service, or SaaS), the cloud has its sights on larger quarry. Commentator Richie Etwaru urges fellow tech entrepreneurs to stop thinking about "the cloud" as a noun and to begin to use "clouding" as a verb. Now everything can be clouded and, presumably, made more efficient and profitable: as Etwaru writes, "Airbnb are modern versions of housing clouds delivering housing as a service, and similarly, Zipcar and Uber are car clouds."[1] Eventually, he tells us, we will have a pool of human labor "unshackled" from the confines of specific jobs ("Human as a Service"); eventually, he writes, we will have everything as a service.

Etwaru's futurism reveals a simple truth about the cloud: it has never really been about computing, because computing is just one part of a larger cultural fantasy. Specifically, I have shown that the cloud is a neoliberal fantasy about user participation that is so widespread and so ambient as to be universal, but that project is always founded on a volatile layer of insecurity. Thus Etwaru implies that regulations and organized labor threaten his vision of Human as a Service; yet as this book demonstrated, those threats and others, such as hackers, the war on terror, viruses, and so forth, are animated by a larger discourse of unfreedom. Alternately attempting to preempt these threats and survive them, the cloud both activates a paranoid reflex and also a melancholia that dwells on its imagined loss. The one temporality that users of the cloud are barred from reflecting upon, it seems, is that of the present.

To answer that problem, I have located the cloud within the sewers, railroads, televisions, bunkers, and archives that both constitute the prehistory of its infrastructure and also allow us to see its discursive underpinnings. This is a difficult task, because the digital cloud actively erases its own historicity; like its namesake, it constructs itself through "pure fluctuation and cyclicity," as Steven Connor describes the temporality of air.[2] This erasure is crucial to producing a sense of limitlessness within the digital environment: just as a pipe creates a sense of water as an infinite resource that can be summoned at the turn of a tap, the cloud creates a sense of computing power as a virtually unlimited resource. To do so, however, causes two things to happen.

First, the cloud is a resource-intensive, extractive technology that converts water and electricity into computational power, leaving a sizable amount of environmental damage that it then displaces from sight. But it also turns human labor into a resource, as the vision of Human as a Service indicates, making it possible to hire Bangladeshi workers to solve one thousand CAPTCHA problems, those "enter the word in the picture here" forms that verify a user is human, for less than $1.50 a batch. Assuming eight straight hours in a "workday," such a worker can expect to earn from $1 to $3 a day.[3] The mind-numbing repetition of proving that one is human and not a computer every ten seconds reveals the slow violence of the information economy, which extracts bare life out of its "human resources." To understand this idea, I have set out a framework I term the *sovereignty of data*, which describes the variable ways that sovereign power interfaces with data-centric tools. Sovereign power has historically decided what counts as human, who is included and who is excluded, when the protection of law can be withdrawn, and therefore who can be discarded or killed. But sovereignty is not a static force; it is now applied differentially and flexibly, anthropologist Aihwa Ong argues, as in China's carving out of special economic zones to offer multinationals a pool of laborers exempt from legal protection.[4] The cloud codifies this flexibility—as well as sovereignty's ghastly imagination—into its cultural logic.

The sovereignty of data further explains how the cloud induces its users to become freelancers for the state's security apparatus. This project of security often bears little resemblance to the historical look and feel of sovereign power; just as the cloud masks hardware with software—as in the software-created "cloud drive"—the cloud veils hard power with the look and feel of soft power.[5] Thus the act of data-mining satellite imagery to send targets to NATO, for example, comes to resemble any other act of online crowdsourcing.

Indeed, such actions are even billed as a way of empowering American users to participate in what the Department of Homeland Security's cybersecurity division terms their "shared responsibility" for their country's security. Yet we would do well to remember that underneath these data-centric interfaces is a familiar politics of death.

Second, when the violence that comes out of this politics rears its head— when targeted marketing crosses over into military targeting—it is far easier to assign blame to external agents and agencies, such as the NSA or foreign cybercriminals, against which users can supposedly fight back, than to critically assess our own complicity with its logic. This is because the cloud causes its users to ascribe a strange agency to its technologies, which allows us to displace our own involvement in the cloud's effects. In actuality, the sovereignty of data is activated by our desire; we supply the data, the free labor, and the participation. Yet it seems easier to "fight back" with technological tools because the cloud produces users rather than publics, and therefore individual rather than collective action.

To return to my comparison of water pipes with piping in computer power, water is still largely regarded as a public resource, while the cloud is almost entirely owned by private companies. When there is a drought, it does not seem unreasonable to invoke collective solutions, such as water conservation and water rationing; yet when digital culture runs into a snag— for example, over privacy—the default response in the United States is to appeal to Silicon Valley start-ups to build better apps. This is what happens when today's dominant metaphor for digital space, "the cloud," is actually a metaphor for private ownership. What gathering spaces emerge within the cloud are closest to the ambiguously named privately owned public open spaces found in an American city's financial district. Though the landscaping of these pocket parks and rooftop gardens bears a superficial resemblance to public space, these overly tidy zones are nevertheless administered by banks, insurance companies, and the like. The eventual consequence is that the lived knowledge essential for imagining and discussing public space has begun to atrophy.

A sense of our involvement in the politics of digital culture was once easier to see back when technology was more scarce. As my chapter on time-sharing indicated, networked computers were once a highly limited (and highly coveted) resource. I remember many days of chatting with strangers on a server because a small hard drive we shared was getting full, or because we had to arrange a time to run a computationally intensive job. The strange intimacy of this cooperation is surely outdated now, but I use it to illustrate a simple point. What has changed is less a wholesale form in which power manifests itself than the way the cloud increasingly masks that sense of a shared space with plenitude, even though it is rooted in, and continuous with, the same landscapes, environments, and architectures that have been used for centuries. To think of the cloud as a limitless, all-encompassing medium that is simply there, inevitable, or—worse—actively out to get us is to discount our own involvement in any sort of shared debate or project. I offer this book to you so that we might return the cloud to the scarcest space of all: the space of public life.

NOTES

Introduction

1. The first part of my provisional definition, the system of networks, is technically what is known as a "network of networks": there are multiple kinds of disparate networks, from fiber to wireless to copper, within it. The Internet was so named because it moved data between satellite, packet radio, and telephone networks (inter-networks). To take the example of video streaming, when the video moves from a computer network operated by, say, Netflix or Amazon, to a different network, the cellular network, this is a "network of networks."

2. Businesses, in contrast, typically date the term's introduction to 2006, when it was used by Google to describe a new business model. Finally, researchers often list the date as 1996: the *MIT Technology Review* finds a reference to a patent for "cloud computing," an unrealized model, in 1996, while the research studio Metahaven incorrectly cites 1996 as the first use of the word "the cloud" as it refers to network design. See Antonio Regalado, "Who Coined 'Cloud Computing?'" and Metahaven, "Captives of the Cloud, Part I."

3. Lewis Fry Richardson's *Weather Prediction by Numerical Process* (1922), as identified in Seb Franklin, "Cloud Control, or the Network as Medium," 452–453.

4. Perhaps the only other legacy of Picturephone, which has been discontinued and is now a relic, is the "pound" or "number" key (#) on the phone, pressed to differentiate Picturephone calls from voice calls.

5. As Allan Sekula writes, most cargo still takes the same amount of time to travel across the Pacific Ocean—eight to twelve days. Sekula, "Dismal Science, Part I," 50.

6. Scholars Lisa Gitelman and Geoffrey Pingree have suggested that a new medium engages in a period of "discursive conflict" with an older medium in order to define its uses for society. A medium is successful, they note, when we naturalize it and view it as completely transparent to our historical frame—when it seems to become "unmediated." As a result, the cloud is simultaneously transparent—it feels completely natural—and opaque—it hides the things that are unnatural to us behind its user-friendly interface. Gitelman and Pingree, "Introduction," xiv.

7. Scholars who think this way often base their argument on John Arquilla and David Ronfeldt, *Networks and Netwars*, producing studies such as Samuel Weber, *Targets of Opportunity*, and Manuel Castells, *The Power of Identity*, which asks: "How can states fight networks?"

8. James Boyle, "Foucault in Cyberspace."

9. This idea is forcefully voiced in Michael Hardt and Antonio Negri, *Empire*: "The fundamental principle of Empire as we have described it throughout this book is that its power has no actual and localizable terrain or center. Imperial power is distributed in networks, through mobile and articulated mechanisms of control" (384). This extends a strain of thinking most typically exemplified by communications scholar Manuel Castells in *The Rise of the Network Society*, and by Yochai Benkler in *The Wealth of Networks*.

10. Michel Foucault, *Discipline and Punish*, 201.

11. This Deleuzian argument about control is most clearly laid out in books such as Alexander Galloway, *Protocol*, Wendy Chun, *Control and Freedom*, and Raiford Guins, *Edited Clean Version*, and embraced by scholars in more "traditional" disciplines, such as D. N. Rodowick, *Reading the Figural, or, Philosophy after the New Media*.

12. Gilles Deleuze, "Postscript on the Societies of Control," 4. For more on this shift, see Franklin, "The Limits of Control."

13. Deleuze, "Postscript on the Societies of Control," 7.

14. Most critiques of Deleuze's historicity have centered on the relationship between disciplinary and control societies, perhaps because they are more obviously coterminous in time. Sovereignty receives rather less attention. In response to this common line of thought among technologists, Geert Lovink has commented that "Internet protocols are not ruling the world . . . In the end, G. W. Bush is." This rejoinder, sent by email to Alexander Galloway and

Eugene Thacker, is what opens their book *The Exploit* (1); they propose that sovereignty and networks may be related, most notably in examples such as Al Qaeda and the "swarm." What differentiates our approaches is one of method: they focus on the technological mediation of wars, while my study, directed at its historical precedents, suggests that this mediation is largely a construct. Despite this disagreement, this book's line of thinking is very much a response to Lovink (via Galloway and Thacker)'s challenge.

15. Michel Foucault, *Security, Territory, Population*, 143. As Judith Butler writes, political theorists Wendy Brown and Giorgio Agamben have productively "refuse[d] the chronological argument that would situate sovereignty prior to governmentality" (Butler, *Precarious Life*, 60).

16. Jean Baudrillard, Paul Virilio, and James Der Derian are perhaps the best-known scholars of this school.

17. John Horvath, "Freeware Capitalism."

18. David E. Sanger, "Mutually Assured Cyberdestruction?"

19. Achille Mbembe, "Necropolitics."

20. Davey Alba, "It's Time to Fight for Your Digital Privacy."

21. The term "medium specificity" comes from art history and generally refers to theories of Greenbergian modernism, though the idea ultimately dates back to ancient Greek philosophers, the Renaissance *paragone* between painting and sculpture, and Enlightenment texts such as Gotthold Ephraim Lessing's *Laocoon, or the Limits between Painting and Poetry* (1766). The phrase has been reappropriated in places such as N. Katherine Hayles, "Print Is Flat, Code Is Deep: The Importance of Media-Specific Analysis," and Lev Manovich, *The Language of New Media*, which (though Manovich does not use the term explicitly) attempts to map the specific attributes of new media through several organizing principles, such as the database. Numerous ever more specific subfields—such as "critical code studies" and "software studies"—have now internalized this method of study, to the point where it has become one of the dominant (if not the default) methods of analyzing new media. Thinking about the attempts by film scholars to define the "medium specific" properties of film from the 1890s to the 1930s—is film a (photo)play? is it an art? is it science?—one quickly understands the parallel impulse to find the "newness" of new media.

22. Such studies, particularly in English, are relatively rare. One recent exception is Anita Chan's study of Peruvian digital culture; see Chan, *Networking Peripheries*.

23. Marshall McLuhan, *Understanding Media*, 3.

24. The term "tactical media," originating in 1993, refers to a set of unconventional artistic practices organized around opposition, and often describes artist groups such as Critical Art Ensemble, Yes Men, Electronic Disturbance Theater, and eToy. Perhaps the clearest definition of the term comes from Rita Raley as "a mutable category" that revolves around "disturbance"; examples include "reverse engineering, hacktivism, denial-of-service attacks, the digital hijack," and so forth (Raley, *Tactical Media*, 6).

25. This point is made most succinctly in David Joselit, *Feedback*. For more, see my discussion in chapter 1 on the Ant Farm collective.

26. Technological determinism has been embedded in the very foundation of "new media" studies, at least since Marshall McLuhan. Lev Manovich offers a typical example: "Today we are in the middle of a new media revolution—the shift of all culture to computer-mediated forms of production, distribution, and communication . . . Mass media and data processing are complementary technologies; they appear together and develop side by side, making modern mass society possible" (Manovich, *The Language of New Media*, 19, 23). Wendy Chun offers an important corrective to the scholar's assignation of too much power to technology: "Thus, in order to understand control-freedom, we need to insist on the failures and the actual operations of technology" (Chun, *Control and Freedom*, 9).

27. On walling off the commons, see James Boyle, "The Second Enclosure Movement and the Construction of the Public Domain." On rhizome, see John E. Newhagen and Sheizaf Rafaeli, "Why Communication Researchers Should Study the Internet."

28. Tiziana Terranova, *Network Culture*, 120.

29. Matthew Kirschenbaum, *Mechanisms*.

30. Rob Nixon, *Slow Violence and the Environmentalism of the Poor*.

31. Ibid., 200.

32. Peter Lunenfeld, *User*.

1   The Shape of the Network

1. Marianne Costantinou, "Septa Working on the Railroad."

2. Jean-Paul Rodrigue, Claude Comtois, and Brian Slack, "Rail Track Mileage."

3. Other telecommunications companies also run fiber on railroad tracks. Level 3 cut a deal with the Union Pacific Railroad to supply roughly half of their rights-of-way; others used CSX and Amtrak routes. In a nod to this heritage, America's new fiber-optic research network has been named LambaRail: lamba for light; rail for a fiber network's nineteenth-century predecessor, the railroad.

4. As Lisa Parks writes in "Around the Antenna Tree": "Most people notice infrastructures only when they are put in the wrong place or break down. This means that public knowledge of them is largely limited to their misplacement or malfunction."

5. Lisa Parks, "Falling Apart."

6. Vincent Cerf, quoted in Jessie Holliday Scanlon and Brad Wieners, "Guest Column: The Internet Cloud."

7. Manny Jalonschi, "Occupy Wall Street's Crowd Democracy—the Anti-Mob"; Stefania Milan, "Cloud Protesting."

8. Etienne Balibar's *Europe Constitution Frontière* (2005), as translated and quoted in Stuart Elden, *Terror and Territory*, 34.

9. Horace H. Nance, "Engineering the Transcontinental Cable," 219.

10. As Kleinrock relates, ARPAnet was designed to be an early form of resource sharing between these specialized labs. "An Interview with Leonard Kleinrock," 7. Scientist David Retz has even commented that "in retrospect, you have to admit, the original concept was 'cloud computing'!" Retz, "ARPANET, as I Recall."

11. Paul Baran, "On Distributed Communications Networks," 4.

12. For more on this myth, which Kazys Varnelis calls the "foundation myth for the Internet," see Varnelis, "Conclusion: The Rise of Network Culture."

13. Stephen J. Lukasik, "Why the Arpanet Was Built," 10.

14. Indeed, communications scholar Mark Andrejevic has termed this concentration of data in the data centers of Google, Microsoft, and so on a recentralization. Andrejevic, "Surveillance in the Digital Enclosure."

15. These are AT&T, Sprint, Verizon/MCI, Level 3/Global Crossing, and Qwest (a sixth company, XO, operates a much smaller network built on top of Level 3's conduit).

16. The reference is to Gilles Deleuze and Felix Guattari's criticism of arboreal thinking in "Rhizome."

17. Here one thinks of Samuel Weber, *Targets of Opportunity*; Michael Hardt and Antonio Negri, *Empire*; and Alexander Galloway, "Global Networks and the Effects on Culture." There, Galloway sees the 9/11 attacks on the World Trade Center as a moment of historical rupture, the last moment of the old way of thinking; even its architecture, "a tower, a center, a pillar, an icon, a hub," is swept away by a terrorist network most exemplary of an age of cloud computing (28).

18. Elden, *Terror and Territory*, xxix; also Giovanna Borradori, "Autoimmunity: Real and Symbolic Suicides," 124.

19. Galloway, "Global Networks and the Effects on Culture," 28. Compare also to Hardt and Negri, *Empire*: "The original design of the Internet was intended to withstand military attack. Since it has no center and almost any portion can operate as an autonomous whole, the network can continue to function even when part of it has been destroyed" (299).

20. Galloway, "Global Networks and the Effects on Culture," 28.

21. Peter Galison, "War against the Center."

22. Paul Baran, "Reliable Digital Communications Systems," 1.

23. Baran, "On Distributed Communications Networks," 2.

24. Galloway, "Global Networks and the Effects on Culture," 29, and Patricia Mellencamp, "Ant Farm Redux."

25. Constantinos Doxiadis, "The Two-Headed Eagle," 2.

26. Ibid., 18.

27. Mark Wigley, "Network Fever."

28. "Mystery Blasts," *Newsweek*, 32.

29. U.S. Senate Subcommittee to Investigate the Administration of the Internal Security Act and Internal Security Laws, Committee on the Judiciary, "A Bill to Safeguard Communications Facilities," Hearing on S.B. 1990, 87th Congress, June 7, 1961, 7 (hereafter "Safeguard Communications Facilities").

30. George A. Phelps, "The Wendover Blast," 13.

31. "Mystery Blasts," *Newsweek*, 32.

32. Darin Barney has also noticed this linkage in *Prometheus Wired*, 68.

33. Gerald W. Johnson, "Plots and Counter-plots," 18.

34. "Safeguard Communications Facilities," 18, 22.

35. Amy Gardner, "Metro Dig at Tysons Stirs Underground Intrigue."

36. General DuPlantis is deputy director of communications and warning systems for the OCDM, Office of Civil and Defense Mobilization. "Safeguard Communications Facilities," 31.

37. Ibid., 34.

38. Ibid., 32.

39. Katie Hafner and Matthew Lyon, *Where Wizards Stay Up Late*, 52.

40. "Safeguard Communications Facilities," 31.

41. U.S. Senate, "Investigation of Administration of Internal Security Act of 1950."

42. Wendy Chun, *Control and Freedom*. Avital Ronell has also observed that telephone and fiber-optic networks may be metaphors for fevered knowledge. Ronell's schizophrenic subject understood telephone wires as a series of electric currents running through its bodies. Ronell, *The Telephone Book*. For more on the Senate's targeting of queer employees of the State Department, see David K. Johnson, *The Lavender Scare*.

43. "Safeguard Communications Facilities," 19.

44. PTT, *Le Cri Postal*.

45. Chun, *Control and Freedom*, 268.

46. Richard Hofstadter, "The Paranoid Style in American Politics," 85.

47. Parmy Olson, "Egypt's Internet Blackout Cost More Than OECD Estimates."

48. Warigia Bowman, "Dictators and the Internet."

49. Borradori, "Autoimmunity: Real and Symbolic Suicides," 99.

50. Ibid., 103.

51. Ibid., 94.

52. David E. Sanger, "Mutually Assured Cyberdestruction?"

53. Zusha Elinson, "BART Cut Cell Service on Spur of the Moment, Emails Show."

54. It is particularly striking that the BART system was created in 1972, the same year that Doxiadis was writing his manifesto about realigning urban transportation networks; BART, after all, was part of a new urban planner's vision, initially a way of rationalizing the public transit systems of all counties in the region into one unified network. In many ways, adding wireless to BART was the final realization of Doxiadis's vision, an apt motto for those under the spell of network fever: "We must coordinate *all* of our Networks *now*. All networks, from roads to telephones."

55. "Phone Sabotage Brings $4000 in Reward Offers," *Los Angeles Times*, 2.

56. John McCarthy, "The Home Information Terminal." I discuss McCarthy's proposal, which grew out of his research in time-sharing systems, in chapter 2.

57. Raindance Corporation, "The Alternative Television Movement," 19.

58. David Joselit, "Tale of the Tape," 196.

59. Joan Didion, "Slouching Towards Bethlehem."

60. A contemporary scholar studying the newspaper industry may have little to say to a contemporary scholar studying network protocols. But at one point, the two senses of the word were inseparable. In the words of German media theorist Hans Magnus Enzensberger, writing in 1970, "The media are making possible mass participation in a social and socialized productive process, the practical means of which are in the hands of the masses themselves . . . In its present form, equipment like television or film does not serve communication but prevents it." Enzensberger, "Constituents of a Theory of the Media," 48.

61. In addition to scholarly studies such as David Joselit, *Feedback*, and Deirdre Boyle, *Subject to Change*, there are numerous books by the video collectives themselves, including Michael Shamberg and the Raindance Corporation, *Guerrilla Television*, and Videofreex, *Spaghetti City Video Manual*.

62. Ant Farm, "Media Van: Ant Farm Video," in Felicity D. Scott, *Living Archive 7*, 224. Photocopy, three-hole-punched, two pages, 1970.

63. Steve Seid, "Tunneling through the Wasteland," 25.

64. Jonathan Crary, "Eclipse of the Spectacle," 289.

65. Ibid., 290.

66. Kirsten Olds, "Networked Collectivities," 125.

67. Felicity Scott, *Living Archive 7*, 99.

68. Ant Farm, "Truckstop Network," in Scott, *Living Archive 7*, 226–227. Collage, n.d.; also see Scott, *Living Archive 7*, 104.

69. Mark Wasiuta, "Ant Farm Underground," 92.

70. This reference occurs in Ant Farm's drawing "3D Truckstop" and is likely a misspelled version of Wendover, Utah, as there is a reference to art being faster if it were situated in neighboring Bonneville Salt Flats, home of the Bonneville Speedway. There is no town named Wendato.

71. Ant Farm, "Truckstop Network."

72. Ant Farm, "Put Energy into a System You Can Believe In," in Scott, *Living Archive 7*, 176. Drawing, 1971.

73. Thanks to Finn Brunton for suggesting this idea.

74. Don Nielsen, "The SRI Van and Computer Internetworking." Some cellular phones continue to use the acronym GPRS (General Packet Radio Service) for this technology.

75. Retz, "ARPANET, as I Recall."

76. Nielsen, "The SRI Van and Computer Internetworking," 3.

77. Ant Farm, "Truck Stop Fantasy One," in Scott, *Living Archive 7*, 174. A single typescript page, 1971.

78. Ant Farm, "Put Energy into a System You Can Believe In."

79. Chip Lord and Curtis Schreier, "Media Van—Ant Farm Interview."

80. Kris Paulsen, "Half-Inch Revolution."

81. To the first claim, Friedrich Kittler writes that "a digital base will erase the very concept of medium," an idea echoed and even expanded by other new media scholars, such as Lev Manovich, subscribing to what might be termed the "convergence hypothesis." Kittler, *Gramophone, Film, Typewriter*, 1. To the second claim, refer to Yochai Benkler, *The Wealth of Networks*.

82. My reference to "reparative reading" is from Eve Kosofsky Sedgwick, "Paranoid Reading and Reparative Reading, Or, You're So Paranoid, You Probably Think This Essay Is about You."

83. Theodore Roszak, *From Satori to Silicon Valley*; John Markoff, *What the Dormouse Said*.

84. Fred Turner, *From Counterculture to Cyberculture*.

85. Newton Minow, "Television and the Public Interest."

2 Time-Sharing and Virtualization

1. Stewart Brand, "Spacewar," 50.

2. Ibid., 58.

3. Paul Ceruzzi, *A History of Modern Computing*, 208.

4. Ibid., 208. The Spacewar article is often considered the first time that news of interactive computing reached a popular audience, but Douglas Engelbart's December 9, 1968, demo of work from the Stanford Research Institute—including a computer mouse, windows, hypertext, and networking—was arguably even more revelatory to observers within the industry. Engelbart opened his presentation with the haunting words: "What if, in your office, you as an intellectual worker were supplied with a computer display backed up by a computer that was alive for you all day and was instantly responsive?" This chapter focuses on the lead-up to both events, choosing to focus less on computer interfaces and graphical interaction (which have been relatively well-studied by other scholars) than on the idea of time-sharing itself.

5. A number of new media scholars have built on Ceruzzi's point: Wendy Chun has used it to remind us that the operating system's software creates what we think of as the user—and not the other way around. This same insight has also led David Golumbia to describe this illusory sense of the user's mastery as central to the cultural logic of computation. Tarleton Gillespie uses the example of a prison's architecture to argue that software's affordances do not just confine or restrict a user's behavior; they also "install a world view by which behaviors they encourage or erase." The distinction I am drawing is that software is not the primary motivator; it is a symptom of a economic transformation. See Wendy Chun, *Programmed Visions*; David Golumbia, *The*

Cultural Logic of Computation, 184, 188; Tarleton Gillespie, "The Stories Digital Tools Tell," 114.

6. Counterexamples, such as AOL's 1,000-free-hours trial CDs that clogged up mailboxes nationwide, or the advent of Free/Open Source Software (F/OSS), such as Linux, serve as exceptions that prove the rule: in the 1980s and 1990s, users typically paid explicitly for hardware products and software. (Before the Tymshare era of the 1970s, computer companies gave away software with the price of the computer; software was not seen as a product to be sold.) This 1980s/1990s model grew out of the idea of digital information as property, which, as Tom Streeter tells us, coalesced in the late 1970s with the confluence of two discourses: first, the legal doctrine of "intellectual property," and second, a consensus that technological development should best be left to market (i.e., neoliberal) forces, rather than explicit government support. Streeter, "Missing the Net," in *The Net Effect*, particularly 76–80.

7. Amazon does not report a breakdown of revenue from its Amazon Web Services (cloud) division, but bundles it in the "other" category. Estimates by Technology Business Research analysts put the AWS division at 84 percent of its "other" revenue that added roughly $3.2 billion to the company's revenue in 2013. In contrast to AWS's "cash cow" status, the rest of Amazon is generally understood as having a negative profit margin. Charles Babcock, "Amazon Web Services Revenue"; Arie Shpanya, "Do Profits Matter?"

8. This concept has reached the general audience via Eli Pariser, *The Filter Bubble*. For a theoretical explanation, see John Cheney-Lippold, "A New Algorithmic Identity."

9. Richard Serra with Carlotta Schoolman, *Television Delivers People*.

10. Art Eisenson and Gary Feldman, *Ellis D. Kropotechev and Zeus, A Marvelous Time-Sharing System*.

11. Jennifer S. Light, "When Computers Were Women."

12. Initially, the woman painter occupies a space of leisure separate from the workplace, but as the film continues, the Zeus computer reveals to Kropotechev that it can be used for leisure, too. By demonstrating a computer art program that shows it can draw and paint, Zeus fuses the two spaces together. Thus, we might observe, the time-shared computer Zeus is actually

part of a larger economic transformation that turns both leisure and work into tasks to be processed.

13. Fernando J Corbató, Marjorie Merwin-Daggett, and Robert C. Daley, "An Experimental Time-Sharing System," 336.

14. J. C. R. Licklider, "Man-Computer Symbiosis," 4.

15. As the traditional division of labor became desexualized, writing turned into "word processing," just as a time-sharing device turned the computer operator into a "data processor." Friedrich Kittler, *Film, Gramophone, Typewriter*, 184.

16. Martin Campbell-Kelly, "The Airy Tape," 22.

17. Shirish Chavan, *Advanced Techniques in Virtual Basic .NET*, 473.

18. Here I am responding to Anne Friedberg's claim that the virtual window is analogous to an "open window" onto a landscape elsewhere. This is typically true, but these exceptional moments—such as debugging—turn the windows inward. Anne Friedberg, *The Virtual Window*.

19. M. V. Wilkes (1951), as quoted in Martin Campbell-Kelly, "The Airy Tape," 24.

20. John McCarthy, "Reminiscences on the Theory of Time-Sharing."

21. Concurrently, Christopher Strachey used the term "time-sharing" to account for the fact that some programs needed to wait for peripheral input. A letter to McCarthy, however, suggests that he was referring to another part of the puzzle, a technique known as multiprogramming. See McCarthy, "Reminiscences on the Theory of Time-Sharing."

22. Douglas Parkhill, *The Challenge of the Computer Utility*, 133.

23. John A. N. Lee and Robert Rosin, "The Project MAC Interviews," 29.

24. Ibid., 29–30.

25. "CTSS foe" Tom Knight, as recorded by Steven Levy, *Hackers*, 94.

26. The study's results were inconclusive, but observers noticed one pattern: "When a programmer is good, / He is very, very good, / But when he is bad, / He is horrid." Harold Sackman, "Man-Computer Communication," 6.

27. Maurizio Lazzarato, "Immaterial Labour," 134.

28. Licklider, "Man-Computer Symbiosis," 7.

29. I discuss the fictive basis of real time in more detail in Tung-Hui Hu, "Real Time/Zero Time."

30. Scholars estimate that we spend as much as 40 percent of an analog film in the dark, looking at black film leader. For this reason, cinema scholar Laura Mulvey dubs the seeming liveness of film "death 24 times a second"— except that in 1961, with the reaction of a human on a typewriter judged a little slower than the eye looking at a movie screen, time-sharing was merely death five times a second.

31. Kaja Silverman, *The Subject of Semiotics*, 141.

32. The distinction between the supposedly passive viewer of television and the active user of a computer is largely fictional, however; it comes down to a historically contingent devaluation of the activities of consumption as "women's work." Feminist scholarship not only offers us a way of critically revisiting that distinction, but also underscores the forms of immaterial labor online that are similarly unrecognized or unacknowledged as work. Actively "using" the Internet may seem to mark a wholesale shift in viewing practices, but constructing the active/passive binary is exactly the goal of a form of capitalism that wants, as Maurizio Lazzarato puts it, "to construct the consumer/communicator—and to construct it as 'active'" for the purposes of seeming self-empowerment (Lazzarato, "Immaterial Labour," 142).

In recalling viewers and television, I mean to invoke the "blindspot debate" of the 1970s, when Marxist communications studies scholars, most notably Dallas Smythe and Richard Maxwell, debated the precise nature of how the audience of radio and television could be understood as a commodity. This debate, Tom Streeter convincingly argues in *Selling the Air*, can be resolved through the understanding of radio/TV audiences—and, as I would suggest, the user—as performing a kind of "women's work" or immaterial labor. (I am indebted to Megan Ankerson for her expertise on this point.)

33. Paul Edwards, *The Closed World*, 258–259.

34. This point is reiterated by Corbató in an article in which he reflected on time-sharing. Fernando Corbató, "Time Sharing."

35. Compare this to the ways that the idea of "free" in the F/OSS (Free/Open Source Software) movement has changed over time, away from the definition of "free as in free beer" before the mid-1990s to "free as in free speech." Gabriella Coleman, *Coding Freedom*, 37–40. Despite the liberatory coding of its

contemporary resonance, the original definition of "free"—"free as in free beer"—indicates that the foundations of liberal freedom in computer history may be largely economic.

36. Les Earnest, as quoted in Brand, "Spacewar," 51.

37. As we have seen, the idea of time-stealing was one in which the user was implicitly encouraged to steal time "for themselves." This moment thus fore-shadowed labor practices in today's Silicon Valley, such as Google's widely imitated "20% time" policy, in which workers are given one day off each week to work on whatever project they want. In a recent visit to Google, my handler was happy to inform me that it was a Google tradition for employee to participate in off-site, "recreational" activities such as Burning Man, since it increased their productivity at the office.

38. Tiziana Terranova, *Network Culture*, 74.

39. I take this from anthropologist Ilana Gershon's model of neoliberal agency, in which freedom is the agent's "ability to act on one's own calculations," to decide for oneself which risks to invest in. Ilana Gershon, "Neoliberal Agency," 540.

40. Maurizio Lazzarato, "Invisible Labour," 134.

41. Here I am recalling Kara Keeling's evocation of ways that queer theory can productively interface with studies of new media, for instance by noting queer malfunctions within normative systems of media. Kara Keeling, "Queer OS."

42. John Horvarth, "Freeware Capitalism," as quoted in Tiziana Terranova, *Network Culture*, 100.

43. For example, one file-sharing site explains that "asking about the risks associated with downloading copyright material is a bit like wondering whether the guy or girl in the bar tonight is likely to result in a 'good time', or whether that will be followed up by [a] call from the local clinic." "Andy," "Don't Download That, Bro."

44. U.S. Supreme Court, *Lawrence v. Texas*, 539 U.S. 558 (2003), 13.

45. Raiford Guins, *Edited Clean Version*.

46. Lauren Berlant, "Introduction," 283.

47. Steven Levy, *Hackers*, 97.

48. Alan Kay, as quoted in Brand, "Spacewar," 52.

49. Paul Baran, "The Future Computer Utility," 79.

50. In 1966, the FCC would, in what is now known as the "First Computer Inquiry," hold a hearing to decide whether or not data processing should be regulated.

51. Martin Greenberger, "The Computers of Tomorrow"; "Sharing the Computer's Time," *Time*.

52. Robert Fano and Fernando Corbató, "Time-Sharing on Computers."

53. John W. Macy, "The New Computer Age."

54. R. D. Jones, "The Public Planning Information System and the Computer Utility," 557.

55. Responds Baran: "It is a new problem. It is one that we have generally been unaware of in the computer field. It is so new we have just not built a large body of people concerned about the problem" (U.S. House of Representatives, *The Computer and Invasion of Privacy*, 133).

56. Testimony by Burton E. Squires Jr. in ibid., 135.

57. Testimony by Baran in ibid., 125, 125, 124.

58. Martin Greenberger, "The Two Sides of Time Sharing," 15.

59. Kenneth Karst, "'The Files,'" 360–361.

60. Ronald Kline, *Consumers in the Country*, 46.

61. These conversations occurred at conferences such as Technology and the City Matrix, Engineering Foundation Research Conference, Santa Barbara, CA, August 22–26, 1966 and The City of Tomorrow, IEEE International Convention, March 20–23, 1967. For an example of a talk given at these conferences, see Paul Baran and Martin Greenberger, "Urban Node Information Network."

62. Jussi Parikka, *Digital Contagions*, 50.

63. Testimony by Baran in U.S. House of Representatives, *The Computer and Invasion of Privacy*, 127.

64. Arthur R. Miller, "Personal Privacy in the Computer Age," 1111.

65. Kenneth Karst, "'The Files,'" 360.

66. Dominique Laporte, *History of Shit*, 56.

67. Baran, "The Future Computer Utility," 77–78.

68. J. C. R. Licklider and Robert Taylor, "The Computer as a Communication Device," 41. The model of communicative intimacy here is built on a sort of in-person debugging; communication *is* debugging.

69. Harold Sackman, "Man-Computer Communication," 6.

70. L. S. Tuomenoksa and W. Ulrich, "Problems of Programming for Time-Shared Systems," 9.

71. Licklider, "Man-Computer Symbiosis," 7.

72. Ibid., 7.

73. John McCarthy, "Recursive Functions of Symbolic Expressions and Their Computation by Machine, Part I."

74. Thomas Osborne, "Security and Vitality," 114.

75. From my experience, programming languages with garbage collection (such as McCarthy's LISP) were once considered "academic" or "teaching" languages, unsuitable for skilled programmers who wanted to manually allocate memory. But the commercial success of Java and C# since the late 1990s and early 2000s has meant widespread acceptance for garbage-collecting languages. More traditional languages, such as C and C++, do not have garbage collection.

76. Fred Cohen, "On the Implications of Computer Viruses," 169.

77. Cohen, "Computer Viruses: Theory and Experiments," 33.

78. Cohen, "On the Implications of Computer Viruses and Methods of Defense," 167.

79. Ibid., 175.

80. Martin Campbell-Kelly, *From Airline Reservations to Sonic the Hedgehog*, vii.

81. Thomas Osborne, "Security and Vitality," 114–115.

82. Wendy Brown, "Neoliberalism and the End of Liberal Democracy," 43.

83. Ulrich Beck, "The Open City."

84. Finn Brunton, *Spam*, 52.

85. Steven Connor, *The Matter of Air*, 275.

86. Martin Heidegger, "The Question Concerning Technology," 16.

87. For more on infrastructure, see Lisa Parks, "Around the Antenna Tree."

88. Anna Munster, *An Aesthesia of Networks*; Alexander Galloway, *The Interface Effect*; Tiziana Terranova, "Failure to Comply."

89. Thomas Ristenpart, Eran Tromer, Hovav Shacham, and Stefan Savage, "Hey, You, Get Off of My Cloud."

90. Ibid., 210.

91. Rob Horning, "Structuring the Self as Inherently Entrepreneurial, Facebook as Neoliberal State."

3   Data Centers and Data Bunkers

1. Due to construction errors by its data center partner, such as leaking roofs, Twitter later moved many of its servers to Sacramento, CA.

2. Greenpeace, "How Clean is Your Cloud?"; see also Allison Carruth, "The Digital Cloud and the Micropolitics of Energy," for more on the "greenwashing" of data centers.

3. James Bamford, "The NSA Is Building the Country's Biggest Spy Center (Watch What You Say)."

4. Major Howard Egan, of the Nauvoo Legion militia (ancestor to the Utah National Guard).

5. The Bunker, "Why the Bunker?"

6. This point was presciently analyzed by the collective Critical Art Ensemble long before the term "cloud computing" came into existence. In *The Electronic Disturbance*, the collective likens the utilization of "electronic information-cores overflow[ing] with files of electronic people (those transformed into credit histories, consumer types, patterns and tendencies, etc.)" to bunkers: "In line with the feudal tradition of the fortress mentality, the bunker guarantees safety and familiarity in exchange for the relinquishment of individual sovereignty. It can act as a seductive agent offering the credible illusion of consumptive choice and ideological peace for the complicit, or it can act as an aggressive force demanding acquiescence for the resistant . . . The electronic form is witnessed as media; as such it attempts to colonize the private residence" (16, 27–28).

7. President Barack Obama, as quoted in the mission statement of Stop. Think. Connect., http://www.stopthinkconnect.org/about-us/.

8. The interested reader can also find amateur PSAs on YouTube that stage the problem of firewalls by recording battle scenes from shooter video games.

9. http://www.onguardonline.gov/stop-think-connect.

10. U.S. Department of Defense, "Report of the Defense Science Board Task Force on Mission Impact of Foreign Influence on DoD Software."

11. Leon Panetta, "Remarks by Secretary Panetta on Cybersecurity to the Business Executives for National Security, New York City."

12. Hillary Clinton, "Remarks on Internet Freedom."

13. Hillary Clinton, "Secretary Clinton's Remarks on Internet Freedom."

14. William J. Clinton, "The Age of Participation."

15. Wendy Brown, *States of Injury*, 6.

16. David Murakami Wood, "'The Internet Must Be Defended!'"

17. Leerom Medovoi, "Global Society Must Be Defended," 62.

18. Lisa Nakamura, "'I WILL DO EVERYthing That Am Asked'"; see also Graham Parker, "419 (occasional 420)."

19. Other Western online communities have also adopted the practice of Orientalizing "risky," non-normative Internet practices; the online Silk Road marketplace for illegal passwords and stolen digital goods was, in fact, started by a white hacker working out of a San Francisco public library. To adopt Brunton's description of 419 e-mails, the narrative of a corrupt, shadow Internet has often been self-consciously constructed to give credulous consumers of such Orientalizing narratives what they expect to find.

20. For more on Nigerian spammers, see Finn Brunton, *Spam*, 109. Per Brunton, the other main sources of spam are China, Russia, the United Kingdom, and Brazil.

21. Ibid., 102.

22. See, for example, James Fontanella-Khan and Richard Waters, "Microsoft to Shield Foreign Users' Data."

23. Emma Barnett and Iain Hollingshead, "The Dark Side of Facebook."

24. Nicole Starosielski, *The Undersea Network*, 107–108.

25. Ibid., 106.

26. Barrett Lyon. "The Story Behind the Mastercard and VISA DDoS Attacks."

27. Michael Geist, "All Your Internets Belong to US, Continued"; also Metahaven, "Captives of the Cloud: Part I."

28. Andy Greenberg, *This Machine Kills Secrets*, 482.

29. Specifically, I refer to Foucault's 1977–1978 lectures, which continue his exploration of biopolitics by examining the shift away from sovereign power and toward power exercised over a population. Michel Foucault, *Security, Territory, and Population*.

30. Jim Bell, "Assassination Politics."

31. Julian Assange, "Conspiracy as Governance," as quoted in Andy Greenberg, *This Machine Kills Secrets*, 248.

32. Wendy Hui Kyong Chun, "Crisis, Crisis, Crisis, or Sovereignty and Networks," 103.

33. In other words, this "you" is a fictional subject position. New media's sovereignty is illusory; as Chun (reading Butler) puts it, new media only evokes only the "fantasies of sovereign . . . structures," which goes hand-in-hand with a desire for "'simpler and more reassuring map of power.'" Chun, quoting Judith Butler, in ibid., 101–102.

34. James Boyle, "Foucault in Cyberspace."

35. One example comes from the group Anonymous's violent confrontation with the Los Zetas drug cartel in Veracruz, Mexico, which threatened to behead a digital leaker. Anonymous members are known for wearing Guy Fawkes masks in public to disguise their identity; yet, the consulting group Stratfor points out, the "amorphous nature of Anonymous can also cut the other way, however. If Los Zetas abduct and execute random patrons at an Internet cafe, behead them and place Guy Fawkes masks on their heads, it will be very difficult to prove that they were not associated with Anonymous." Stratfor, "Anonymous vs. Zetas Amid Mexico's Cartel Violence."

36. For an example of this shift: after World War II, "a disciplinary society was what we already no longer were, had ceased to be." Gilles Deleuze, "Postscript on the Societies of Control," 3.

37. Foucault, *Security, Territory, Population*, 105.

38. Judith Butler, *Precarious Life*, 54; italics in original.

39. Susan Sontag, "The Imagination of Disaster," 42; Iron Mountain, "Data Backup."

40. For more on Iron Mountain and other such storage facilities, see Brian Murphy, "Bomb-Proofing the Digital Image."

41. David F. Bell, "Bunker Busting and Bunker Mentalities, or Is It Safe to Be Underground?"

42. Bell's article was written before Barack Obama's inauguration, but the Obama administration's reliance on national security reasons for justifying its decision to withhold records on CIA and NSA operations has arguably only continued this climate of secrecy.

43. Bell adds that shortly after Cheney's disappearance from public view, Osama bin Laden was also hiding, ostensibly in the shadowy network of caves and tunnels in the Tora Bora desert. This secret location justified the Bush administration's obsessive pursuit of a new "bunker buster" nuclear weapon.

44. The National Audio-Visual Conservation Center's website is at http://www.loc.gov/avconservation/packard/.

45. Bell, "Bunker Busting and Bunker Mentalities, or Is It Safe to Be Underground?," 224.

46. Ibid., 224.

47. This is anticipated by Sontag, who writes that the imagination of disaster comes out of an age that combines "two equally fearful, but seemingly opposed, destinies: unremitting banality and inconceivable terror." Sontag was writing about a Cold War era where aerial or nuclear attack could lead to "extinction which could come at any time, virtually without warning," and yet where citizens were stupidly being asked to be constantly watching and vigilant. Sontag, "The Imagination of Disaster," 42, 48. Though her work was on science fiction films, it is nevertheless keen cultural analysis: the phrase "real time" was a Cold War invention, and real-time computer systems initially came out of military artillery calculations.

48. Paul Virilio, *Bunker Archaeology*, 12.

49. Ibid., 39.

50. Ibid., 201.

51. Ibid., 11.

52. Ibid., 10.

53. Ibid., 21.

54. Ibid., 11.

55. The monument: "Something that reminds, warns." Ibid., 11–12.

56. Ibid., 46.

57. Ibid., 34.

58. Ibid., 39.

59. I address this point in more detail elsewhere, arguing that real time is not an innate quality of digital media, but rather a construct that suppress the delays, glitches, and even moments of stillness at its center ("dead time"). Real time produces a feeling of "liveness" by continually covering over "dead time"; seen correctly, real time is not the the present tense, but the melancholic imagination of the present from the perspective of the future that is just milliseconds away. Tung-Hui Hu, "Real Time/ Zero Time."

60. Virilio, *Bunker Archaeology*, 16.

61. Paul Virilio, "Cryptic Architecture," 16.

62. Planets Consortium, "Planets TimeCapsule Deposit."

63. Nels Olson and Jian Zheng, "NIST/LoC Final Report to ODAT."

64. See, for instance, the CAMiLEON Project, which reverse-engineered the BBC's Domesday Book with emulation technology, and, more generally, CAMiLEON lead Margaret Hedstrom's article "Digital Preservation."

65. Planets Consortium, "Preservation and Long-Term Access via NETworked Services."

66. Planets Consortium, "TIME CAPSULE—A Showcase for Digital Preservation."

67. Planets Consortium, "Report on Emerging Digital Art Characterisation Technique."

68. Paul Duguid, "Material Matters," 66.

69. Bruce Sterling, "The Life and Death of Media."

70. Charles R. Acland, *Residual Media*, xx. Though the term "living dead" is not explored in any depth, the metaphor of media on its deathbed is made central in Paolo Cherchi Usai's book *The Death of Cinema*, where the film preservationist is likened to a surgeon watching over its patient.

71. Recently, scholars have begun to complicate this distinction: for example, Raiford Guins's *Game After* considers the aftereffects of outmoded video games in today's digital culture. However, I note, they continue to operate using a historiography of living/dead media.

72. As quoted in Ian Daly, "Nuclear Bunker Houses World's Toughest Server Farm."

73. Sigmund Freud, "Mourning and Melancholia."

74. Abraham and Torok, "Poetics of Psychoanalysis," 4.

75. Virilio, *Bunker Archaeology*, 46.

76. Jacques Derrida, "Fors," xvi.

77. Derrida: "What a crypt commemorates, as the incorporated object's 'monument' or 'tomb,' is not the object itself, but its exclusion." Ibid., xvii.

78. Bonnie Weddle, "PLANETS Digital Genome TimeCapsule."

79. Virilio, *Bunker Archaeology*, 16. As he writes, there is an "implicit empathy between the inanimate object and visitor" (14).

4   Seeing the Cloud of Data

1. Sandvine, "Global Internet Phenomena Report."

2. Caren Kaplan, "Precision Targets," 696.

3. Ibid., 694.

4. Greg Elmer, *Profiling Machines*; Joseph Turrow, *Niche Envy*; John Cheney-Lippold, "A New Algorithmic Identity."

5. Paul Virilio, *War and Cinema*, 3.

6. "For most people in the United States, war is almost always elsewhere," writes Caren Kaplan; "our gaze is almost always fixed on representations of war that come from places perceived to be remote from the heartland." Kaplan, "Precision Targets," 693.

7. James Der Derian, *Virtuous War*. The shift is toward the "soft" forms of war that he identifies, such as cyberwarfare, viruses, etc. And these forms of remote seeing, as Paul Virilio elaborated in his study *War and Cinema*, in turn came out of older technologies of capturing targets at a distance: the "shot" of cinema is named after Etienne-Jules Marey's 1882 chronophotographic gun, while color film grew out of military reconnaissance flights. On the visual aspect of war, see also Harun Farocki's film *Images of the World and the Inscription of War*.

8. Tiziana Terranova, "Failure to Comply."

9. David Knoke, "It Takes a Network."

10. The quote here is from Harun Farocki's *War at a Distance*.

11. Reciprocally, the data targeted by government agencies are no longer just "private" data, such as cell phone metadata, but public sources; facilities such as the CIA's Open Source Center and the Department of Homeland Security's Social Network Monitoring Center have begun sifting through hundreds of millions of messages on Twitter, Facebook, and Google.

12. Caren Kaplan, "Precision Targets," 708.

13. Eve Kosofsky Sedgwick, "Paranoid Reading and Reparative Reading," 140.

14. To be sure, there are a virtually infinite number of subtler instances of control available for study online. But by restricting their study to code itself, scholars risk naturalizing the ideological tendencies of software to mask the real spaces it inevitably affects. For as we have seen, the cloud's effects reach us even when we are not explicitly using digital media. We may receive targeted advertisements based on our shopping history, or different mortgage rates depending on our credit history.

15. This "passive/active" distinction is in fact a product of new media historiography, which attempts to define the newness of new media by positing historical breaks or ruptures. I critique this binary later in the chapter.

16. Richard Norton-Taylor and Nick Hopkins, "Libya Air Strikes."

17. NOS, "Door Twitter geen verrassingsaanvallen op Libië."

18. The Libyan conflict also spurred a number of professionally planned acts of cyberwarfare. A Libyan hacker by the nom de guerre Tariq bin Ziyad Brigade calling for "electronic jihad" unleashed a worm against the US Army and US corporations in 2010, while April 2011 saw a group of cybersecurity

specialists draft a classified report, *Project Cyber Dawn: Libya*. This report spelled out Libya's vulnerabilities to cyberattacks and detailed a potential plan for the US government to disable an oil refinery at Ras Lanouf with a virus. (The United States ultimately decided not to go ahead with this plan.) As blurry as the line between hacktivism and cyberwarfare may be—the former is nominally less destructive than the latter—this chapter focuses on hacktivism as a potential avenue for amateur and public engagement.

19. E-mail from Huub to *Wired*, in Noah Schachtman, "Listen: Secret Libyan Psyops, Caught by Online Sleuths."

20. NOS, "Werkwijze Dirk de Jager." My translation.

21. Jeff Gilmore, "Where Is Lt Zuckerberg?"

22. "Audio of USAF aircraft on HF radio warning a Libyan ship to stay in port or be attacked & destroyed. http://t.co/5lEOoyQ via @FMCNL."

23. John Pollock, "People Power 2.0."

24. David Cenciotti, "Operation Odyssey Dawn Explained (Day 3)."

25. Adam Gabbatt, "Nato, Twitter, and Air Strikes in Libya."

26. Gabriella Coleman and Alex Golub have shown that critics often elide the complexity of political beliefs held by disparate hacker communities by using reductive terms such as "hacker ethics." Coleman and Golub, "Hacker Practice."

27. Michael Reed, "Re: [tor-talk] Iran Cracks Down on Web Dissident Technology."

28. Geert Lovink and Ned Rossiter, as quoted in Rita Raley, *Tactical Media*, 81.

29. Alexander Galloway and Eugene Thacker, *The Exploit*, 115.

30. Thacker and Galloway continue: "Forms of informatic play should be interrogated not as a liberation from the rigid constraints of systems of exchange and production but as the very pillars that prop those systems up." Ibid., 115.

31. Joshua Kapstein, "How the NSA Recruits in a Post-Snowden World." The NSA also sponsors a slightly outmoded website to recruit the next generation, "CryptoKids," which features games and kitschy cartoon characters such as Crypto Cat, Decipher Dog, and so on, and a button that tells them how to work for the NSA.

32. William Boddy, *New Media and Popular Imagination*, 43, as quoted in David Morley, *Media, Modernity and Technology*, 244.

33. Paul Taylor and Tim Jordan, *Hacktivism and Cyberwars*.

34. Schachtman, "Listen: Secret Libyan Psyops, Caught by Online Sleuths."

35. Keith Alexander, "DEF CON 20 by General Keith B Alexander Shared Values Shared Response."

36. See Quentin Hardy, "Wealth Managers Enlist Spy Tools to Map Portfolios."

37. Gabriella Coleman, *Coding Freedom*, 129, 131.

38. Figures from Peter Eavis, "Twitter's Market Valuation Suggests Wall St. Sees Huge Growth Potential." Twitter itself trumpeted its ability to monetize conflict and activism; the third sentence of its IPO prospectus reads: "A local resident in Abbottabad, Pakistan unknowingly reported the raid on Osama Bin Laden's compound on Twitter hours before traditional media and news." For a discussion of the uncomfortable relationship between activism and corporate-owned social networks, see Tiziana Terranova and Joan Donovan, "Occupy Social Networks."

39. Maurizio Lazzarato, "Immaterial Labor," 134.

40. Lisa Lynch, "'As I Photograph the Night Sky, the Other Night Sky Photographs Back.'"

41. Priest, as quoted in Lynch, ibid.

42. Sedgwick, "Paranoid Reading and Repetitive Reading," 140.

43. Fredric Jameson, "Cognitive Mapping," 356.

44. Sedgwick, "Paranoid Reading and Repetitive Reading," 131.

45. John Arquilla and David Ronfeldt, *Networks and Netwars*, 11.

46. Stanley McChrystal, "Becoming the Enemy," 66.

47. Alexander Galloway, *The Interface Effect*, 98–99.

48. Ibid., 92.

49. John Schwartz, "Satellite Spotters Glimpse Secrets, and Tell Them"; W. Patrick McCray. *Keep Watching the Skies!*

50. Schwartz, "Satellite Spotters Glimpse Secrets, and Tell Them."

51. Trevor Paglen, *Blank Spots on the Map*," 137.

52. Tom Vanderbilt and Trevor Paglen, "Trevor Paglen Talks about the 'Other Night Sky,' 2007–," 225.

53. Amanda Happé, "The Other Night Sky," 5.

54. Ibid., 5.

55. The company name Keyhole, Inc. was a tongue-in-cheek reference to the spy satellite (and, specifically, fiction writer Tom Clancy's propensity to use the term *keyhole* in his books). Failing in its attempts to develop civilian applications, Keyhole, Inc., was then—in a curious twist of fate—bailed out by the very agencies responsible for analyzing the actual Keyhole satellites. For more background on Keyhole, Inc., see Craig M. Dalton, "Sovereigns, Spooks, and Hackers."

56. Sartre's parable is in *Being and Nothingness*, 259. Thanks to Lara Shalson for this idea.

57. Happé, "The Other Night Sky," 5. This is an assertion that Paglen elsewhere complicates, in, for example, Paglen and Keenan, "Fog of Wars."

58. Thomas Keenan, "Disappearances," 42.

59. "Seeing Is Believing: An Interview with Trevor Paglen," by Seth Curcio, February 24, 2011.

60. Karen Beckman, "Telescopes, Transparency, and Torture," 66.

61. Paglen, *Blank Spots on the Map*, 248.

62. Altman Siegel Gallery, press release for "Trevor Paglen: *Unhuman*."

63. "Interview: Walead Beshty," by Mikkel Carl, July 2010, 13.

64. "TD Blog Interview with Trevor Paglen," by The Talking Dog, December 10, 2006.

65. Paglen, *Blank Spots on the Map*, 15.

66. Ibid., 16.

67. Christopher Mims, "Fear-Based Psychology of the 'Internet Kill Switch.'"

68. U.S. Senate, "Protecting Cyberspace as a National Asset Act of 2010."

69. Anita Gohdes, "Pulling the Plug."

70. Ibid., 13.

71. Leerom Medovoi, "Global Society Must Be Defended," 54.

72. Ibid., 72.

73. Ibid., 74.

74. Ibid., 54.

75. While Medovoi begins by claiming that the framework for contemporary war is properly regulation rather than sovereignty (the war on terror is a new type of crime fighting, in his view), he acknowledges that the "reverse" is true: for example, the logic of the prison is remapped onto the detention camps of the war on terror, such as Guantanamo.

76. Paglen, *Blank Spots on the Map*, 15.

77. Slavoj Zizek, "Biopolitics," 270–271.

78. Paul Halliday, *Habeas Corpus*, 174.

79. Judith Butler, *Precarious Life*, 59.

80. Gilles Deleuze, "Postscript on the Societies of Control," 5.

81. David H. Petraeus, as quoted in Knoke, "It Takes a Network," 7.

82. Giorgio Agamben, "Bodies without Words," 169.

83. Foucault's investigation into how society "makes life" seems worlds away from Agamben's analysis of killing. Given a choice between Agamben and Foucault, new media scholars have, by and large, chosen Foucault's "soft" power as the more powerful framework, just as they have generally gravitated toward "software studies" over "hardware studies." As Rey Chow writes, "Foucault's work resonates most readily with the high tech, medical, and political manipulations of contemporary human existence, from the ostracization and incarceration of the insane and the criminal, to the surveillance of sexual practices . . . For Agamben, on the other hand, coercion is really a matter of extermination . . . [as in] his primary example of the Nazi camps." Chow, "Sacrifice, Mimesis, and the Theorizing of Victimhood (A Speculative Essay)," 133. It is only recently that the other side—the power to kill—has been reexamined seriously, for example, in the figure of the suicide bomber that creates a new politics of death. Stuart Murray, "Thanatopolitics," 204.

84. See, for example, Giorgio Agamben, *Homo Sacer*.

85. Kip Hawley, *Permanent Emergency*.

Conclusion

1. Richie Etwaru, "Enough of the Cloud Already, What Is Next for Enterprise Technology?"

2. Steven Connor, *The Matter of Air*, 274.

3. Prices for one thousand CAPTCHA problems solved are currently from 80 cents to $1.50 as of the time of this writing (Freelancer.com); calculations for speed of CAPTCHA solving are from Brian Krebs, "Virtual Sweatshops Defeat Bot-or-Not Tests," and also Finn Brunton, *Spam*, 170.

4. Aihwa Ong, "Powers of Sovereignty."

5. The term "soft power"—taken out of its international relations context—is imprecise, but I believe it offers a useful mnemonic device here. A more accurate explanation is the role of culture in Antonio Gramsci's writings on hegemony; it is through culture that the state engineers the active consent of its citizens. The cloud, in my argument, is the fluctuating, dynamic, and always rewired mechanism of symbolic values for producing this culture (which we know as "digital culture").

BIBLIOGRAPHY

Abraham, Nicolas, and Maria Torok. "Poetics of Psychoanalysis: 'The Lost Object: Me.'" *SubStance* 13, no. 2 (1984): 3–18.

Acland, Charles R., ed. *Residual Media*. Minneapolis: University of Minnesota Press, 2007.

Agamben, Giorgio. "Bodies without Words: Against the Biopolitical Tatoo." *German Law Journal* 5, no. 2 (2004): 167–169.

Agamben, Giorgio. *Homo Sacer: Sovereign Power and Bare Life*. Stanford: Stanford University Press, 1998.

Alba, Davey. "It's Time to Fight for Your Digital Privacy," *Popular Mechanics* 191, no. 2 (February 2014): 56–63.

Alexander, Keith. "DEF CON 20 by General Keith B Alexander Shared Values Shared Response." YouTube video, filmed July 27, 2012. http://youtube.com/watch?v=Rm5cT-SFoOg.

Altman Siegel Gallery. Press release for "Trevor Paglen: *Unhuman*," February 10, 2011. http://www.altmansiegel.com/tpaglen2show/tpaglen2show.pdf.

Andrejevic, Mark. "Surveillance in the Digital Enclosure." *The Communication Review* 10 (2007): 295–317.

"Andy." "Don't Download That, Bro, You're Going to Get Busted." torrentfreak.com, March 16, 2013. https://torrentfreak.com/dont-download-that-bro-youre-going-to-get-busted-130316/.

Arquilla, John, and David Ronfeldt. *Networks and Netwars: The Future of Terror, Crime, and Militancy*. Santa Monica, CA: RAND Corporation, MR-1382, 2001.

Babcock, Charles. "Amazon Web Services Revenue: New Details." *Information Week*, October 24, 2013. http://www.informationweek.com/cloud/infrastructure-as-a-service/amazon-web-services-revenue-new-details/d/d-id/1112068?

Bamford, James. "The NSA Is Building the Country's Biggest Spy Center (Watch What You Say)." *Wired*, March 15, 2012. http://www.wired.com/2012/03/ff_nsadatacenter/.

Baran, Paul. "The Future Computer Utility." *National Affairs* 8 (Summer 1967): 75–87.

Baran, Paul. "On Distributed Communications Networks." Santa Monica, CA: RAND Corporation, P-2626, 1962.

Baran, Paul. "Reliable Digital Communications Systems Using Unreliable Network Repeater Nodes." Santa Monica, CA: RAND Corporation, P-1995, 1960.

Baran, Paul, and Martin Greenberger, "Urban Node Information Network." Santa Monica, CA: RAND Corporation, P-3562, 1967.

Barnett, Emma, and Iain Hollingshead. "The Dark Side of Facebook," *The Daily Telegraph* (March 3, 2012): 23.

Barney, Darin. *Prometheus Wired: The Hope for Democracy in the Age of Network Technology*, Chicago: University of Chicago Press, 2000.

Beck, Ulrich. "The Open City: Architecture in Reflexive Modernity." In *Democracy without Enemies*, 115–121. Cambridge: Polity Press, 1998.

Beckman, Karen. "Telescopes, Transparency, and Torture: Trevor Paglen and the Politics of Exposure." *Art Journal* 66, no. 3 (Fall 2007): 62–67.

Bell, David F. "Bunker Busting and Bunker Mentalities, or Is It Safe to Be Underground?" *South Atlantic Quarterly* 107, no. 2 (Spring 2008): 213–229.

Bell, Jim. "Assassination Politics." cryptome.org. April 3, 1997. http://cryptome.org/ap.htm.

Benkler, Yochai, *The Wealth of Networks: How Social Production Transforms Markets and Freedom*. New Haven: Yale University Press, 2006.

Berlant, Lauren, "Introduction to Special Issue on Intimacy." *Critical Inquiry* 24, no. 2 (Winter 1988): 281–288.

Beshty, Walead. "Interview: Walead Beshty," by Mikkel Carl, 2010. http://www.konsthall.malmo.se/upload/pdf/Walead_Beshty_Interview.pdf.

Boddy, William. *New Media and Popular Imagination*. New York: Oxford University Press, 2004.

Borradori, Giovanna. "Autoimmunity: Real and Symbolic Suicides—A Dialogue with Jacques Derrida." In *Philosophy in a Time of Terror: Dialogues with Jürgen Habermas and Jacques Derrida*, 85–136. Chicago: University of Chicago Press, 2003.

Bowman, Warigia. "Dictators and the Internet." *Cairo Review of Global Affairs*, March 25, 2011. http://www.aucegypt.edu/gapp/cairoreview/pages/articleDetails.aspx?aid =34.

Boyle, Deirdre. *Subject to Change: Guerrilla Television Revisited*. New York: Oxford University Press, 1996.

Boyle, James. "Foucault in Cyberspace: Surveillance, Sovereignty, and Hardwired Censors." *University of Cincinnati Law Review* 66 (1997): 177–205.

Boyle, James. "The Second Enclosure Movement and the Construction of the Public Domain." *Law and Contemporary Problems* 66 (2003): 33–74.

Brand, Stewart. "Spacewar: Fanatic Life and Symbolic Death among the Computer Bums." *Rolling Stone*, December 7, 1972, 50–58.

Brown, Wendy. "Neoliberalism and the End of Liberal Democracy." In *Edgework: Critical Essays on Knowledge and Politics*, 37–59. Princeton: Princeton University Press, 2005.

Brown, Wendy. *States of Injury: Power and Freedom*. Princeton: Princeton University Press, 1995.

Brunton, Finn. *Spam: A Shadow History of the Internet*. Cambridge, MA: MIT Press, 2013.

Bunker, The. "Why the Bunker?" January 2013 (link since removed). https:// web.archive.org/web/20130109021718/http://www.thebunker.net/why-the-bunker.

Butler, Judith. *Precarious Life: The Powers of Mourning and Violence*. London: Verso, 2004.

Campbell-Kelly, Martin. *From Airline Reservations to Sonic the Hedgehog: A History of the Software Industry*. Cambridge, MA: MIT Press, 2003.

Campbell-Kelly, Martin. "The Airy Tape: An Early Chapter in the History of Debugging." *IEEE Annals of the History of Computing* 14, no. 4 (1992): 16–26.

Carruth, Allison. "The Digital Cloud and the Micropolitics of Energy." *Public Culture* 26, no. 2 (Spring 2014): 339–364.

Castells, Manuel. *The Power of Identity*, 2nd ed. Oxford: Blackwell, 2010.

Castells, Manuel. *The Rise of the Network Society*. Vol. 1: *The Information Age: Economy, Society and Culture*. Malden, MA: Blackwell Publishers, 1996.

Cenciotti, David. "Operation Odyssey Dawn Explained (Day 3)." *The Aviationist* (blog), March 22, 2011. http://theaviationist.com/2011/03/22/operation-odyssey-dawn -explained-day-3/.

Ceruzzi, Paul. *A History of Modern Computing*. Cambridge, MA: MIT Press, 2003.

Chan, Anita. *Networking Peripheries.* Cambridge, MA: MIT Press, 2013.

Chavan, Shirish. *Advanced Techniques in Visual Basic .NET.* Delhi: Pearson Education India, 2004.

Cheney-Lippold, John. "A New Algorithmic Identity: Soft Biopolitics and the Modulation of Control." *Theory, Culture & Society* 28, no. 6 (November 2011): 164–181.

Cherchi Usai, Paolo. *The Death of Cinema: History, Cultural Memory, and the Digital Dark Age.* London: BFI Press, 2001.

Chow, Rey. "Sacrifice, Mimesis, and the Theorizing of Victimhood (A Speculative Essay)." *Representations* 94, no. 1 (Spring 2006): 131–149.

Chun, Wendy Hui Kyong. *Control and Freedom: Power and Paranoia in the Age of Fiber Optics.* Cambridge, MA: MIT Press, 2006.

Chun, Wendy Hui Kyong. "Crisis, Crisis, Crisis, or Sovereignty and Networks." *Theory Culture & Society* 28, no. 6 (2011): 91–112.

Chun, Wendy Hui Kyong. *Programmed Visions: Software and Memory.* Cambridge, MA: MIT Press, 2011.

Clinton, Hillary. "Remarks on Internet Freedom." Speech delivered January 21, 2010, Newseum, Washington, DC.

Clinton, Hillary. "Secretary Clinton's Remarks on Internet Freedom." Speech delivered December 8, 2011, Fokker Terminal, The Hague, Netherlands.

Clinton, William J. "The Age of Participation." YouTube video of panel discussion with Hillary Clinton, Michael Crow, Manal Al-Sharif, Shree Bose, John McCain, and Jimmy Wales at the Clinton Global Initiative conference, March 21, 2014. https://www.youtube.com/watch?v=u00kWmZ8WQg.

Cohen, Fred. "Computer Viruses: Theory and Experiments." *Computers & Security* 6 (1987): 22–35.

Cohen, Fred. "On the Implications of Computer Viruses and Methods of Defense." *Computers & Security* 7 (1988): 167–184.

Coleman, Gabriella. *Coding Freedom: The Ethics and Aesthetics of Hacking.* Princeton: Princeton University Press, 2012.

Coleman, Gabriella, and Alex Golub. "Hacker Practice: Moral Genres and the Cultural Articulation of Liberalism." *Anthropology Today* 8, no. 3 (2008): 255–277.

Connor, Steven. *The Matter of Air: Science and Art of the Ethereal.* London: Reaktion Books, 2010.

Corbató, Fernando. "Time Sharing." In *Encyclopedia of Computer Science*, 4th ed., 1778–1782. Chichester, UK: John Wiley and Sons Ltd., 2003.

Corbató, Fernando J., Marjorie Merwin-Daggett, and Robert C. Daley. "An Experimental Time-Sharing System." In *Proceedings of the AFIPS Spring Joint Computer Conference*, vol. 21, 335–344. Palo Alto: National Press, 1962.

Costantinou, Marianne. "Septa Working on the Railroad: Steel-Driving Men Tear Up Old Tracks to Lay New Ones." *Philadelphia Daily News*, April 6, 1992: 5.

Crary, Jonathan. "Eclipse of the Spectacle." In *Art after Modernism: Rethinking Representation*, ed. Brian Wallis, 283–294. New York: New Museum, 1984.

Critical Art Ensemble. *The Electronic Disturbance*. Brooklyn: Autonomedia, 1994.

Dalton, Craig M. "Sovereigns, Spooks, and Hackers: An Early History of Google Geo Services and Map Mashups." *Cartographica* 48, no. 4 (2013): 261–274.

Daly, Ian. "Nuclear Bunker Houses World's Toughest Server Farm." *Wired (UK)*, October 5, 2010. http://www.wired.co.uk/magazine/archive/2010/11/features/20-thousand -terabytes-under-the-ground/.

Deleuze, Gilles. "Postscript on the Societies of Control." *October* 59 (Winter 1992): 3–7.

Deleuze, Gilles, and Felix Guattari. "Rhizome." In *A Thousand Plateaus: Capitalism and Schizophrenia*, trans. Brian Massumi, 3–25. Minneapolis: University of Minnesota Press, 1987.

Der Derian, James. *Virtuous War: Mapping The Military-Industrial-Media-Entertainment Network*. New York: Basic Books, 2001.

Derrida, Jacques. "Fors." In Nicholas Abraham and Maria Torok, *The Wolf Man's Magic Word: A Cryptonymy*, trans. Nicholas Rand, xi–xlvii. Minneapolis: University of Minnesota Press, 1986.

Didion, Joan. "Slouching Towards Bethlehem." *Saturday Evening Post* 240, no. 19 (September 23, 1967): 25–94.

Dorros, Irwin. "The Picturephone System: The Network." *Bell System Technical Journal* 50, no. 2 (February 1971): 221–233.

Doxiadis, Constantinos. "The Two-Headed Eagle (From the past to the future of human settlements)." *Ekistics* 33, no. 198 (May 1972): 406–420. http://www.doxiadis.org/Downloads/the_two_headed_eagle.pdf.

Duguid, Paul. "Material Matters: The Past and Futurology of the Book." In *The Future of the Book*, ed. Geoffrey Nunberg, 63–102. Berkeley: University of California Press, 1996.

Eavis, Peter. "Twitter's Market Valuation Suggests Wall St. Sees Huge Growth Potential." "Dealb%k" (blog), *New York Times*, November 6, 2013. http://dealbook .nytimes.com/2013/11/06/twitters-market-valuation-suggests-wall-st-sees-huge -growth-potential/.

Edwards, Paul. *The Closed World: Computers and the Politics of Discourse in Cold War America*. Cambridge, MA: MIT Press, 1997.

Eisenson, Art, and Gary Feldman. *Ellis D. Kropotechev and Zeus, A Marvelous Time-Sharing Device*. 16mm B&W film, March 1967 (15 minutes). Stanford Department of Computer Science; held in the Computer History Museum, Mountain View, CA.

Elden, Stuart. *Terror and Territory: The Spatial Extent of Sovereignty*. Minneapolis: University of Minnesota Press, 2009.

Elinson, Zusha. "BART Cut Cell Service on Spur of the Moment, Emails Show." *Bay Citizen*, October 11, 2011. http://www.baycitizen.org/bart-protests/story/ bart-cut-cell-service-spur-moment-emails/.

Elmer, Greg. *Profiling Machines: Mapping the Personal Information Economy*. Cambridge, MA: MIT Press, 2003.

Enzensberger, Hans Magnus. "Constituents of a Theory of the Media" (1970). In *Critical Essays*, ed. Reinhold Grimm and Bruce Armstrong, 46–76. New York: Continuum, 1982.

Etwaru, Richie. "Enough of the Cloud Already, What Is Next for Enterprise Technology?" March 31, 2014. http://www.huffingtonpost.com/richie-etwaru/enough-of -the-cloud-alrea_b_5056275.html.

Fano, Robert, and Fernando Corbató. "Time-Sharing on Computers." *Scientific American* 215, no. 3 (1966): 129–140.

Farocki, Harun. *Images of the World and the Inscription of War*. 16mm film, 1988.

Farocki, Harun. *War at a Distance*. Video, 1993.

Fontanella-Khan, James, and Richard Waters. "Microsoft to Shield Foreign Users' Data." *Financial Times*, January 23, 2014, 1.

Foucault, Michel. *Discipline and Punish: The Birth of the Prison*. New York: Vintage, 1975.

Foucault, Michel. *Security, Territory, Population: Lectures at the College de France*. Basingstoke, UK: Palgrave Macmillan, 2007.

Franklin, Seb. "Cloud Control, or the Network as Medium." *Cultural Politics* 8, no. 3 (2012): 443–464.

Franklin, Seb. "The Limits of Control." *Cultural Politics* 7, no. 2 (2011): 311–320.

Freud, Sigmund. "Mourning and Melancholia" (1917). In *The Standard Edition of Complete Psychological Works of Sigmund Freud*, 237–258. New York: Norton, 1976.

Friedberg, Anne. *The Virtual Window: From Alberti to Microsoft*. Cambridge, MA: MIT Press, 2006.

Gabbatt, Adam. "Nato, Twitter and Air Strikes in Libya." *The Guardian* (blog), June 15, 2011. http://www.theguardian.com/help/insideguardian/2011/jun/15/nato-twitter -libya.

Galison, Peter. "War against the Center." *Grey Room* 4 (Summer 2001): 5–33.

Galloway, Alexander. "Global Networks and the Effects on Culture." *Annals of the American Academy of Political and Social Science* 597 (January 2005): 19–31.

Galloway, Alexander. *The Interface Effect*. Cambridge: Polity Press, 2012.

Galloway, Alexander. *Protocol: How Control Exists after Decentralization*. Cambridge, MA: MIT Press, 2004.

Galloway, Alexander, and Eugene Thacker. *The Exploit: A Theory of Networks*. Minneapolis: University of Minnesota Press, 2007.

Gardner, Amy. "Metro Dig at Tysons Stirs Underground Intrigue." *Washington Post*, May 31, 2009, A1.

Geist, Michael. "All Your Internets Belong to US, Continued: The Bodog.com Case." March 6, 2013. http://www.michaelgeist.ca/2012/03/bodog-case-column-post/.

Gershon, Ilana. "Neoliberal Agency." *Current Anthropology* 52, no. 4 (August 2011): 537–555.

Gillespie, Tarleton. "The Stories Digital Tools Tell." In *New Media: Theories and Practices of Digitextuality*, ed. John Caldwell and Anna Everett, 107–126. New York: Routledge, 2003.

Gilmore, Jeff. "Where Is Lt Zuckerberg? An Advocacy for Social Media and Digital Collaboration in the Military." *Small Wars Journal*, January 9, 2013. http:// smallwarsjournal.com/jrnl/art/where-is-lt-zuckerberg.

Gitelman, Lisa, and Geoffrey Pingree. "Introduction." In *New Media, 1740–1915*, ed. Lisa Gitelman and Geoffrey Pingree, i–xxii. Cambridge, MA: MIT Press, 2003.

Gohdes, Anita. "Pulling the Plug: Network Disruptions and Violence in Civil Conflict." *Journal of Peace Research* (2015): 1–16. Advance online publication, doi: 10.1177/ 0022343314551398.

Golumbia, David. *The Cultural Logic of Computation*. Cambridge, MA: Harvard University Press, 2009.

Greenberg, Andy. *This Machine Kills Secrets*. New York: Penguin, 2012.

Greenberger, Martin. "The Computers of Tomorrow." *The Atlantic* 213 (May 1964): 63–67.

Greenberger, Martin. "The Two Sides of Time Sharing." Cambridge, MA: MIT Sloan School of Management, Paper 127-65, 1965.

Greenpeace. "How Clean Is Your Cloud?" April 2012. http://www.greenpeace.org/international/Global/international/publications/climate/2012/iCoal/HowCleanisYourCloud.pdf.

Guins, Raiford. *Edited Clean Version: Technology and the Culture of Control*. Minneapolis: University of Minnesota Press, 2009.

Guins, Raiford. *Game After: A Cultural Study of Video Game Afterlife*. Cambridge, MA: MIT Press, 2014.

Hafner, Katie, and Matthew Lyon. *Where Wizards Stay Up Late: The Origins of the Internet*. New York: Simon and Schuster, 1996.

Halliday, Paul. *Habeas Corpus: From England to Empire*. Cambridge, MA: Harvard University Press, 2010.

Happé, Amanda. "The Other Night Sky." *SWITCH* 3 (Spring 2010): 4–5.

Hardt, Michael and Antonio Negri. *Empire*. Cambridge, MA: Harvard University Press, 2000.

Hardy, Quentin. "Wealth Managers Enlist Spy Tools to Map Portfolios." *New York Times*, August 4, 2014, B1.

Hawley, Kip. *Permanent Emergency: Inside the TSA and the Fight for the Future of American Security*. New York: Palgrave Macmillan, 2012.

Hayles, N. Katherine. "Print Is Flat, Code Is Deep: The Importance of Media-Specific Analysis." *Poetics Today* 25, no. 1 (2004): 67–90.

Hedstrom, Margaret. "Digital Preservation: A Time Bomb for Digital Libraries." *Computers and the Humanities* 31, no. 3 (1997): 189–202.

Heidegger, Martin. "The Question Concerning Technology." In *The Question Regarding Technology, and Other Essays*, trans. William Lovitt, 3–35. New York: Harper, 1982.

Hofstadter, Richard. "The Paranoid Style in American Politics." *Harpers*, November 1964, 77–86.

Horning, Rob. "Structuring the Self as Inherently Entrepreneurial, Facebook as Neoliberal State." *Marginal Utility Annex* (blog), March 1, 2011. http://marginal-utility.blogspot.com/2011/03/structuring-self-as-inherently.html.

Horvath, John. "Freeware Capitalism." Post on nettime.org mailing list, February 5, 1998. http://www.nettime.org/Lists-Archives/nettime-l-9802/msg00026.html.

Hu, Tung-Hui. "Real Time/Zero Time." *Discourse: Journal for Theoretical Studies in Media and Culture* 34, no. 2 (2012): 163–184.

Iron Mountain. "Data Backup." http://www.ironmountain.com/Services/Data -Management/Cloud-Backup-Services.aspx.

Jalonschi, Manny. "Occupy Wall Street's Crowd Democracy—the Anti-Mob." *The Indypendent* (blog), October 8, 2011. http://www.indypendent.org/2011/10/08/ crowd-democracy-antimob/.

Jameson, Fredric. "Cognitive Mapping." In *Marxism and the Interpretation of Culture*, ed. Cary Nelson and Lawrence Grossberg, 347–360. Urbana: University of Illinois Press, 1980.

Johnson, David K. *The Lavender Scare: The Cold War Persecution of Gays and Lesbians in the Federal Government*. Chicago: University of Chicago Press, 2004.

Johnson, Gerald W. "Plots and Counter-plots." *The New Republic* 145, no. 1 (July 3, 1961): 18.

Jones, R. D. "The Public Planning Information System and the Computer Utility." In *Proceedings of the ACM 1967 22nd National Conference*, ed. Solomon Rosenthal, 553–564. New York: ACM Press, 1967.

Joselit, David. *Feedback: Television against Democracy*. Cambridge, MA: MIT Press, 2006.

Joselit, David. "Tale of the Tape." *Artforum* 40, no. 9 (May 2002) 152–155, 196.

Kaplan, Caren. "Precision Targets: GPS and the Militarization of U.S. Consumer Identity." *American Quarterly* 58, no. 3 (Sept. 2006): 693–713.

Kapstein, Joshua. "How the NSA Recruits in a Post-Snowden World." *The Daily Beast* (blog), January 17, 2014. http://www.thedailybeast.com/articles/2014/01/17/how -the-nsa-recruits-in-a-post-snowden-world.html.

Karst, Kenneth. "'The Files': Legal Controls over the Accuracy and Accessibility of Stored Personal Data." *Law and Contemporary Problems* 31, no. 2 (1966): 342–376.

Keeling, Kara. "Queer OS." *Cinema Journal* 53, no. 2 (Winter 2014): 152–157.

Keenan, Thomas. "Disappearances: The Photographs of Trevor Paglen." *Aperture* 191 (Summer 2008): 36–42.

Kirschenbaum, Matthew. *Mechanisms: New Media and the Forensic Imagination*. Cambridge, MA: MIT Press, 2008.

Kittler, Friedrich. *Gramophone, Film, Typewriter*. Stanford: Stanford University Press, 1999.

Kleinrock, Leonard. "An Interview with Leonard Kleinrock," by Judy O'Neill. April 3, 1990, Charles Babbage Institute, University of Minnesota. http://conservancy .umn.edu/bitstream/handle/11299/107411/oh190lk.pdf?sequence=1.

Kline, Ronald. *Consumers in the Country: Technology and Social Change in Rural America*. Baltimore: Johns Hopkins University Press, 2000.

Knoke, David. "It Takes a Network: The Rise and Fall of Social Network Analysis in U.S. Army Counterinsurgency Doctrine." *International Network for Social Network Analysis* 33, no. 1 (July 2013): 1–10.

Krebs, Brian. "Virtual Sweatshops Defeat Bot-or-Not Tests." *Krebs on Security* (blog), January 2012. http://krebsonsecurity.com/2012/01/virtual-sweatshops-defeat-bot -or-not-tests/.

Laporte, Dominique. *History of Shit*. Trans. Nadia Benabid and Rodolphe el-Khoury. Cambridge, MA: MIT Press, [1978] 2002.

Lazzarato, Maurizio. "Immaterial Labour." Trans. Paul Colilli and Ed Emory. In *Radical Thought in Italy*, ed. Paolo Virno and Michael Hardt, 132–146. Minneapolis: University of Minnesota Press, 1996.

Lee, John A. N., and Robert Rosin. "The Project MAC Interviews: October 18, 1988." *IEEE Annals of the History of Computing* 14, no. 2 (1992): 14–35.

Levy, Steven. *Hackers: Heroes of the Computer Revolution*. Sebastopol, CA: O'Reilly Media, 2010.

Lewallen, Constance M., and Steven Seid, eds. *Ant Farm 1968–1978*. Exhibition catalog. Berkeley: University of California Press, 2004.

Licklider, J. C. R. "Man-Computer Symbiosis." *IRE Transactions on Human Factors in Electronics*, vol. HFE-1 (March 1960): 4–11.

Licklider, J. C. R., and Robert Taylor. "The Computer as a Communication Device." *Science and Technology* (September 1968): 20–41.

Light, Jennifer S. "When Computers Were Women." *Technology and Culture* 40, no. 3 (July 1999): 455–483.

Lord, Chip, and Curtis Schreier. "Media Van—Ant Farm Interview: Jimmy Stamp." *Floater Magazine*, no. 2 (January 2009). http://floatermagazine.com/issue02/pdfs/ Media_Van.pdf.

Lukasik, Stephen J. "Why the Arpanet Was Built." *IEEE Annals of the History of Computing* 33:3 (July–September 2011): 4–21.

Lunenfeld, Peter. *User: InfoTechnoDemo*. Cambridge, MA: MIT Press, 2005.

Lynch, Lisa. "'As I Photograph the Night Sky, the Other Night Sky Photographs Back': Surveillance, Transparency, and the Frenzy of Disclosure." Paper presented at the Society for Cinema and Media Studies, New Orleans, LA, March 10–13, 2011.

Lyon, Barrett. "The Story Behind the Mastercard and VISA DDoS Attacks." *Blyon* (blog), December 8, 2010. http://verbophobia.blyon.com/mastercard-ddos/.

Macy, John W. "The New Computer Age: Automated Government," *Saturday Review*, July 23, 1966, 23–25, 70.

Manovich, Lev. *The Language of New Media*. Cambridge, MA: MIT Press, 2001.

Markoff, John. *What the Dormouse Said: How the Sixties Counterculture Shaped the Personal Computer Industry*. New York: Penguin, 2006.

Mbembe, Achille. "Necropolitics." *Public Culture* 15, no. 1 (2003): 11–40.

McCarthy, John. "Recursive Functions of Symbolic Expressions and Their Computation by Machine, Part I." *Communications of the ACM* 3, no. 4 (1960): 184–195. Reprinted with author's commentary in 2000. http://www-formal.stanford.edu/jmc/recursive.pdf.

McCarthy, John. "Reminiscences on the Theory of Time-Sharing." 1983. http://jmc.stanford.edu/computing-science/timesharing.html.

McCarthy, John. "The Home Information Terminal." In *Man and Computer, Proceedings of the International Conference, Bordeaux, 1970*, ed. Maurice Marois, 48–57. Basel: Karger, 1972. Reprinted June 1, 2000. http://www-formal.stanford.edu/jmc/hoter2.pdf.

McChrystal, Stanley. "Becoming the Enemy: To Win in Afghanistan, We Need to Fight More Like the Taliban." *Foreign Policy* 185 (March–April 2011): 66–70.

McCray, W. Patrick. *Keep Watching the Skies!: The Story of Operation Moonwatch and the Dawn of the Space Age*. Princeton: Princeton University Press, 2008.

McLuhan, Marshall. *Understanding Media: The Extensions of Man*, New York: McGraw-Hill, 1964.

Medovoi, Leerom. "Global Society Must Be Defended: Biopolitics without Boundaries." *Social Text* 25, no. 2 (Summer 2007): 53–79.

Mellencamp, Patricia. "Ant Farm Redux: Pyrotechnics and Emergence." *Journal of Film and Video* 57, nos. 1–2 (Spring/Summer 2005): 40–56.

Metahaven [Daniel van der Velden and Vinca Kruk]. "Captives of the Cloud: Part I." *e-flux*, 2012. http://www.e-flux.com/journal/captives-of-the-cloud-part-i/.

Milan, Stefania. "Cloud Protesting: Dissent in Times of Social Media." *The Citizen Lab* (blog), Munk School of Global Affairs, University of Toronto, October 18, 2011. http://citizenlab.org/2011/10/cloud-protesting-dissent-in-times-of-social-media/.

Miller, Arthur R. "Personal Privacy in the Computer Age: The Challenge of a New Technology in an Information-Oriented Society." *Michigan Law Review* 67, no. 6 (April 1969): 1089–1246.

Mims, Christopher. "The Fear-Based Psychology of the 'Internet Kill Switch.'" *Technology Review* (blog), August 18, 2010. http://www.technologyreview.com/view/420288/the-fear-based-psychology-of-the-internet-kill-switch/.

Minow, Newton. "Television and the Public Interest." Speech delivered May 9, 1961, National Association of Broadcasters, Washington, DC.

Morley, David. *Media, Modernity and Technology: The Geography of the New.* New York: Routledge, 2007.

Mulvey, Laura. *Death 24x a Second: Stillness and the Moving Image.* London: Reaktion Books, 2006.

Munster, Anna. *An Aesthesia of Networks.* Cambridge, MA: MIT Press, 2014.

Murakami Wood, David. "'The Internet Must Be Defended!'" *Notes from the Ubiquitous Surveillance Society* (blog), December 7, 2010. http://ubisurv.wordpress.com/2010/12/07/the-internet-must-de-defended/.

Murphy, Brian. "Bomb-Proofing the Digital Image: An Archaeology of Media Preservation Infrastructure." *Media-N* 10, no. 1, 2014. http://median.newmediacaucus.org/art-infrastructures-hardware/bomb-proofing-the-digital-image-an-archaeology-of-media-preservation-infrastructure/.

Murray, Stuart. "Thanatopolitics: Reading in Agamben a Rejoinder to Biopolitical Life." *Communication and Critical/Cultural Studies* 5, no. 2 (June 2008): 203–207.

"Mystery Blasts." *Newsweek*, June 12, 1961, 32.

Nakamura, Lisa. "'I WILL DO EVERYthing That Am Asked': Scambaiting, Digital Show-Space, and the Racial Violence of Social Media." *Journal of Visual Culture* 13, no. 3 (December 2014): 257–274.

Nance, Horace H. "Engineering the Transcontinental Cable." *Bell System Magazine* 20, no. 4 (November 1941): 207–221.

Newhagen, John E., and Sheizaf Rafaeli. "Why Communication Researchers Should Study the Internet: A Dialogue," *Journal of Computer-Mediated Communication* 1, no. 4 (March 1996): 4–13.

Nielsen, Don. "The SRI Van and Computer Internetworking." *Core* 3, no. 1 (February 2002): 2–7. A publication of the Computer History Museum.

Nixon, Rob. *Slow Violence and the Environmentalism of the Poor*. Cambridge, MA: Harvard University Press, 2011.

Norton-Taylor, Richard, and Nick Hopkins. "Libya Air Strikes: Nato Uses Twitter to Help Gather Targets." *The Guardian*, June 15, 2011. http://www.theguardian.com/world/2011/jun/15/libya-nato-gathers-targets-twitter.

NOS [Nederlandse Omroep Stichting, Dutch Broadcast Foundation]. "Door Twitter geen verrassingsaanvallen op Libië," March 21, 2011. http://nos.nl/artikel/227449-door-twitter-geen-verrassingsaanvallen-op-libie.html.

NOS [Nederlandse Omroep Stichting, Dutch Broadcast Foundation]. "Werkwijze Dirk de Jager," March 22, 2011. http://nos.nl/artikel/227453-werkwijze-dirk-de-jager.html.

Olds, Kirsten. "Networked Collectivities: North American Artists' Groups, 1968–1978." Ph.D. diss., University of Michigan, 2009.

Olson, Nels, and Jian Zheng. "NIST/LoC Final Report to ODAT." Presentation to the meeting of the Government Information Preservation Working Group (GIPWoG), January 30, 2007.

Olson, Parmy. "Egypt's Internet Blackout Cost More Than OECD Estimates." *Forbes* blog, February 3, 2011. http://www.forbes.com/sites/parmyolson/2011/02/03/how-much-did-five-days-of-no-internet-cost-egypt/.

Ong, Aihwa. "Powers of Sovereignty: State, People, Wealth, Life." *Focaal—Journal of Global and Historical Anthropology* 64 (2012): 24–35.

Osborne, Thomas. "Security and Vitality: Drains, Liberalism and Power in the Nineteenth Century." In *Foucault and Political Reason: Liberalism, Neo-liberalism, and Rationalities of Government*, ed. Andrew Barry, Thomas Osborne, and Nikolas Rose, 99–122. Chicago: University of Chicago Press, 1996.

Paglen, Trevor. *Blank Spots on the Map: The Dark Geography of the Pentagon's Secret World*. New York: Dutton, 2009.

Paglen, Trevor. "Seeing Is Believing: An Interview with Trevor Paglen," by Seth Curcio. *Daily Serving*, February 24, 2011. http://dailyserving.com/2011/02/interview-with-trevor-paglen/.

Paglen, Trevor. "TD Blog Interview with Trevor Paglen," by The Talking Dog. *The Talking Dog* (blog), December 10, 2006. http://thetalkingdog.com/archives2/000724.html.

Paglen, Trevor, and Thomas Keenan. "Fog of Wars." *Bidoun* 1, no. 8 (2006): 36–39.

Panetta, Leon. "Remarks by Secretary Panetta on Cybersecurity to the Business Executives for National Security, New York City." October 11, 2012. http://www.defense.gov/transcripts/transcript.aspx?transcriptid=5136

Parikka, Jussi. *Digital Contagions: A Media Archaeology of Computer Viruses.* New York: Peter Lang, 2007.

Pariser, Eli. *The Filter Bubble: What the Internet Is Hiding from You.* New York: Penguin Press, 2011.

Parker, Graham. "419 (occasional 420): Reston, Virginia & Lagos, Nigeria, 2005." In *Fair Use: Notes from Spam.* London: Book Works, 2009.

Parkhill, Douglas. *The Challenge of the Computer Utility*, Reading, MA: Addison-Wesley, 1966.

Parks, Lisa. "Around the Antenna Tree: The Politics of Infrastructure Visibility." March 6, 2009. http://flowtv.org/2009/03/around-the-antenna-tree-the-politics-of-infrastructural-visibilitylisa-parks-uc-santa-barbara/.

Parks, Lisa. "Falling Apart: Electronics Salvaging and the Global Media Economy." In *Residual Media*, ed. Charles R. Acland, 32–47. Minneapolis: University of Minnesota Press, 2007.

Paulsen, Kris. "Half-Inch Revolution: The Guerilla Video Tape Network." *Amodern* 2, "Network Archaeology," October 2013. http://amodern.net/article/half-inch-revolution/.

Phelps, George A. "The Wendover Blast." *Northeastern Nevada Historical Society* 91, no. 1 (1991): 4–28.

"Phone Sabotage Brings $4000 in Reward Offers: Agents of F.B.I. Checking on Four Reported Cases." *Los Angeles Times*, April 25, 1947, 2.

Planets Consortium. "Planets TimeCapsule Deposit." http://www.planets-project.eu/news/?id=1273674576.

Planets Consortium. "Preservation and Long-Term Access via NETworked Services." http://www.planets-project.eu/docs/comms/PLANETS_BROCHURE.pdf.

Planets Consortium. "Report on Emerging Digital Art Characterisation Technique." http://www.planets-project.eu/docs/reports/Planets_PC5-D5_Emerging_Digital_Art_Tech.pdf.

Planets Consortium. "TIME CAPSULE—A Showcase for Digital Preservation." http://www.ifs.tuwien.ac.at/dp/timecapsule/home.html.

Pollock, John. "People Power 2.0." *Technology Review* 115, no. 3 (June 2012): 62–71.

PTT [Postmen and Telegraphers' Union]. *Le Cri Postal*, April 1907, as quoted in Emile Pouget, *Sabotage*, trans. Arturo Giovannitti. Chicago: Charles H. Kerr & Co., [1911] 1913.

Raindance Corporation. *Radical Software* 1, no. 1 (1970).

Raley, Rita. *Tactical Media*. Minneapolis: University of Minnesota Press, 2009.

Reed, Michael. "Re: [tor-talk] Iran Cracks Down on Web Dissident Technology." cryptome.org mailing list, March 22, 2011. http://cryptome.org/0003/tor-spy.htm.

Regalado, Antonio. "Who Coined 'Cloud Computing?'" *Technology Review*, October 31, 2011. http://www.technologyreview.com/news/425970/who-coined-cloud-computing/.

Retz, David. "ARPANET, as I Recall." April 5, 2010. http://comware.us/Content/internetrecollections.

Ristenpart, Thomas, Eran Tromer, Hovav Shacham, and Stefan Savage. "Hey, You, Get Off of My Cloud: Exploring Information Leakage in Third-Party Compute Clouds." In *CCS '09: Proceedings of the 16th ACM Conference on Computer and Communications Security*, ed. Somesh Jha, Angelos D. Keromytis, and Hao Chen, 199–212. New York: ACM Press, 2009.

Rodowick, D. N. *Reading the Figural, or, Philosophy after the New Media*. Durham, NC: Duke University Press, 2001.

Rodrigue, Jean-Paul, Claude Comtois, and Brian Slack, "Rail Track Mileage and Number of Class I Rail Carriers, United States, 1830–2008." http://people.hofstra.edu/geotrans/eng/ch3en/conc3en/usrail18402003.html.

Ronell, Avital. *The Telephone Book: Technology—Schizophrenia—Electric Speech*. Lincoln: University of Nebraska, 1991.

Roszak, Theodore. *From Satori to Silicon Valley: San Francisco and the American Counterculture*. San Francisco: Don't Call It Frisco Press, 1986.

Sackman, Harold. "Man-Computer Communication: Experimental Investigation of User Effectiveness." In *Proceedings of the Sixth SIGCPR Conference on Computer Personnel Research*, ed. Robert Blechen, 93–105. New York: ACM Press, 1968.

Sandvine. "Global Internet Phenomena Report: 2H 2013." https://www.sandvine.com/downloads/general/global-internet-phenomena/2013/2h-2013-global-internet-phenomena-report.pdf.

Sanger, David E. "Mutually Assured Cyberdestruction?" *New York Times*, June 3, 2012, 4.

Sartre, Jean-Paul. *Being and Nothingness*. Trans. Hazel E. Barns. New York: Washington Square Press, [1943] 1993.

Scanlon, Jessie Holliday, and Brad Wieners. "Guest Column: The Internet Cloud." *Computerworld*, July 16, 1999. http://www.computerworld.com.au/article/104942/ guest_column_internet_cloud/.

Schachtman, Noah. "Listen: Secret Libyan Psyops, Caught by Online Sleuths." *Wired* (blog), March 2011. http://www.wired.com/2011/03/secret-libya-psyops/.

Schwartz, John. "Satellite Spotters Glimpse Secrets, and Tell Them." *New York Times*, February 5, 2008, A1.

Scott, Felicity D. *Living Archive 7: Ant Farm: Allegorical Time Warp: The Media Fallout of July 21, 1969*. Barcelona: Actar Publishing, 2008.

Sedgwick, Eve Kosofsky. "Paranoid Reading and Reparative Reading, Or, You're So Paranoid, You Probably Think This Essay Is about You." In *Touching Feeling: Affect, Pedagogy, Performativity*, 123–151. Durham, NC: Duke University Press, 2003.

Seid, Steve. "Tunneling through the Wasteland: Ant Farm Video." In Constance M. Lewallen and Steven Seid, *Ant Farm 1968-1978*, 22–37. Exhibition catalog. Berkeley: University of California Press, 2004.

Sekula, Allan. "Dismal Science, Part 1." In *Fish Story*, 41–54. Rotterdam and Düsseldorf: Witte de With Center for Contemporary Art/Richter Verlag, 1995.

Serra, Richard, with Carlotta Schoolman. *Television Delivers People*. Video, 1973, originally broadcast on an Amarillo, TX, public television.

Shamberg, Michael, and the Raindance Corporation. *Guerrilla Television*. New York: Henry Holt & Co., Inc., 1971.

"Sharing the Computer's Time." *Time* 86, no. 20 (November 12, 1965): 116.

Shpanya, Arie. "Do Profits Matter? The Curious Case of Amazon.com." *Venturebeat*, October 24, 2013. http://venturebeat.com/2013/10/24/do-profits-matter-the -curious-case-of-amazon-com/.

Silverman, Kaja. *The Subject of Semiotics*. New York: Oxford University Press, 1983.

Sontag, Susan. "The Imagination of Disaster." *Commentary* 40 (October 1965): 42–48.

Starosielski, Nicole. *The Undersea Network*. Durham, NC: Duke University Press, 2015.

Sterling, Bruce. "The Life and Death of Media." Electronic Frontier Foundation, 2003. http://w2.eff.org/Misc/Publications/Bruce_Sterling/Dead_Media_Project/.

Stratfor. "Anonymous vs. Zetas Amid Mexico's Cartel Violence." November 3, 2011, via WikiLeaks. http://wikileaks.org/gifiles/docs/51/51091_anonymous-vs-zetas-amid-mexico-s-cartel-violence-.html.

Streeter, Tom. *Selling the Air: A Critique of the Policy of Commercial Broadcasting in the United States.* Chicago: University of Chicago Press, 2006.

Streeter, Tom. *The Net Effect: Romanticism, Capitalism, and the Internet.* New York: NYU Press, 2011.

Taylor, Paul, and Tim Jordan, *Hacktivism and Cyberwars: A Rebel with a Cause?* New York: Routledge, 2004.

Terranova, Tiziana. "Failure to Comply: Bioart, Security, and the Market." European Institute for Progressive Cultural Politics, June 2007. http://eipcp.net/transversal/1007/terranova/en.

Terranova, Tiziana. *Network Culture: Politics for the Information Age.* London: Pluto Press, 2004.

Terranova, Tiziana, and Joan Donovan. "Occupy Social Networks: The Paradoxes of Corporate Social Media for Networked Social Movements." In *Unlike Us Reader: Social Media Monopolies and their Alternatives,* ed. Geert Lovink and Miriam Rasch, 296–311. Amsterdam: Institute for Network Cultures, 2013.

Tuomenoksa, L. S., and W. Ulrich. "Problems of Programming for Time-Shared Systems." *IEEE Transactions on Communication Technology* 15, no. 1 (February 1967): 5–10.

Turner, Fred. *From Counterculture to Cyberculture: Stewart Brand, the Whole Earth Network, and the Rise of Digital Utopianism.* Chicago: University of Chicago Press, 2008.

Turrow, Joseph. *Niche Envy: Marketing Discrimination in the Digital Age.* Cambridge, MA: MIT Press, 2006.

U.S. Department of Defense. "Report of the Defense Science Board Task Force on Mission Impact of Foreign Influence on DoD Software." September 2007. http://www.acq.osd.mil/dsb/reports/ADA486949.pdf.

U.S. House of Representatives. *The Computer and Invasion of Privacy.* Hearings of the House of Representatives Special Subcommittee on Invasion of Privacy, Committee on Government Operations, July 26–28, 1966. Washington, DC: Government Printing Office, 1966.

U.S. Senate. "Investigation of Administration of Internal Security Act of 1950." S. Res. 366, 81st Cong., 2nd Sess. (1950).

U.S. Senate. "A Bill to Safeguard Communications Facilities," by the Subcommittee to Investigate the Administration of the Internal Security Act and Internal Security Laws, Committee on the Judiciary, Hearing on S.B. 1990, 87th Cong., 1st Sess., June 7, 1961.

U.S. Senate. "Protecting Cyberspace as a National Asset Act of 2010." S. 3480, 111th Cong., 2nd Sess. (2010).

U.S. Supreme Court. *Lawrence v. Texas*, 539 U.S. 558 (2003).

Vanderbilt, Tom, and Trevor Paglen. "Trevor Paglen Talks about the 'Other Night Sky,' 2007–." *Artforum* 47, no. 7 (March 2009): 225.

Varnelis, Kazys. "Conclusion: The Rise of Network Culture." In *Networked Publics*, ed. K. Varnelis, 145–163. Cambridge, MA: MIT Press, 2008.

Videofreex. *Spaghetti City Video Manual*. New York: Praeger, 1973.

Virilio, Paul. *Bunker Archaeology*, trans. George Collins. New York: Princeton Architectural Press, [1975] 1994.

Virilio, Paul. "Cryptic Architecture." In *Architecture Principe* (1966), trans. George Collins. Bensancon: Les Editions de l'Imprimeur, 1997. Reprinted in *The Virilio Reader*, ed. Steve Redhead, 15–18. New York: Columbia University Press, 2004.

Virilio, Paul. *War and Cinema: The Logistics of Perception*. London: Verso, [1984] 1989.

Wasiuta, Mark. "Ant Farm Underground." *Cabinet* 30 (Summer 2008): 92–93.

Weber, Samuel. *Targets of Opportunity: On the Militarization of Thinking*. New York: Fordham University Press, 2005.

Weddle, Bonnie. "PLANETS Digital Genome TimeCapsule." *L'Archivista* (blog), May 18, 2010. http://larchivista.blogspot.com/2010/05/planets-digital-genome-timecapsule.html.

Wigley, Mark. "Network Fever." *Grey Room* 4 (Summer 2001): 82–122.

Žižek, Slavoj. "Biopolitics: Between Abu Ghraib and Terri Schiavo." *Artforum* 44, no. 4 (December 2005): 270–271.

INDEX

Note: Page numbers in *italics* refer to illustrations.